EXPLORATIONS IN SOCIO

British Sociological Associatior

Sami Zubaida (editor)		
Richard Brown (editor)	2	*Knowledge, Education and Cultural Change*
Paul Rock and Mary McIntosh (editors)	3	*Deviance and Social Control*
Emanuel de Kadt and Gavin Williams (editors)	4	*Sociology and Development*
Frank Parkin (editor)	5	*The Social Analysis of Class Structure*
Diana Leonard Barker and Sheila Allen (editors)	6	*Sexual Divisions and Society: Process and Change*
Diana Leonard Barker and Sheila Allen (editors)	7	*Dependence and Exploitation in Work and Marriage*
Richard Scase (editor)	8	*Industrial Society: Class, Cleavage and Control*
Robert Dingwall, Christian Heath, Margaret Reid and Margaret Stacey (editors)	9	*Health Care and Health Knowledge*
Robert Dingwall, Christian Heath, Margaret Reid and Margaret Stacey (editors)	10	*Health and the Division of Labour*
Gary Littlejohn, Barry Smart, John Wakeford and Nira Yuval-Davis (editors)	11	*Power and the State*
Michele Barrett, Philip Corrigan, Annette Kuhn and Janet Wolff (editors)	12	*Ideology and Cultural Production*
Bob Fryer, Alan Hunt, Doreen MacBarnet and Bert Moorhouse (editors)	13	*Law, State and Society*
Philip Abrams, Rosemary Deem, Janet Finch and Paul Rock (editors)	14	*Practice and Progress: British Sociology 1950–80*
Graham Day, Lesley Caldwell, Karen Jones, David Robbins and Hilary Rose (editors)	15	*Diversity and Decomposition in the Labour Market*
David Robbins, Lesley Caldwell, Graham Day, Karen Jones and Hilary Rose (editors)	16	*Rethinking Social Inequality*

Eva Gamarnikow, David Morgan, June Purvis and Daphne Taylorson (editors)	17	*The Public and the Private*
Eva Gamarnikow, David Morgan, June Purvis and Daphne Taylorson (editors)	18	*Gender, Class and Work*
* Gareth Rees, Janet Bujra, Paul Littlewood, Howard Newby and Teresa L. Rees (editor)	19	*Political Action and Social Identity: Class, Locality and Ideology*
* Howard Newby, Janet Bujra, Paul Littlewood, Gareth Rees, Teresa L. Rees (editors)	20	*Restructuring Capital: Recession and Reorganization in Industrial Society*
* Sheila Allen, Alan Waton, Kate Purcell and Stephen Wood (editors)	21	*The Experience of Unemployment*
* Kate Purcell, Stephen Wood, Alan Waton and Sheila Allen (editors)	22	*The Changing Experience of Employment: Restructuring and Recession*
* Jalna Hanmer and Mary Maynard (editors)	23	*Women, Violence and Social Control*
* Colin Creighton and Martin Shaw (editors)	24	*The Sociology of War and Peace*
* Alan Bryman, Bill Bytheway, Patricia Allott and Teresa Keil (editors)	25	*Rethinking the Life Cycle*
* Patricia Allott, Teresa Keil, Alan Bryman and Bill Bytheway (editors)	26	*Women and the Life Cycle*

* Published by Macmillan

The Sociology of War and Peace

Edited by

Colin Creighton

and

Martin Shaw

Lecturers in Sociology, University of Hull

MACMILLAN
PRESS

First published 1987

Published by
THE MACMILLAN PRESS LTD
Houndmills, Basingstoke, Hampshire RG21 2XS
and London
Companies and representatives
throughout the world

Typeset by Wessex Typesetters
(A Division of Eastern Press Ltd)
Frome, Somerset

Printed in Hong Kong

British Library Cataloguing in Publication Data
The Sociology of war and peace.—(Explorations in sociology; 24)
1. Pacificism 2. War and society
I. Creighton, Colin II. Shaw, Martin
III. Series
303.6′6 JX1938
ISBN 0-333-41838-7 (hardcover)
ISBN 0-333-41839-5 (paperback)

Contents

Acknowledgements vii

Notes on the contributors viii

Introduction 1
Martin Shaw and Colin Creighton

PART I THE SOCIOLOGY OF WAR

1 Violence, Peace and War in 'Early' Human Society: The Case of the Eskimo 17
David Riches

2 War and the Rise of the West 37
John A. Hall

3 War and Social Theory: Into Battle with Classes, Nations and States 54
Michael Mann

4 Hi-Tech Armaments, Space Militarisation and the Third World 73
Paul W. Hoag

PART II MILITARISM, THE STATE AND SOCIAL CHANGE

5 Militarisation and the South African State 99
Mark Mitchell and Dave Russell

6 Israel: Conflict, War and Social Change 121
Avishai Ehrlich

7 The Rise and Fall of the Military–Democratic State: Britain 1940–85 143
Martin Shaw

8 The People's War and the People's Theatre: British Socialist Theatre 1939–45 159
Don Watson

9 What did you do in the War, Mam? Women Steelworkers at the Consett Iron Company during the Second World War 178
Kath Price

PART III THE SOCIOLOGY OF PEACE MOVEMENTS

10 The Sociology of CND 199
John Mattausch

11 Activists for Peace: The Social Basis of a Local Peace Movement 218
Graham Day and David Robbins

Index 237

Acknowledgements

This book is one of two based on papers offered at the 1985 conference of the British Sociological Association, held at the University of Hull on the theme, 'War, Violence and Social Change'. It would not have been possible without the efforts of our co-organisers, Jalna Hanmer and Mary Maynard, who also helped to select the papers for this volume, and of the BSA officers, Anne Dix and Mike Milotte. Equally essential at all stages was the secretarial support we received, from Melanie Bucknell, Stella Rhind and Pat Wilkinson. We would like to thank all of them, together with all the delegates who took part in the discussions which led to this book.

COLIN CREIGHTON
MARTIN SHAW

Hull

Notes on the Contributors

Colin Creighton and **Martin Shaw** are Lecturers in Sociology, University of Hull.

Graham Day is Lecturer in Sociology, University College of Wales, Aberystwyth. **David Robbins** was Lecturer in Sociology, University College of Wales, Aberystwyth, until his tragic death in a climbing accident in 1986.

Avishai Ehrlich is Lecturer in Sociology, University of Tel Aviv.

John A. Hall is Senior Lecturer in Sociology, University of Southampton.

Paul W. Hoag is a Research Associate at Wichita State University, Kansas, USA, and chair of the annual scholarly program of the Union for Radical Political Economics.

Michael Mann is Reader in Sociology, London School of Economics and Political Science.

John Mattausch is a postgraduate student in sociology, University of Edinburgh.

Mark Mitchell and **Dave Russell** are Senior Lecturers in Sociology, Portsmouth Polytechnic.

Kath Price is a Tutor with the Open University, Northern Region.

David Riches is Lecturer in Social Anthropology, University of St Andrews.

Don Watson is Research Officer with the Coronary Prevention Group, London.

Introduction

Martin Shaw and Colin Creighton

It has been customary, among the relatively small band of sociologists who have started to write about war and peace, to open almost any article by bemoaning the absence of these issues in our discipline. When the British Sociological Association decided to hold its 1985 Conference on the theme, 'War, Violence and Social Change', there was some doubt as to whether the volume of ongoing work – in a field which hardly existed in British sociology before the present decade – was sufficient to justify devoting a major national event to it. One contributor, who has since published an expanded version of his paper elsewhere, took up the familiar refrain of sociology's 'neglect and betrayal' in its treatment of violence and war (Marsland, 1985). And yet, while the Conference certainly called forth important work on other forms of social violence – particularly, as will be seen from the companion volume edited by Jalna Hanmer and Mary Maynard, on *Gender and Violence* – it also proved a landmark in the reinstatement of the central issues of war and peace in British sociology. This book will show, we hope, the vitality of the discipline, and something of the range of work being produced by both established writers and younger researchers. With this volume, it should be possible to end the complaint of neglect, and to begin to mark out the substantive areas of concern to which the 'sociology of war and peace' is devoting itself.

The emerging sociological approach to war and peace (at this stage we can still talk of a broad common area of interest, even if there are divergences as there must always be in the social sciences) can partly be defined by contrasting it with those from other disciplines. A large part of the field is occupied by subjects which are fairly closely allied to military practice. Strategic and defence studies are typically quite narrowly concerned with political, institutional and technical problems; while military history is often more interesting because at its best it shows an ability to bring together social and political with military knowledge. A smaller corner is contested by peace studies, which in part is a kind of defence-studies-in-reverse. Although also concerned with the wider conditions of peace, it is not always informed by a deep understanding of war as a socio-historical problem. Another relevant domain is that of international relations, which broadens the perspective to consider the political and diplomatic aspects, but is not generally interested in the relationship of these issues to underlying questions of social structure.

Within sociology itself the traditional field is that of military sociology, well represented at the 1985 BSA (although unfortunately not in this volume) by contributions from the United States and continental Europe. This area of work has demonstrated sociology's relevance by examining the social relations of the military themselves, in a cross-cultural perspective (see the survey by Harries-Jenkins and Moscos, 1981). Military sociology can be seen, however, as but a relatively small sub-area of the sociology of war and peace as conceived by most of the contributors to this volume. For sociology is taking on the much broader questions of the impetus to, and implications of, warfare for societies as wholes – not only for specialised military institutions and their members – and of the social factors which may prevent war.

The sociology of war and peace is much closer to some work in social anthropology and, more especially, social history than it is to any of the studies of war so far mentioned. Riches's chapter shows the relevance of the former, while the chapters by Mann, Hall, Shaw, Watson and Price represent variants of historical sociology. There is a large measure of agreement between sociologists and social historians on the affinities of their subjects, the remaining differences being largely those of method and style. Of the chapters mentioned above, the first three exhibit the typically sociological stance of 'theoretical history'; but the contributions of Watson and Price, based on archive research and oral history, are close in method to those of social historians, while using sociological concepts. Other chapters too, demonstrate how uncertain the academic boundaries must be in this field: Mattausch's and Day and Robbins's studies of contemporary peace movements are bound to become source materials for future social historians – as the earlier sociological study of CND by Parkin, which they discuss, has already become.

The sociology of war and peace can be defined, then, as the theoretical, historical and empirical study of war, war-preparation and the effects of war in their social context, together with the social processes which inhibit and may (in the future) prevent war. Peace, as David Riches comments in these pages, is almost incapable of objective definition except as the absence of war. So rather than embracing any of the more positive concepts of peace adopted by its enthusiasts, the writers in this volume generally make the assumption that war is the problem. In defining the social and political conditions which may make it possible to avoid war, we may make a more substantial contribution to a lasting peace than by an *a priori* definition of this goal. Certainly, as the final chapters in this book show, it is necessary to make a critical – if sympathetic – sociological examination of the 'peace movements' themselves.

What, then, are the key issues for a historical sociology of war and peace? The chapters in this book suggest a number of major themes, around which ongoing theory and research could develop. Inevitably, since the problems are very large and the attention devoted to them is still modest, any attempt to define an agenda will expose large gaps in the work so far carried out – not least in the coverage of this book. But part of the task at this stage must be to outline the questions that need to be asked, even if the answers are extremely provisional where they exist at all.

SOCIOLOGY OF VIOLENCE AND WAR

The first large set of issues concerns the roots of social violence and its relationship to warfare. This is an area in which an enormous amount of popular simplification occurs, and part of the task is the basic job of sorting out the concepts. Aggression is not force, force is not violence, violence is not killing, killing is not war; and yet the contexts in which it is assumed that these are all one and the same thing are quite innumerable. Not only must we deny that these terms are interchangeable; we must question any assumption of automatic connections between them. It really is quite absurd to suppose that it follows from the fact that individual people show aggression to each other in certain social situations, that superpower states must prepare to annihilate each other's populations with thermonuclear weapons. No such link makes any logical or scientific sense.

Within the social sciences, anthropologists have long had an important role in insisting that things are vastly more complex – by showing that this is so even in the more 'simple' societies in which one might assume that any 'basic' tendencies towards violence and/or warfare would manifest themselves. Riches's chapter continues this tradition by reviewing both the general evidence for small-scale societies, and (in more detail) the particular pattern among the Eskimos. This is especially interesting because it shows peoples who do have socially recognised, indeed legitimate, violence and killing – which, moreover, can be socially explained – but who lack any definable form of warfare.

Riches's chapter is the only one included here to address an issue of general importance, which is apparently much more difficult to deal with in the context of modern industrial societies. The problem is the relationship between 'external' violence (war) and 'internal' social violence. In a small-scale society, the difference between the two may be less marked – indeed external violence may not take the form of corporate conflict. In modern capitalist and state-socialist industrial societies, there are sharp institutional demarcations. War is vastly extended as a legitimate sphere of violence – with a scope for killing and destruction unimaginable before the present historical period – even if it is formally more regulated than ever before. Within societies (particularly Western democracies), however, even states which possess immense powers of coercion are circumscribed in their resort to violence. Equally individuals and non-state organisations or social groups are typically denied virtually any legitimate use of physical force, and killing is legally excluded in almost all circumstances. This has been explained in terms of the 'internal pacification' of societies by nation-states (Giddens, 1985). Social conflicts, along lines of class, race and gender especially, are however still acute, and result in violence and sometimes killing, often in expressive rather than instrumental forms.

In several areas of our society, the forms of both social and state violence, and the complex relationships between them have become central areas of social debate. No one could doubt the importance of the 'battles' on the miners' picket lines, the violence both by and against the police in the inner-city riots, or, to take a very different sort of violence, the pattern of rapes and other physical assaults against women and children. The 1985 BSA Conference was well supplied with papers on all these themes. And yet hardly any of the research in progress investigates the links between these forms of violence and the external violence of war. The Falklands war has cast a considerable shadow over the Thatcher years, which have also seen the recrudescence of violence in class and urban conflicts. But despite some fine research on the Falklands war in the media, which was a highlight of the 1985 BSA (reported in Glasgow University Media Group, 1985), no one has yet attempted to deal with the relationship of this war experience to our other social troubles.

One reason for this is that, tempting as the equation of war and social violence may be, there are no simple connections between the two. War is a very different social phenomenon from internal social conflict (which itself takes sharply varying forms). Although they are both violent, the one does not necessarily produce the other. Sociologists have often seen violence within society, since Durkheim's study of suicide, as dependent on social cohesion. Total war, in 1939–45 especially, actually increased many forms of social cohesion, and narrowed the range of social and political conflict. The 'increasing violence' of society since the 1960s (itself a notion which requires critical examination) is often seen as a form of social disintegration, and can be identified with the decline of national solidarity from its wartime peak. How the Falklands war fits into this pattern is something which needs investigation, for as the chapter by Shaw reminds us it represents a sort of war experience which contrasts with that of 1939–45.

THE HISTORICAL SOCIOLOGY OF WAR

The state is the social institution which explains the dichotomous relationship of modern societies to violence. The experience which we have been discussing, in which the scope of war has widened while that of legitimate violence within societies has narrowed, has its roots in the state's ever more successful assertion of its legal monopoly of force. This was seen as a defining characteristic of states by both Weber and Marx (although neither of them identified the central role of the process of war in realising the state's control over society).

Marx in particular opened up a tradition of social thought in which the state (as it is still widely referred to: in fact there is not one state but many, in a 'state system') is seen as dependent on society. The sequence of mode of production, class formation and class struggle was thought of as explaining the forms of state power which developed. The state was seen as an institution of coercion within society, responding to the rising social violence between classes and establishing a framework within which class domination might be exercised.

The sociology of war has necessarily revised this view of the state, which was dominant in the early revival of state theory in the late 1960s and early 1970s. At the very least it has reinstated the dimension of external coercion as a defining characteristic, and in most cases writers have gone further to suggest a dynamic role for inter-state conflict in the determination of social and political relations within societies. This revision has come from other sources too, but the development of a historical sociology of war has certainly reinforced the case for a different view of the state. Evidence of a 'revisionist' view will be found directly or indirectly in many of these chapters, notably those of Mann, Hall, Mitchell and Russell, Ehrlich, Shaw and Mattausch. Giddens's work (1985), which appeared after this book was prepared, is in many ways the fullest statement of this view, although its argument would not necessarily be accepted on all issues by the present writers.

The concern to emphasise the significance of external violence has tended to overshadow, amongst sociologists, the study of another category of wars, fought either for control of or secession from the state, namely, civil wars. Such wars occupy an important place in the analysis of social change, representing crucial moments in the historical development of many states and societies. They also remind us of the need to retain some hold, in our treatment of war, upon divisions of class, race, religion, region, tribe and nation. The chapter by Mitchell and Russell analyses the development of the South African state as a response to internal as well as external conflict.

There is, indeed, a case for saying that the historical sociology of war, on the evidence of these chapters, is really a new form of the sociology of the state. Many contributions are concerned with the implications of changing forms of warfare for the state (and beyond that, economy and society) rather than the changing forms of warfare *per se*. But this tendency is generally a matter of emphasis, reflecting the direction from which a lot of the new sociological work on warfare has come, and the wider milieu to which its arguments must be relevant. Historical sociologists of war are still, partially, at the stage of assimilating the work of social and military historians rather than of independent analyses of warfare.

Within these limitations, however, some important problems have been demarcated. One is the issue of the historical relationship of warfare to capitalism. The influence of state theory has actually been very important here, enabling us to resist the temptation to postulate direct causal links from capitalism to warfare. If Marxist ideas have an influence, it is a position such as Kaldor's (1982), which suggests a Clausewitzian analogy between 'mode of warfare' and 'mode of production' rather than a causal relation. Moreover, there is a good deal of interest in reversing what would seem to be the conventional Marxist terms of debate. The concern is often to investigate the implications of the mode of warfare for the development of capitalism (and state socialism) rather than vice versa. Hall's chapter takes a broad comparative look at one aspect of this issue, putting forward some radical proposals on the theme of 'warfare and the rise of capitalism'.

A second broad issue is that of the historical forms of warfare and their relationships to social change. Sociologists, like historians, have used the concept of 'total war' to define modern warfare. There is, however, no single model of total war. Warfare has become total in the sense of tending towards a total contest of economies and societies, and at the same time in the different sense of moving towards total destructiveness (Clausewitz's ideal of 'absolute war'). The coming together of these two kinds of totalisation of war reflects the interaction of complex processes – within both the mode of warfare and the mode of production. We need to see total warfare as a rapidly changing mode, the result of extremely dynamic social, political, technological and strategic forces (Shaw, 1987).

Sociologists have so far produced little systematic work on the processes, phases and forms of total war. Three essays in this book provide different sorts of gloss, however, on the problems involved: Mann's historically-guided reflections on the relevance of the concepts of class, nation and state; Hoag's commentary on the insertion of futuristic 'Star Wars' technology in an economically divided world society, especially a Third World which is undergoing rapid military development; and Shaw's analysis of the political implications of the transition to the nuclear age.

STATE SYSTEM AND WORLD SOCIETY

Wars arise, in the modern world, from both conflicts between states and conflicts involving states and other social forces – often national groupings which aspire to statehood, but also class-based political movements which challenge the existing form of state. A sociology of war can hardly discuss the mode of warfare without making assumptions about the world order from which these wars arise. The theories of the world order which have influenced sociology most have been those which see it primarily as an economic system, in which international inequalities are produced by such processes as the functioning of the world market. There are, of course, Marxist theories of the causes of war which posit direct links between international market relations and wars. But few, perhaps even fewer Marxists, would take such theories as adequate bases for explaining most wars since the First World War (which was after all the context in which theories of imperialism were developed). We noted the resistance of sociologists of war to the attempts to reduce warfare to capitalism; part of this argument has tended to be that the international 'state system' is an important and equally irreducible level of reality. Wars do not arise directly out of socio-economic relations, but out of the relations of state and semi-state forces to each other in the state system.

Here sociologists of war might appear to find common ground with the study of international relations – in itself something of a derivative and hybrid subject. Certainly the concern with the state system is a common focus, but sociologists would tend to reject the bias of much 'international relations' towards seeing this as a discrete political, diplomatic and military arena. Sociologists would want to stress the relationships between the state system and the world economy, and also between states as actors in an international system and their economic and social basis in the national societies. Wars, after all, do not arise solely from inter-state differences but also from conflicts of politics and cultures (especially nationalisms) within states. Civil wars are the most obvious manifestation of these. National economy and class relations are also central to the ability of states (and non-state forces) to pursue wars: they both affect and are profoundly affected by wars. The study of the state system must be located in his context of world economy and society and their national segments.

Sociologists have not devoted a great deal of attention to these issues, but as Michael Mann's chapter shows at a conceptual level, the interrelations of states, nations and classes are critical to issues of war and peace today. The state system is not the most likely subject for sociological study, but without an understanding of it all sociological work on wars and their social effects will be lacking a crucial dimension. (A beginning of a sociological contribution to these issues can be found in some of the papers in Banks (1986).)

COMPARATIVE SOCIOLOGY OF MILITARISM

A more specific set of issues is that of the variable experience by national societies of the processes of total war. In virtually every country, at every point in the twentieth century, war or war-preparation has had a major significance for economy, society, politics and ideology. And yet this has differed markedly, not only between periods of actual war and those of war-preparation, or between particular wars, but also between individual societies. A major problem, then, is to identify the factors involved in varying experiences of militarism, and the relationships between them.

Here there is massive scope for comparative research, and the chapters in this book only scratch the surface of the problems, although we hope in a stimulating way. The very concept of 'militarism' tends of course to be value-loaded, and to be used in a pejorative sense to refer to societies which positively glory in war-preparation. This usage has its value, in enabling us to discriminate between different types of war-preparations (although it also opens up the possibility of rather dubious distinctions between 'their' war effort which is militaristic and 'ours' which is not). It deprives us, however, of generic terms for war-preparation (militarism) and for the increasing influence of war-preparation on society (militarisation), both of which are needed. Using these terms in the more inclusive sense need not prevent us from discriminating between contrasting types of militarism and militarisation.

To do just this is indeed the main purpose of placing alongside, in the second section of this volume, chapters about contemporary South Africa and Israel and about Britain in the Second World War and after. South Africa, as Mitchell and Russell show, is a case in which an equation between militarisation and repression is fairly easily made. In Israel, Ehrlich suggests, while many of the forms of Western democratic society exist (at least for the Jewish population), these can be seen as limited by the context of external relations and militarism. In Britain in 1939–45, in contrast, militarisation can be seen as involving an expansion of the democratic content of the state, in line with the thesis of a 'military participation ratio' key to social change. The interesting comparative questions, perhaps, are the extent to which a 'democratic' element co-exists with even the more repressive forms of militarism, and to which constraints on 'democratisation' remain within the British case. Watson considers the relationship between radical political theatre and official war policies for the arts;

Price qualifies the wartime participation thesis by showing the limitations of the changes in women's lives as a result of war work.

These chapters, taken together, suggest a wider order of questions about state and war, for future research. Are repressive (or totalitarian) states more prone to war than liberal democracies? Are capitalist states more militarist than state-socialist, or vice versa? Or does militarism have much more to do with the economic strength and geopolitical position of states than with their political system? And instead of the simple question of whether or not militarisation leads to repression, we might ask: under what circumstances does it tend mainly to reinforce authoritarian tendencies in the state, and under which other conditions is war actually associated with democratisation? Asking more complex questions invites, of course, more complex answers. The relationships between the experience of war and militarism and wider socio-political change might be seen to depend on a wide range of factors: type of war, military technology, war-mobilisation; existing economy, class structure, political system; and – not least – actual experience of war both on the battlefield and in society. This sort of comparative study should both gain direction from, and provide feedback to, the sort of general historical sociology of war suggested in the previous section.

SOCIOLOGY AND PEACE

There is, as we have already noted, a great deal more difficulty with the concept of 'peace' than with that of 'war'. Peace can be defined as absence of war; but can we ever say that war is absent in any modern society? 'Peace' since 1945 has meant the absence of a major war in the Northern hemisphere; but this has been a period of unprecedented war preparations, combined with numerous wars fought in the Third World. Not surprisingly, then, many seek a more securely based peace, but there are wide divergences in how this is to be achieved, and even on what it means. The 'peace movements' are more accurately described as nuclear disarmanent movements, since this is where most of their specific aims lie, but the broader label indicates the coalescence of nuclear disarmanent and anti-militarism with more general ideas of social change. Peace, for many, means the creation of a freer, more just, egalitarian and ecologically responsible society: it describes a larger goal.

There is some argument among sociologists as to whether we should even be concerned with peace (a new study group on war and peace was established at the 1985 BSA, but not without some opposition to this title from those who wanted to confine it to war and military organisation). Certainly, even among those sociologists who would welcome work in this field, there is little as yet written to express what the possible scope of sociology's contribution should be. Undoubtedly a sociological approach would work from a basis that lasting peace requires more than specific measures of disarmament and *détente*, necessary as these surely are. Sociologists would want to examine the cultural, ideological and political forces at work in the reproduction of modes of warfare. There have been frequent suggestions, for example, of the role of male domination in generating and reinforcing militarism – a theme of the women's peace movement. Given the broad basis (as our companion volume shows) of research on gender and violence, there is scope for more substantial work on the relationship between patriarchy and militarism (this is an obvious gap in the present book). More thorough research on the social and ideological supports for war-preparation would enable us to outline much more clearly the social changes which might assist the more narrowly focused processes of disarmament and international political change.

If sociologists have hardly addressed themselves directly to the large issues of the social conditions for peace, they have paid some attention to the social bases of the 'Peace movements'. The chapters by Mattausch and by Day and Robbins give a useful basis for an understanding of the British peace movement (it would of course be valuable to compare this with similar movements in other countries: see Kaltefleiter and Pfaltzgraff, 1985). Mattausch makes a provocative revision of sociological thinking with his argument that there is a 'state class', which provides the social support for CND. Day and Robbins come closer to the wider issue of social foundations for peace, which we have just broached, in their analysis of a local peace movement in terms of the influence of a 'new politics'. Both chapters, however, indicate that a restricted social basis is one of the fundamental problems of the British peace movement. As that movement passes from its massive successes in mobilisation in the early 1980s to the more difficult task of maintaining and extending its influence over a longer term, sociological research can identify underlying factors which influence its development.

Any agenda for a new field of study can only be provisional: but we hope that these notes, and more importantly the varied work in this book, indicate exciting possibilities which will attract more sociologists to work around the issues which have been raised. For the study of war and peace has a bearing on all the really big questions of sociology: the nature of industrial societies, both capitalist and state-socialist; the nature and functions of modern states; and the causes and directions of social conflict. Not only this, but the issue of war is the overriding problem of society today: a sociology which does not address itself to this is begging a fundamental question – the very survival of human society – upon which all other social questions depend.

Sociologists are human beings: we cannot remain indifferent to a problem which concerns all members of human society. This does not mean that sociologists must adopt one particular political stance, but that sociologists may wish to bring their expertise to bear on the practical issues, and that individuals and groups within sociology may express their views in their work. Marsland (1985), for example, has urged the view that sociology should identify more closely with national defence, with NATO and against 'the Soviet enemy'. Other sociologists working in this field might accept the need for a military defence of society, but question whether – in the nuclear age – war is still possible, or the risk of deterrence justifiable. Judgements on theoretical issues clearly affect political stances: Marsland assumes 'the inherently peaceable impulses of liberal democracy and the military-political expansionism which is inseparable from socialism' (p. 40). Others might reverse the comparison (substituting 'capitalism' for liberal democracy); while Mann, in this volume, argues that class is increasingly separable from geopolitics in the international system as a whole. On his argument, there is no simple connection, either way, between political system and military propensity.

It might be thought, of course, that all three theoretical positions actually reflect prior political commitments: that in matters such as this, sociologists are victims of their prejudices. And yet, while we all have our values which influence our formulations, these are matters on which evidence is possible. Argument should be as careful with respect to facts and the positions of others as in any other field.

The commitment of sociology as a discipline must be to clarifying the fundamental issues which face society, and to informing – with others – the choices which individuals and social groups make. There can be no sociology of peace which does not rest on a sociology of war and other forms of social violence, and which is not prepared to subject ideologies of peace and peace movements to critical examination. Equally, however, there can be no sociology of war which does not consider the qualitative changes in warfare which have taken place in our own time, with their appalling potential for the destruction of individual lives and of human society as a whole. The avoidance of war between the superpowers, and the creation of social, political and military institutions which more permanently inhibit war, must surely be tasks which any sociologist can accept, even if there is wide disagreement on the means. In this sense, a sociology of war must entail a sociology of peace, and sociologists, as thinking human beings with special skills and knowledge, may see their work as contributing to general social awareness. This book, like the conference on which it is based, may be seen as a modest contribution along these lines, as well as marking the point at which the sociology of war and peace emerges as a real component of British sociology.

REFERENCES

Banks, M. (1986) *The State in International Relations*, Brighton: Wheatsheaf.

Giddens, A. (1985) *The Nation-State and Violence*, Volume 2, of *A Contemporary Critique of Historical Materialism*, Cambridge: Polity.

Glasgow University Media Group (1985) *War and Peace News*, Milton Keynes: Open University Press.

Harries-Jenkins, G. and Moscos, C. (1981) 'Armed Forces and Society', *Current Sociology*, vol. 29, no. 3, Winter.

Kaldor, M. (1982) 'Warfare and Capitalism', in E. P. Thompson *et al.*, *Exterminism and Cold War*, London: Verso.

Kaltefleiter, W. and Pfaltzgraff, H. (1985) *The Peace Movements in Europe and the United States*, London: Croom Helm.

Marsland, D. (1985) *Neglect and Betrayal: War and Violence in Modern Sociology*, London: Institute for European Defence and Strategic Studies.

Shaw, M. (1987) *Dialectics of Total War: An Essay on the Social Theory of War and Peace*, London: Pluto.

Part I
The Sociology of War

1 Violence, Peace and War in 'Early' Human Society: The Case of the Eskimo

David Riches

This chapter is offered as a contribution of social anthropology to grasping certain matters about peace and war which preoccupy members of my own (middle-class urban) society. Since what follows addresses the interests of ordinary people, it is their definition of war which is present as background to the discussion. War is understood as 'the authorised employment of physical force against other persons, as a means by which groups competing for control of public resources and benefits attempt to influence the outcome of the competition in their favour'. This definition evidently leaves as unspecified the identity and boundaries of the groups concerned, but implies that their structure is corporate.[1]

The interests of ordinary people which are approached in what follows revolve around the question as to whether or not there are societies for whom the experience of war is absent. The study of supposedly peaceful societies, it might reasonably be suggested, may offer insights into a manner of conducting social relations from which 'our' society may benefit. Social anthropologists are asked this sort of question because they are known to engage in 'comparative sociology', by which is meant the cross-cultural study of human social systems. They are also asked because they are known to specialise particularly in the study of societies whose social structures and technologies are 'simple', the analysis of which may therefore be expected to offer insights into whether or not there is something intrinsically 'warlike' or 'peaceful' in the human social condition.

The popular view about peace and war in such simple societies is contradictory. On the one hand, there is the well-known case of the Yanomamö, the so-called fierce people, rudimentary agriculturalists and hunters of the Brazilian–Venezuelan border, among whom combat between groups is at such a level that 24 per cent of adult males meet death by violent means (Chagnon, 1977). On the other hand, there are the pre-Neolithic peoples such as the Eskimo of the North American Arctic, the Pygmies of central Africa, and the Bushman of the Kalahari, who are familiarly known as 'harmless people' (Marshall Thomas, 1969) since they (so it is believed) eschew violence of all kinds. The possible scientific interest in such specialised nomadic hunting and gathering peoples as relics of a pristine Palaeolithic age, and their vulnerability in a rapidly changing world, has meant that their way of life has been protected against depredations in some countries; this happened, for example, with the Eskimo in eighteenth- and nineteenth-century Greenland, and with certain pygmoid peoples (as well as the recently 'discovered' Tasaday) in the historical Philippines (Jenness, 1967; Rosaldo, 1982). But such protection has hardly been won everywhere. The alcohol-related violence with which the present-day Eskimo or Australian Aborigine is associated, and the way in which Bushmen in Namibia have been brutalised by their military employment as 'trackers' by the South African security forces (Lee and Hurlich, 1982), would appear to contrast poignantly with these peoples' supposedly peaceful past.

Where analysis is concerned, the employment of terms like peace, war and violence is fraught with difficulty. Peace, for example, is a state of affairs which is objectively almost impossible to define, except as the absence of something (i.e. war, violence). Violence commonsensically refers to the rendering of physical hurt, yet physical force wielded against people by arms of government is often spoken of as social control, or the maintenance of order (cf. Radcliffe-Brown, 1940, p. xiv). Evidently, all these terms have strong ideological connotations (cf. Riches, 1986). Certainly, where the traditional[2] Eskimo is concerned (to take an example of a society which has been mentioned), the peacefulness which supposedly prevailed is normally assessed not in terms of the absence of war, but in terms of the absence of violence: physical force between people is popularly believed to have occurred neither within nor between social groups. A central aim of this chapter is dispassionately to review the data from one society in which war is reputed to be absent, and the method by which this is achieved is indeed through examining and explaining all customary social interaction in this society which might, in the commonsense terms cited above, be labelled as violent.[3] It is concluded that while – against the popular view – one would be exercised to call this a peaceful society, the criteria for war are not met through the data considered. What is quite clear is that the social structure of the society concerned is a major factor underlying this absence of war. The chosen society is the Canadian Eskimo. The present writer conducted fieldwork in the Canadian Arctic in the early 1970s, but this chapter draws only to a small extent on this research. The focus here is instead put on the condition of Eskimo society at the time of contact with Europeans, for which there is abundant information in the anthropological literature;[4] such contact effectively occurred around sixty years ago over much of the Canadian Arctic.

But there is another aim in this chapter. Implicit in what follows is a debate between social anthropologist and ethologist about analytic approaches to war and violence. Commentators (such as the present writer) who tackle problems about war and violence in human societies from the perspective of mainstream social anthropology find the field aggressively preempted by advocates of a biological basis of human social behaviour (e.g. Lorenz, 1966; Eibl-Eibesfeldt, 1979; cf. Tiger and Fox, 1972). These ethologists' suggestion that a propensity for violence is imprinted at a very early stage in a child's development, or that it is underlain, in whole or part, by innate mechanisms or capacities, is, of course, a highly attractive notion to ordinary people, for whom violence appears so irrational, intractable – and inevitable. In the argument that has ensued, ethologists have undoubtedly been victims of unfair criticism from social anthropologists: eager to emphasise the culturally-specific and purposive nature of violence, social anthropologists have often crudely represented the ethological position as 'instinct-reductionist', when it is clear that *both* learning and heredity are incorporated in ethological models (Eibl-Eibesfeldt, 1979, p. 14; cf. Montagu, 1968). All the same, the unfortunate outcome for social anthropologists is that they have come to debate the issue on the ethologists' terms. Much may still be worrying about ethological procedure – for example, the way in which complex cultural elaborations are researched through focus on such evidence as tendencies in human infancy, the behaviours of the both deaf and blind, and the performances of people in conditions of artificial experiment, and the way, too, in which superficial parallels between human cultural practice and animal behaviour lead rapidly to the conclusion that aspects of the former have at least innate components.[5] However, the recommendation here is that, sidestepping these worries, social anthropologists should relentlessly and exhaustively pursue a distinctively sociological approach to violent practice in human society; the ball will then be in the dissenting ethologists' court: it will be their turn to identify the shortcomings in the analysis.

In the battle between social anthropology and ethology, social anthropology's strength may well come from the stressing of the *meaning* that is intrinsic to all human social life: what distinguishes human social actions and representations is that they have a conscious, purposive and knowledgeful basis. Committed to drawing both homologies and analogies between human and animal behaviour, ethologists are obliged to reject an explanatory focus on meaning. Eibl-Eibesfedt explicitly remarks that '. . . we do not know to what extent animals are guided by conscious purposes' (1979, p. 30). Confined to the objectively observable, this latter writer elects to focus on the social patterns which *result* from violent action – and thereby entrusts himself to functional explanations, with all the perils these entail (Hempel, 1959).

In the controversies about war and violence in human societies, the importance of the focus on meaning is significantly evident in the muddled reasoning of those – both ethologist and non-ethologist – who neglect it. Nowhere is this more plain than in some of the recent discussions on the supposedly peaceful societies. A review of some of the problematics that have arisen looks forward to the Eskimo analysis which follows shortly. Two matters will be considered here. First, there is the question as to what is really meant (if anything) by the statement that some societies are 'peaceful'. Second, there is the question of the relevance (or otherwise) of certain tendencies in the social and emotional training of young children in these societies.

The first point effectively considers whether or not the characterisation of societies by ordinary people as 'peaceful' or 'warlike' can foster analytical – as opposed to broadly descriptive – purposes. The difficulties evident when understanding is directed through the employment of such categories as 'peaceful society' suggest that it cannot so serve (cf. Heelas, 1982). Thus, a close examination of 'peaceful societies' quickly reveals that recorded incidents of violence are by no means absent. Discussion is then forced to consider such sterile concerns as how infrequent these incidents have to be for the characterisation of the society as peaceful to hold. This state of affairs has recently been reached by anthropologists working on Bushman society. For example, seeking to counter Marshall Thomas's stereotyping of the Bushmen as 'harmless people', Lee has calculated that the level of homicide in this society is well above the domestic level that obtains in the United States (1979, p. 398). But he then maintains that, statistics notwithstanding, the Bushmen may be regarded at least as *relatively* peaceful, for the United States figures do not include the massive number of deaths resulting in war (e.g. from the war in Vietnam), and the Bushman are without the state control structures and medical facilities which in the industrial world substantially dampen down the levels of physical assault and considerably reduce the numbers of such assaults which turn into deaths.

Consonant with the question of the peacefulness of certain societies is the impressive body of documentation which has emerged in recent years on the affectual training of children in these societies (the Bushman included[6]). The contributions of Turnbull on Zairean Pygmies (1978) and Briggs on the Canadian Eskimo (1970; 1975) are the most impressive here. For example, Briggs gives a detailed account of how Eskimos are brought up to repress the outward expression of anger. It is when writers suggest that a generally peaceable social existence in adult life results from such practices that controversy arises. Such is evidently the position of the editor of a useful collection of papers, who hints strongly that if we were all raised like Eskimos the world would be a less violent and warlike place (Montagu, 1978, pp. 6–9). That there is a serious problem with such an assertion is immediately revealed in the astute riposte of one of the contributors to the collection, who provides a discussion on the Semai, a tribal minority in peninsular Malaysia. He reveals that while it may be that Semai children are trained to be non-aggressive, one can certainly expect Semai adults to be extremely violent if threatened by 'outsider' Malays and with little chance to withdraw (Dentan, 1978, p. 95).

Asking whether societies are 'peaceful', or enquiring into the emotional training of children, will not reveal very much about the *meaning* of violent social acts in human society because, in both instances, the focus is on inappropriate units of analysis. To discern the meaning of social acts, analysis must ultimately rest on the purpose of such acts, and this, in turn, requires a *context of the social relation* which articulates the link between the actor and the person to whom the act is directed. Not to specify a structure of social relations is likely to render the understanding of violence and war in human society impossible. Thus to speak of *societies* as 'peaceful' is analytically not helpful, since, as highly abstract categories, 'societies' do not act purposively. In much the same way, a focus on general emotional training may be expected to promise rather little as regards subsequent social interactions in adult life; *per se*, the training in appropriate emotional controls appears not to incorporate in any prominent fashion the fact that in adult life, different behaviour, with different emotional loads, is appropriate to different people – varying according to the category of social relation in which these people are incumbent. One is forced to conclude (by default) that the specific social relations on behalf of which Eskimo children are trained to repress anger are those in which socialiser and socialisee will be incumbent when both are adults, namely some sort of close kinship relation. But this will not reveal whether Eskimo adults are prepared to entertain violence *vis-à-vis* distant kin or non-kin. Germane to this is Eibl-Eibesfeldt's pertinent comment about the extreme pacificism of the recently-discovered Tasaday of the Philippines. The discouragement of aggression and violence in Tasaday culture cannot be unconnected to the fact that, numbering only twenty-five individuals, this 'society' effectively amounts to a close knit (kinship) group (1979, p. 162).

Before considering the social acts of the traditional Canadian Eskimo which might qualify as violence, a review of the social structure of Eskimo society would seem to be appropriate. This review draws on an enormous literature, and more especially on the analysis of this literature in Riches (1982).

Traditional Canadian Eskimo social structure was politically non-centralised and highly flexible. Institutions of government were not present, and the organisation of leadership was marked by its fluidity: people were incumbent in leadership positions (*isumataaq*) only in so far as their fellows were prepared to acquiesce in the decisions they made in some field of activity (normally, hunting) in which they excelled. In this context, the Eskimo nuclear family had considerable autonomy. For economic purposes, this unit was obliged to ally with several others in groups of up to one hundred people, but the choice of precisely with which others was wide, with the result that, as the seasons and years passed, a given family could change several times the group with which it was associated on the nomadic round. In the context of the nuclear family, there was a marked asymmetry in gender roles. In political and public life, the man represented the family and the woman played no formal part. Where the woman exercised informal influence over her husband's political decisions, this was achieved within the (private) confines of the family household.

In the traditional Eskimo society, three basic categories of social relationship were important. The most significant of these was the kinship relationship. An Eskimo would normally have a large network of kin, by virtue of the fact that kin up to the collateral range of second or third cousin on both father's and mother's sides were reckoned socially; for a married Eskimo, the spouse's kin were also of importance. What was 'important' about Eskimo kinship was the social obligation of rendering mutual support, assistance and protection, especially as regards sharing the food from the hunt. Eskimos dissatisfied with their kinsfolks' performance in this respect might be able to separate from them and join another group, but the sparsity of population could mean that this would entail a long journey, and this was not always feasible. Against this, the absence of formal procedures of social control – gentle ridicule was the main method by which miscreants might be brought into line – meant that kin were highly constrained to engage in reticent and emotionally-controlled behaviour (see above). 'Strangership' was the obverse of the kinship relationship. With strangership, the norms of support, sharing and emotional control did not apply. Finally, there was a relationship intermediate between kinship and strangership. This was the so-called 'ancillary relationship' (Guemple, 1972), of which there were several sub-varieties – the spouse–exchange relationship is the best known of these. Ancillary relationships were, in effect, honorary kinship relationships; they would typically be negotiated by strangers who wished to subscribe to norms of support and assistance; for example, the husband of a destitute family arriving at a camp in which there were no kin might establish a spouse–exchange relationship with one of the camp members, providing he was first able to convince his host-to-be of his good intentions.

For the purpose of this chapter, the spatial distribution of people incumbent in these social categories is important, and most especially as regards the kinship relationship. The most salient constraint in this respect was the very low population densities across the Arctic, and the fact that the rudimentary sledge technology meant that overland travel was effectively 'on foot'. Spatially this meant that the overwhelming bulk of a person's kin lived within a fairly restricted area of territory, since marriage – from which the kinship relationship is generated – was invariably contracted among people who lived within a reasonable distance of one another

(Damas, 1975). More than this, the repeated marriages which ensued within a given territorial area meant that few people within this area could not claim either a direct kinship relationship, or else a kinship connection with a common intermediary. The obverse of this was, of course, that strangers – people not formally connected by kinship – mainly lived outside one another's normal territorial range; people did not encounter strangers very often.

In what follows, all activities in traditional Eskimo life which to the Western mind could possibly qualify as violence are considered and explained. Close attention will be paid to the meaning intrinsic to the social acts concerned, especially as regards the purpose, or goal, for which they are consciously performed.

(i) FEMALE INFANTICIDE

As among very many hunting and gathering societies, infanticide was prevalent in at least some sub-groups within the traditional Eskimo society; in contrast to some hunting and gathering peoples, females were invariably selected. The level of female infanticide reached its peak among the Netsilik Eskimo of the Canadian Central Arctic, where around one-in-five new-born female children would be killed, by exposure. The explanation of Eskimo female infanticide is a matter of some controversy (Riches, 1982, pp. 60–1). The tempting suggestion is to relate its practice to dire environmental pressures, and to argue that girls, because they do not procure food in the hunt, are especially expendable when there is too little food to go around. However, it is by no means clear that, *for the Eskimo*, making a living in the Arctic was particularly precarious. Moreover, to cite the respective Eskimo gender roles to account for female infanticide is contradictory in its own terms: women had *indispensible* roles to perform within the domestic domain, by way of fabricating clothing, preparing food and bringing up children. Far more likely, female infanticide relates to something positive about the woman's capabilities, specifically her unique ability to bear children. In this regard, it is crucial to note that it was not the family which brought up the girl child that benefited from her reproductive and domestic services; rather, it was the family into which she married. And to be noted here is that this latter family was likely to be related by kinship either tenuously, or not at all, to the girl's natal family, since in most Eskimo sub-groups, marriage rules required people to select their spouses from outside the collateral range of second cousin. A more promising suggestion about female infanticide is that it is a strategy by which people in distantly related groups (who might have married the female child who was killed) may be denied reproductive potential, and therefore the full chance to maximise their population levels: to practise female infanticide may be a means by which the girl's natal group restricts the number of females available in marriage to other groups, with whom it is in competition for economic resources.[7]

(ii) EXECUTION

The most striking act of physical hurt which Eskimos customarily practised in pre-contact society was the formal execution. When this occurred, executor and executed were invariably related very closely by kinship. Execution was an exceptional measure of social control. Ridicule and shaming, or failing these, ostracism, were the main positive measures of drawing miscreants 'into line', if simply moving away from them was inexpedient. But people who showed themselves to be immune from such subtle pressures, and whose behaviour was sufficiently unacceptable as to constitute a danger to the group, might be liable for physical elimination. Religious practitioners, who abused their spiritual powers, and who imposed excessive sexual or economic demands on the lay populace in return for ritual services, were especially liable to this most extreme of sanctions. A close kinsman of the perpetrator would be detailed to exercise the execution, for good reason. Homicide – it was by no means unknown in Eskimo society – required that the victim's kin exercise vengeance (see below). Thus, where close kin were responsible for the death, the question of vengeance could not arise.

(iii) VENGEANCE AND PRE-EMPTIVE HOMICIDE

Between distant kin and stranger Eskimos, acts of violence very commonly related to the abduction, or the fear of abduction, of women. The absence of a firm kinship relationship between, in this instance, a woman's husband and her abductor, meant that norms of consideration and respect did not have to be upheld between the men concerned. The vital importance of a wife to perform domestic services provided the most usual motive for abduction. Men prepared to entertain such a dangerous course of action – which might involve journeying to distant parts where the local residents would be strangers – were typically those who had lost their spouses through death or divorce. Vengeance killing in connection with the abduction of women typically arose when – as usually happened – the woman's husband was killed or seriously injured when the abduction took place. The expectation was that the murdered man's kin would exercise like treatment *vis-à-vis* the abductor or his kin, though it is clear that this duty was quite often neglected. At any rate, the consequence of these norms and strategies was that, should a stranger Eskimo wander into a camp, for whatever reason, he might well be set upon and killed by the residents, who suspected his intentions, fearing that to abduct a woman was his plan. Burch (1975, p. 25) describes this happening when a hunter got marooned on an ice floe and was carried by wind and tide into distant parts. The potential for violence in the relationship between stranger Eskimos is confirmed in instances when it was accepted, unlike in this last case, that the interloper's intentions were peaceful and that he was genuinely in need of assistance. Before admittance to the camp, a ritual would be performed between host and newcomer, dramatising the suspicions which lay just beneath the surface: violence would be metaphorically enacted in the ritual, which might take the form of a boxing bout.

(iv) ESKIMO–INDIAN AND ESKIMO–EUROPEAN RELATIONS

At the time of the first contact with Europeans, the Eskimos' relations with both the Indians and with the Europeans themselves, were characterised by occasional outbreaks of violence in which killing was quite often the result. As one might expect of ethnic groups located in adjacent geographic regions, both mutual suspicion and sporadic trading marked the relations between Eskimos, who in Canada lived in Arctic (tundra) regions, and the Indians of the northern coniferous forests (e.g. Taylor, 1979). For the extreme southern part of the Arctic, the eighteenth- and nineteenth-century journals of the earliest European explorers report many killings, most usually involving the Indians as aggressors and the Eskimos as victims. As to why the Indians were typically the aggressors is a puzzle, since the social structure of the traditional Indian society in these parts is generally agreed to have been much the same as that of the Eskimo. The plausible suggestion, put by Leacock (1981, p. 169), is that Indian attacks – both on other Indian groups and on Eskimos – were reported at a time when Indian society had already been transformed and 'brutalised' as a result of dealings with Europeans (mainly traders and explorers) with whom they had been in contact for some time. Where Eskimos are reported killing Indians, the purpose would appear to be revenge for past Indian atrocities. This is supported by events on the Labrador coast (eastern Canadian seaboard) in the eighteenth century, where Eskimo and Indian communities were sited closer together than elsewhere, and where the Europeans' intrusion into Eskimo country – as both peasant and commercial fisherman – was more pervasive. The background to the reported incidences of Eskimos killing Indians in these parts is the Eskimos' more brutal treatment at the hands of Indians and Europeans in consort, the bows and arrows of the former proving to be of no match against the firearms of the latter (Jenness, 1965). A history of extreme suspicion and resentment no doubt lay behind the Eskimos' slaughter of the first German Moravians who attempted to establish a mission station on the coast in 1752.

The pattern of violence between Eskimos and Europeans in the high Arctic (well away from Indian country) is rather different. Here the Europeans were explorers in search of the Northwest Passage, commonly suffering from scurvy and from the general rigours of the Arctic, and, almost without exception, the victims of Eskimo attack. Graburn (1969b, pp. 77–94) gives a résumé of such attacks, and argues that the first Europeans to penetrate Eskimo territory in these parts were treated as Eskimos treat migratory game animals – as an economic resource to be opportunistically plundered. This is plausible, and is consonant with the fact that the explorers were certainly robbed of metal and other equipment adaptable to Eskimo technology. It is also consonant with the fact that when the explorers came to establish more formal trading arrangements with the indigenous population (which normally occurred in the history of European–Eskimo relations throughout the Arctic), the Eskimos assumed an entirely peaceable disposition. One speculates that economic plunder was similarly the chief aim of Indians who attacked and killed Eskimos in more southern parts, to which the mutual revenge killings between Indian and Eskimo, mentioned above, may be related.

In spite of these quite definite patterns of violence, it is not unreasonable to dub – purely for descriptive purposes – the traditional Eskimo society as a relatively peaceful one. Statistically-speaking, the sorts of incidents related above do not seem to have happened all that often. In support of this possibly startling conclusion, the salience of the social structure of Eskimo society will be re-emphasised.

In the first place, warfare in this society was absent – if the criteria for warfare advanced at the beginning of this essay be allowed. Thus, a state of affairs in which distinctively corporate groups were pitted in competition for resources did not exist. The extreme fluidity in Eskimo political structure meant that corporate groups, as orthodoxly understood, were not present, and nor, *ipso facto*, were the specific governmental authorities through which the deployment of physical hurt against others might be authorised. To be sure, a measure of cooperation was required in several of the vengeance and plunder activities of which violence was usually a part, for example in retaliatory or pre-emptive homicide and in the abduction of women (see (iii), above). But the cooperation involved was small-scale, and above all, short-lived. The groups concerned were evident only for so long as the particular incident which they were mobilised to meet remained an issue. The memberships of successive groups taking part in a number of such incidents over a period of time would never be the same.

So far as violence was concerned, both the literature and statements from informants strongly give the impression that it was relatively infrequent. Not least because of the sparsity of the population, Eskimos moved in a social world where kinship relations were pervasive and where social dealings were therefore dominated by the importance of mutual support and emotional control. Thus the chance of strangers encountering one another – at least, without the restraining presence of intermediaries who were kin to both – was small, with the likelihood that actual attempts of woman-abduction would occur, correspondingly small. One presumes that encounters with Indians or early European explorers were even more infrequent; indeed, in some parts of the Arctic they will not have occurred at all. It is clear that most other pre-Neolithic (i.e. pre-agricultural/pastoral) societies of which there are historic examples have social structures, and also patterns of violence, which are similar to those of the Eskimo – this is clearly brought out in Lee's studies of the Bushman (1979, ch. 13). The statistical impression is given that some of these societies are/were more peaceful, and others less peaceful, than the Eskimo.

However, evaluations of the presence of violence in these societies may plainly follow those given here for the Eskimo.

The salience of demographic context as a factor predisposing the *frequency* of violence, *given such simple-structured societies*, invites a striking contrast between the nomadic hunting and gathering society – the allegedly 'peaceful' society – and the frequently-cited instance of a supremely 'violent' society, the Yanomamö of the Brazilian–Venezuelan border (Chagnon, 1977). Outstandingly high levels of inter-communal violence, or threats of violence, mean that the Yanomamö local groups forge alliances – albeit highly unstable and shifting alliances – with one another, with the result that offence/defence is coordinated to an extent which might reasonably be described as war. But even so, Yanomamö and (say) Eskimo society are remarkably similar, both in terms of social structure, and also in respect of certain crucial aspects of culture. All that has been said about the politically uncentralised nature of Eskimo society, the flexibility of local grouping, the pre-eminence of kinship as a social articulator and the fluidity of leadership, apply equally to the Yanomamö – though Yanomamö leadership is more about matters of fighting than hunting. The Yanomamö also live an effectively nomadic life, for although a rudimentary agriculture is the mainstay of the economy, considerations of warfare often mean that local groups shift their region of occupation over some distance and at quite short notice, re-establishing a subsistence livelihood in a new area by bringing seedlings from the old place, by calling on the help of nearby allies, and by stressing more the hunting sector of the economy. Again like the Eskimo, major aims in intercommunal warfare (violence) are vengeance and the abduction of women – of whom female infanticide seems to ensure a shortage. But, as one would expect of a basically agricultural society, the Yanomamö population density is much greater than that which prevailed certainly among the Canadian Eskimo. And the high level of Yanomamö violence is plainly predisposed by this. It is not that population 'pressure' itself causes 'problems' which have to be resolved through violence (*pace* Divale and Harris, 1976). Rather, a high population density means that people who are related only distantly by kinship, or not all, are bound to live close by one another, and therefore the geographical logistics of woman abduction and vengeance, and the basic matter of locating one's enemies, are surmountable with rather little difficulty.

That the decision to *perform* violence in a social setting rests fundamentally on the social norms which prevail, and on the cultural values which give meaning to the goals which violence achieves, is underlined in another context, which may be mentioned very briefly. This context is that of the contemporary Canadian Arctic, where Eskimos live relatively sedentary lives in modern villages alongside quite large numbers of European-Canadians whose task it is to socialise them into the mysteries of the industrial world. Through the efforts of missionaries and administrators, none of the patterns of violence which customarily prevailed in the traditional society is in marked evidence today. Yet, as is very well-known, incidents of violence between Eskimos (though not between Eskimo and European) in these villages are at extremely high levels, and normally occur along with the consumption of alcohol. Much of the violence is between kin. The radically changed culture which underpins this evidently new type of Eskimo violence has been aptly characterised by Brody (1977), among others, as a culture of opposition – opposition to the mainstream middle-class Canadian values which the Europeans are attempting to inculcate in the Arctic communities. In this way, as the Europeans deplore the association between alcohol and violence, so the Eskimos, visibly, celebrate it. The corporate character of the Eskimo communities in the modern villages means, indeed, that the Eskimos' violence could be described as 'symbolic warfare'.

Some important comments about a distinctively sociological approach to peace and war in human society (especially early pre-capitalist society) may be drawn from the Eskimo data and discussion. A consideration of two points has, as implicit background, the rival views of the ethologists.

The first point considers the nature of violence in human society, and addresses the question of the possibility of a peaceful social condition. A sociological analysis of the Eskimo material reveals, quite clearly, that distinct, identifiable purposes relating to the course of social interaction are strategically achieved through the practice of violence. The cases from the traditional Eskimo society exemplify the realisation of such purposes through the instrumental use of violence; but this is not to say that, in other societies and settings, important purposes will not be achieved through the deployment of violence as an expressive force – this is hinted at in the brief mention of Eskimo violence in the contemporary scene. The sociological analysis also indicates that the practice of violence usually has a normative aspect: no doubt the recipient in a particular incident, and some witnesses, will consider it quite unwarranted, but through an appeal to some social value the perpetrator will be certain to make the case that it is entirely legitimate. A fundamental, or 'deep' purpose in the practice of violence – which is quite possibly universal in all instances – may indeed be revealed when focus is put on the perpetrator's appeal for legitimacy. This is a matter which has been explored in some detail elsewhere (Riches, 1986), where the suggestion is made that this deep purpose relates precisely to perpetrator's position of having to negate the objections which the recipients and witnesses of the violence will probably raise. In this respect, the right of punitive or pre-emptive retaliation will likely be invoked as the basis for violence's legitimacy: the deep purpose connotes the fact that some aspect of the social performance of the person to whom violence is imparted *has* to be halted; and that the rendering of physical harm is the only available means to achieve this end. At this juncture, a conclusion may be entered. This is that the strategic competence of violence is such that an entirely peaceful condition may not be expected in any social setting. But that to approach explanatorily this universal condition of 'non-peace' does not require an appeal to unconscious or biological dispositions in the human being: an appeal to conscious purpose is entirely sufficient.

A second, distinctively sociological comment about peace and war focuses on aspects of the dynamics of inter-personal and inter-group relations. Of considerable practical and theoretical importance for the understanding of instances where physical hurt is being imparted and received, the concern is with the body of knowledge held by the perpetrator about the nature and character of the recipient. For purpose of debate with the ethologists, attention will be put specifically on that knowledge where the recipient is deemed not-fully-human. The epistemological status of this knowledge is at issue. Ethologists evidently treat it literally – as reflecting 'pseudospeciation' (see below). A sociological approach would likely treat it as in some sense a distortion of what the actors know things to be – as ideology, or as a 'collective representation'. To treat such knowledge in the former sense is the more readily to invite a fatalistic view of war and violence (*pace* Eibl-Eibesfeldt, 1979, pp. 79, 165). To treat it in the latter sense is to allow that inter-personal or inter-group relations where physical hurt is involved may be radically rethought: ideology may be powerful, but it is not immutable.

The Eskimo material may be brought to be bear on this issue, since in two of the cited types of Eskimo violence, the notion that the recipient is not-fully-human is invoked. Where infanticide is concerned, Eskimo dogma holds that the child's death is not that of a properly formed human person. Infanticide is normally imparted within the first few days of a child's life, before the child has received a name. In Eskimo cosmology, the receiving of the name is what makes a child a full human being; with naming, the physical body of the child receives a special spiritual force, which stems from the recently-deceased ancestor after whom the child is named. In the case of violence towards Indians and Europeans, the victims are similarly held not to be human. In common with most tribal people, Eskimo dogma regards Eskimos – and only Eskimos – as real persons (*Inuit*, the name by which Eskimos refer to themselves, means 'genuine people').

The contrast between ethological and sociological approaches here, impinges on the crucial question as to whether knowledge that *alter* is not-fully-human enters directly into relevant perceptions as physical hurt is actually perpetrated, or whether it comprises a set of beliefs brought to bear prior to, or after – but independently of – the event, as a means to justify, rationalise, or impart a moral rectitude to it.

The view that such knowledge constitutes a pseudospeciation is representative of the former position. As a cultural norm, pseudospeciation is described by analogy with the formation of distinct species in the animal world: just as species adapt to different niches, cultures are seen as marking themselves off from each other in much the same way (Eibl-Eibesfeldt, 1979, p. 122). Indeed, in the opinion of most ethologists, aspects of this cultural norm themselves have distinct biological roots – as stemming from an innate rejection of strangers (1979, p. 122).

To treat such knowledge as ideology is, in contrast, to suppose that it constitutes just one, among possibly several, bodies of knowledge which perpetrators of physical hurt hold about their victims. Thus, other knowledge, which seems formally to contradict the perception of the 'other' as not-fully-human, is evident in the perpetrator's total stock of knowledge. For example, during the course of combat the soldier normally sees his opposite number as equally tactically astute and technically skilful as himself – which is hardly the epitome of animality. Whilst it is tempting to regard such contradictory views as governed by the experience of qualitatively different situations, a more persuasive approach is to assert that they reflect evaluations of the same situation for different purposes. As the predicament in a given situation is actually being met, so one body of knowledge is relevant – that the opponent is fully human. When the situation is cogitated about later, and the aggressor confronts the moral question as to how physical hurt, or death, could have been perpetrated, so another body of knowledge is relevant – that the opponent was not-fully-human. Given its social function, 'ideology' is a fair description of this latter type of knowledge (cf. Riches, 1985).

The ideological nature of the Eskimo view that infanticided children are not-fully-human, or that Indians and Europeans might be similarly regarded, is supported in the existence of other knowledge which seems formally to contradict this view. It is clear, for example, that Eskimo mothers would suffer considerable emotional trauma, as they were compelled, often by third-generation family members, to abandon their children. And the many instances when Eskimos and Indians, and Eskimos and early Europeans, eagerly engaged in trade, and (on fewer occasions) intermarried, suggest the existence of a view that the non-Eskimo might have human qualities after all!

A final point remains, and it addresses the important question of the developmental relation between violence and war. This question arises partly from the definition of war offered in the chapter. Whilst reasons have been given for this definition, it remains a fairly arbitrary one: thus, were other definitions employed, much of the Eskimos' 'vengeance' violence might be labelled warfare, without stretching credulity. Something similar may, of course, be said, of the definition of violence. Many would regard a notion of violence as 'the perpetration of physical hurt' as excessively narrow. Others would prefer to absorb such violence into a more inclusive category of 'aggression', which would also comprise behaviour ranging from ritualised threats of violence, to such ostensibly non-violent practices as boundary marking. This is not the place to comment on such definitions, except to remark that, as with all definitions, each rests on particular philosophical premises about the nature of society and social explanation that by no means all writers will share.

The merit of the definitions which guide the discussion in this chapter is that they at least allow the popularly worrying question as to the circumstances under which certain behaviours, where bodily harm is occasionally rendered, become transformed into the large scale, more persistent and more thoroughly organised forms of giving hurt, which are generally known as warfare. The contrast, mentioned earlier, between those hunting and gathering peoples, such as the Eskimo, among whom warfare is absent, and the Yanomamö, where it is virulent, hinted strongly that increased population pressure is a crucial factor in precipitating the emergence of warfare in this way, a point with which many commentators concur (e.g. Tiger and Fox,

1972, p. 224). It is therefore well to re-emphasise here a central theme of this chapter, which is that the crucially contingent factor in this regard is the prevailing culture and structure of social relations. The effect (or otherwise) of population pressure on levels of violence, and on the development of war, must be mediated by the presence of issues to fight about, and by social norms which serve either to limit, or else to facilitate the organisation of, the fighting.

NOTES

1. Other considerations of warfare in the social anthropological literature, grounded in purposes different from those addressed in this chapter, are notably offered by Hallpike (1973), Divale and Harris (1976) and Vayda (1976).
2. 'Traditional' is the anthropologist's handy word to refer to the state of a society before, or at the time of, contact with European Colonialists.
3. The complex sociological discussions about possible broader meanings of violence cannot be tackled in this chapter.
4. Graburn (1969a) is useful background reading.
5. For an excellent critique of this latter procedure, see Fortes (1983).
6. See Draper (1978).
7. Riches (1974) presents a more refined version of this argument, with reference to one particular Eskimo sub-group.

REFERENCES

Briggs, J. (1970) *Never in Anger: portrait of an Eskimo family*, Cambridge, Mass.: Harvard University Press.

Briggs, J. (1975) 'The Origins of Non-Violence: Aggression in two Canadian Eskimo Groups', in W. Muensterberger and A. H. Esman (eds), *The Psychoanalytic Study of Society*, New York: International Universities Press, pp. 134–203.

Brody, H. (1977) 'Alcohol, Change and the Industrial Frontier', *Inuit Studies*, vol. 1, pp. 31–46.

Burch, E. S. (1975) *Eskimo Kinsmen: Changing Family Relationships in Northwest Alaska*, St Paul: West Publishing Co.

Chagnon, N. (1977) *The Yanomamö: the Fierce People*, 2nd edn, New York: Holt, Rinehart & Winston.

Damas, D. (1975) 'Demographic Aspects of Central Eskimo Marriage Practices', *American Ethnologist*, vol. 2, pp. 410–18.

Dentan, R. K. (1978) 'Notes on Childhood in a Non-violent Context: the Semai Case', in A. Montagu (ed.), *Learning Non-aggression*, New York: Oxford University Press, pp. 94–143.

Divale, W. and Harris, M. (1976) 'Population, Warfare, and the Male Supremacist Complex', *American Anthropologist*, vol. 78, pp. 521–38.

Draper, P. (1978) 'The Learning Environment for Aggression – Anti-social Behaviour among the !Kung', in A. Montagu (ed.), *Learning Non-aggression*, New York: Oxford University Press, pp. 31–53.
Eibl-Eibesfeldt, I. (1979) *The Biology of Peace and War*, London: Thames & Hudson.
Fortes, M. (1983) *Rules and the Emergence of Society*, London: Royal Anthropological Institute.
Graburn, N. (1969a) 'Eskimo Law in the Light of Self- and Group-Interest', *Law Society Review*, vol. 4, pp. 45–60.
Graburn, N. (1969b) *Eskimos without Igloos*, Boston: Little, Brown.
Guemple, L. (1972) 'Eskimo Band Organisation and the "DP" Camp Hypothesis', *Arctic Anthropology*, vol. 9, pp. 80–112.
Hallpike, C. (1973) 'Functionalist Interpretations of Primitive Warfare', *Man*, vol. 8, pp. 451–70.
Heelas, P. (1982) 'Anthropology, Violence and Catharsis', in P. Marsh and A. Campbell (eds), *Aggression and Violence*, Oxford: Blackwell.
Hempel, C. (1959) 'The Logic of Functional Explanation', in L. Gross (ed.), *Symposium on Sociological Theory*, New York: Harper & Row.
Jenness, D. (1965) *Eskimo Administration: Labrador*, Montreal: Arctic Institute of North America.
Jenness, D. (1967) *Eskimo Administration: Greenland*, Montreal: Arctic Institute of North America.
Leacock, E. (1981) *Myths of Male Dominance*, New York: Monthly Review Press.
Lee, R. (1979) *The !Kung San: Men, Women and Work in a Foraging Society*, Cambridge: University Press.
Lee, R. and Hurlich, S. (1982) 'From Foragers to Fighters: South Africa's Militarization of the Namibian San', in E. Leacock and R. Lee (eds), *Politics and History in Band Societies*, Cambridge: University Press, pp. 327–45.
Lorenz, C. (1966) *On Aggression*, London: Methuen.
Marshall Thomas, E. (1969) *The Harmless People*, original 1959, Harmondsworth: Penguin.
Montagu, A. (ed) (1968) *Man and Aggression*, New York: Oxford University Press.
Montagu, A. (ed.) (1978) *Learning Non-aggression*, New York: Oxford University Press.
Radcliffe-Brown, A. (1940) 'Preface', in M. Fortes and E. Evans-Pritchard (eds), *African Political Systems*, London: Oxford University Press, pp. xi–xxiii.
Riches, D. (1974) 'The Netsilik Eskimo: a Special Case of Selective Female Infanticide', *Ethnology*, vol. 13, pp. 351–61.
Riches, D. (1982) *Northern Nomadic Hunter-gatherers*, London: Academic.
Riches, D. (1985) 'Power as a Representational Model', in R. Fardon (ed.), *Power and Knowledge*, Edinburgh: Scottish Academic Press.
Riches, D. (ed.) (1986) *The Anthropology of Violence*, Oxford: Blackwell.
Rosaldo, R. (1982) 'Utter Savages of Scientific Value', in E. Leacock and R. Lee (eds), *Politics and History in Band Societies*, Cambridge: University Press, pp. 309–325.

Taylor, J. G. (1979) 'Indian-Inuit Relations in Eastern Labrador', *Arctic Anthropology*, vol. 16, pp. 49–58.
Tiger, L. and Fox, R. (1972) *The Imperial Animal*, London: Secker & Warburg.
Turnbull, C. (1978) 'The Politics of Non-aggression', in A. Montagu (ed.), *Learning Non-aggression*, New York: Oxford University Press, pp. 161–220.
Vayda, A. (1976) *War in Ecological Perspective*, New York: Plenum Press.

2 War and the Rise of the West

John A. Hall

The argument to be made can be highlighted immediately by recalling that John Nef's *War and Human Progress* (1950) argues the strong thesis that war is inimical to human progress. I contest this by saying that war has sometimes played a positive role in human progress. Phrasing the matter in this way perhaps gives too many hostages to fortune. To avoid the discussion of red herrings, let me be specific about my argument: war in Western European history played a significant role in the triumph of capitalism. I begin by analysing the role of warfare in Imperial China, India and in Islam of the arid zone; in these civilisations war did not help capitalist development. In contrast, war played a vital part in allowing and enabling the emergence of an autonomous economic dynamic of broadly capitalist hue in the Occident.

To explain this I shall be most interested in the types of state that wage war. The emphasis on 'states' is deliberate since no single theory of 'the state' in history makes sense, as will become apparent as the result of distinctions that will be made in the course of this chapter (cf. Hall, 1985a; Hall, 1986).

THE CAPSTONE STATE OF IMPERIAL CHINA

How is it possible to integrate large areas in pre-industrial conditions? The economy can only integrate a small area. This is necessarily so in the agrarian age, given that an ox pulling a cart of grain would have eaten its load within a hundred miles. In contrast, military means are capable of integrating a much larger area. Certainly, the Chinese empire was created by the military, and the limit of that empire was marked by the Great Wall. Now there is a standard Marxist answer to this granting of independent autonomy to military/political factors in history, namely that soldiers are inherently parasitic on the producers of wealth. There are two obvious objections to this rather easy formulation. First, an empire could be created cost-free since booty was capable of financing much military expansion. Secondly, the peace brought by imperial rule was not entirely exploitative; a lessening of warfare and banditry combined with the diffusion of knowledge and coinage typically makes for greater productivity within empires than without (Mann, 1977). Nevertheless, neither of these objections is sufficient to hide the great merit of the Marxist question. Empires are not just created by the sword; if they wish to survive then they must also *continue* to possess military might. How was it possible to raise sufficient revenues to maintain the army over time? Some part of the answer lies in the increasing productivity of agriculture within imperial boundaries, but fundamentally it is necessary to confront the question as to the relationship between state and society.

Pre-industrial empires confront a problem when trying to extract taxation. Typically, they do not themselves possess large enough bureaucracies to administer taxation, and are thus forced to do so via local notables. The weakness of the Chinese state can be shown by considering the mandarinate. Quite simply there were never enough mandarins to make 'total control' a possibility (Huang, 1974, ch. 1). The weakness of the state is, however, most graphically illustrated by feudalising tendencies which led to the refusal to pay tax, sometimes at crucial moments of barbarian invasion.

The argument to this point is worth summarising. Military power created progress in establishing an empire, but beyond this point there is uncertainty. On the one hand, it is possible to argue that the empire collapsed for military reasons because it was 'assassinated' from the outside by nomads ever more attracted to its wealth. On the other hand, however, there is great force to the Marxist-inspired contention that this empire collapsed for the essentially internal reason of extreme selfishness on the part of the gentry who would not allow themselves to be taxed sufficiently so as to prevent the conquest of China. In so far as there is truth to the former of these positions, the Marxist canon is dented, as it is, however, by the presence of class conflict which does not lead to social development (Hall, 1985b, ch. 2). Social progress in China did not result from internal class factors; social evolution eventually had to take place for reasons of military competition.

The Chinese empire was restored time and again. This takes us to the key question: in what ways, if any, did the imperial form have deleterious effects upon the Chinese economy? Does the imperial form, created by military means, affect economic life?

Medieval China witnessed considerable economic advance of a broadly capitalist character. Interestingly the greatest expansion took place during a period of *disunity*. This encouraged the Southern Sung to build a navy in order to man all waterways which stood between them and their Northern competitors. Political fragmentation meant that markets and cities gained some autonomy. Furthermore, the quality of coinage provided by competing states tended to improve during disunity since merchants would not return to or trust governments which manipulated the coinage excessively (Elvin, 1973, ch. 14). Disunity also encouraged evolution in military affairs. The Mongols were the first to use gunpowder, and they forced the Sung into adopting it as well. Yet once China was firmly reunited under the native Ming dynasty it proved possible for many decades to *downplay* gunpowder. The nomads to the north, even when they continued to use gunpowder, could always be defeated by sheer logistical weight – and it was best that gunpowder was controlled since it would all too easily aid in further disunification of the empire. Such policy is typical of empires:

> In other societies heavy state expenditure on war has promoted creative investment and the military has constituted a very large market for arms, supplies and ships. This also occurred in the Roman empire, in that the exaction of taxes to pay troops was a major stimulus to long distance trade. But Roman armies never faced an enemy which was significantly superior in equipment, so that this did not act as a spur to imitation or invention. Indeed, because of state power, military demands eventually restricted economic growth. In the late Empire, military supplies were demanded as taxes in kind; for a time, money traders were virtually abolished. The response to increased external pressure from barbarians was thus not invention but a tightening of the screws of state repression. (Hopkins, 1976, p. 77.)

The point being made is this: only an empire free of rivals of equal status could afford this sort of policy. In the Christian West, this policy would have spelt destruction.

It is worth recapitulating at this point. Some economic improvements, particularly the distribution of seeds and the diffusion of knowledge, were caused by imperial peace, although the military exactions of the empire when beleaguered deleteriously affected economic life. Many significant economic advances cannot be credited to the empire, however, for the banal reason that they took place during a period of disunity. But it is now time to turn to the other side of the coin, namely to the impact of the empire when unity was restored upon the Chinese economy.

How did the empire react to capitalist forces created in periods of disunity? The state limited the autonomy of cities while between 1371 and 1567 all foreign trade was banned. Nevertheless, *the* most spectacular way in which politics could affect the economy concerned the fate of the explorations undertaken by the eunuch admiral Cheng-Ho in the 1430s. These expeditions were entirely successful, and they placed China in a position in which she could have reaped the benefits that were shortly to fall to the Portuguese, Dutch and British. The character of politics in China, and in this case largely court politics, determined that none of this was to happen. The mandarins, jealous of the emergence of sources of power alternative to their own, were opposed to Cheng-Ho because he was a eunuch. Sudden nomadic pressure on the Northern frontiers allowed them to argue that resources had to be spent to meet a more immediate problem. In a centralised system, relatively minor conflicts and pressures could have major effects.

Chinese imperial government thus deserves the appellation 'capstone'. The united Chinese élite sat atop a series of separate 'societies', which it did not wish to penetrate or mobilise; perhaps the key to its behaviour was its fear that horizontal linkages it could not see would get out of control. This Chinese capstone government blocked the fully fledged emergence of intensive capitalist relationships.

This is *not* to say that the impact of the state upon capitalism must always be negative. A different type of state, the European organic state, proved capable, once capitalist relationships were established, of providing crucial services for this type of economic system. Chinese capstone government was incapable of providing equivalent services. It was not powerful enough to establish decent currency and credit arrangements. Furthermore there was no legal protection for the businessman, money was scarce, interest rates high and banking undeveloped.

PREDATORY RULE: THE HINDU CUSTODIAL STATE AND THE CYCLICAL STATE OF ISLAM

War was creative in Chinese civilisation through establishing an empire, even though the character of that political form in the end ruled out any capitalist economic dynamic. India and Islam differ from China in having cultures more extensive than the polities which they contained. This meant that the bureaucratic interference of capstone rule was eliminated. But the polities of these civilisations interfered none the less, and they did so habitually in a wholly predatory manner; they were certainly not able to provide any necessary infrastructure for capitalist advance. Warfare in such societies was largely destructive.

Classical Hindu civilisation took a long historical process to gell. Only when the imperial drive of Asoka and the soteriological challenge of Buddhism, the two being of course interrelated, were defeated did the classical synthesis of Hindu India emerge. What was striking about this civilisation was that the Brahmans withdrew from political power and organised much social life themselves through caste. They established and held together a community which was, in a certain sense, an anti-society; for this community was based upon systematically ignoring the claims to reciprocity between human beings (Karve, 1961; Hall, 1985b, ch. 3). This form of hierarchical social organisation had a great deal to do with the defeat of any autonomous economic advance (Hutton, 1963). But caste affected economic life in a second negative manner. Dumont (1957) has argued that power and authority became separated in Indian civilisation. This is not to say that the Brahman does not recognise power; to the contrary, ideological legitimacy is quite easy to come by, and it consists in sacralising individual kings. However, there is no conception of the king as the fount of authority for the social order, nor even as the key giver of laws. All these matters are left to the Brahman, and the king must merely preserve the social order. But how in practice do neo-Brahmanical texts see kingly activity? Left with little positive social function to fulfil, kings are largely ceremonial actors whose main interest seems to be in warfare. Their rule is shortlived and personal, and considerable cynicism is shown towards their motives. The effects of this upon the economy can be seen in a moment. In summary, it can be said that the state in this civilisation is, as Marx realised, fundamentally free floating. It is a weak state because it is merely the 'custodian' of a social order.

The state in Islam is similarly weak, although the mechanism by which it came to be so is very different. A religious vision united the Arab tribes and thereby allowed them great military capacity. The Islamic conquerors brought a monotheism with them; they possessed force *and* value (Cook and Crone, 1977). This inheritance presented problems when rule over conquered land had to be consolidated and regulated. The Umayyads were able to rule for some time on the basis of traditional kinship cohesion, but such politics were far removed from original Islamic purposes. The Arabs did not 'feel at home' in their conquered lands. They were unable to integrate with the settled population; since they were the carriers of their own religious vision they scorned and did not wish to be absorbed by civilisation. Tribesmen had not bargained for, nor were they prepared to accede to, taxation, and they hankered for the simplicity and egalitarianism that had marked the earliest period of Islamic history. It is in these Umayyad years that the experts in the word codified Islam. The ulama were not integrated into the first caliphate and the codification they made harked back to a simpler tribal past, a past in which there was little room for the necessities of power (Crone, 1980). Mainstream Islam, in other words, came to have a distrust for the exercise of political power. Shari'a law was neither a Caesaropapist doctrine supporting imperial power nor one like Christianity, which said that the purpose of religion was purely spiritual, and that accordingly power relations did not matter and could be left to proceed on their own course. Government thus has very slim roots in society, and stability came to depend upon such solidarity as the rulers of society could themselves achieve, as is true of most conquest societies. As such social solidarity tends to be evanescent, government in classical Islam tended to be highly unstable.

Possession of the sacred norms of society did not, however, enable the ulama to turn their backs on political power as had Indian intellectuals. The reason for this divergence lies in the nature of pastoralism. Power was needed because nomads were militarily powerful. Islamic civilisation was not just made in the image of tribal simplicity, but also had to contend with the continuing presence of tribes. Pastoralism combined with the rigour of Islamic ideology in a manner first fully spelt out by Ibn Khaldun.

Nomads are not completely independent. Ibn Khaldun noted that the city is necessary for nomads. Certain craft work, such as tanning and heavier metalwork, requires static equipment which would *per se* invalidate nomad existence; it is much easier to obtain such material by trading, especially as this brings in wealth. Cities require a government so that market transactions can be reliable and regular, but its control is limited to the cities and their surroundings. The essential contrast, to use a Moroccan expression, is between the *Bled el Makhzen*, the area of order, and the *Bled el Siba*, the area of tribal dissidence: it should be noted that the third party, the peasantry, thin on the ground in North Africa but of great historical importance in Egypt, Iran, Iraq, Syria and Anatolia, plays no active role in this picture since tribes, rather than peasants, have military force.

The dynamics of Ibn Khaldunian sociology result from the inability of cities to govern themselves. In European society such self-government ultimately depended upon the ability of cities to raise their own troops or to provide mercenaries able to defeat organised armies operating within a relatively pacified terrain. Muslim society in the arid zone was not at all like this. Urban citizens faced a land of dissidence capable of great military surges. Those who could not defend themselves looked for a defender, and they found it in *one* tribe, capable of fighting off tribal incursions and of providing order for markets. But once a tribe became a ruler of a city it automatically began to suffer moral degeneracy. The predominant quality that had allowed the tribe to come to prominence in the first place was social soldarity, but the ease and luxury of city life undermines this. So although citizens support the tribal rulers at first they become restive, typically by about the third generation of the ruling dynasty. The ulama begin by serving the ruling house as administrators and judges; yet they possess the sacred norms of Islam which, because of their precise codification, are not nearly as much at the mercy of secular power as was the relatively spiritual doctrine of Christianity. Some ulama become discontented with the ruling house as it becomes corrupt. In time, they declare the ruling house to be impious, and invite in one of the tribes from the area of dissidence. It is here that the presence of an ideology shared with the tribesmen matters. This manner of accession to power probably explains why Islamic culture, more extensive than any state, was maintained: a ruling house coming to power as the result of a religious spasm was unlikely to turn against Islam and never had the time to do so. This Ibn Khaldunian circulation of élites suggests the term 'cyclical' polity for the state in classical Islam.

The custodial and the cyclical states did not have deep roots in society, were transient and, as such, predatory. Cities were not autonomous and economic life within them was correspondingly distorted by the power of military leaders. Lapidus's comment is typical:

> Every property owner, merchant or citizen had personally to come to terms with the governors, emirs and officials. Not the office but the man himself became the power to be reckoned with for there could be no appeal to justice, but only to money and to countervailing influences and to protection no less costly than the previous exaction. (1967, p. 56.)

Legal affairs were equally at the mercy of political power in Islam, with a corresponding diminution of the possibility of rational calculation. The predatory nature of rule encouraged hoarding in general and religious endowments, in *waqf* in Islam and in the extraordinary temple economies of Hindu India (Cahen, 1970; Stein, 1960). Vast quantities of land came to be held in this manner and this made the state's revenue all the smaller, and did not in any case encourage productive investment in land. But then neither did other forms of ownership. Land grants were to be held for a short duration and a premium was placed on exploitation (Hodgson, 1974, vol. 2, p. 137; Hall, 1985b, chs 3 and 4).

It is worth spelling out the argument a little further. Islamic and Hindu cultures were both larger than the states that rose and fell within their boundaries. They were thus free from the bureaucratic interference of an empire co-existent with a culture or, more accurately, a polity that created its own culture. In the Indian case, a particular block on economic advance came from the fact that the culture was one which did not recognise all human beings as of equal worth, and this made some impact on the very possibility of long-distance trade: caste regulations meant that such travel was discouraged, for fear of pollution. This can be exaggerated, however, and in India there was *some* feeling of participation in a single civilisation. This feeling was widespread in Islam and in Christianity.

Both Islam and Christianity held together a large area in which equal citizens could recognise each other; in other words, both these civilisations centred themselves on a sense of community. Why then did not Islam similarly help capitalism? In Europe the ability of a merchant to move with his capital away from persecution was allied to the presence of a more organic type of state which was in place over long periods of time. This type of state was forced to provide infrastructural services for society, both because of the pre-existence of a civil society and because of the need to raise revenue to compete in war with other similarly stable states. In Islam, no such organic states existed. The fear of tribesmen meant that urban strata could not rule themselves and a premium was accordingly placed upon military power. Governments elsewhere were unlikely to be more stable, so that the mere moving of one's capital did not matter. The explanation for the difference is probably military. In Europe the emergence of states forced the aristocracy to gain profits from land rather than from warfare, and the reasonably settled character of the core of Europe meant that monarchs *had* to turn to the provision of infrastructural services in order to gain revenue. In Muslim and Hindu society, wars always remained the greatest potential source of profit. In Islam the solidarity of a tribe was the greatest military asset:

> it was with difficulty that [the barons of Europe] could combine really massive armies under one chief for general indiscriminate slaughter; to concentrate power in one hand, the chances of fixed succession, modulated by dynastic marriages or even by the purchase of succession rights, were as important as outright political and military skill. No ruler extended his sway far beyond his hereditary lands . . . [in Muslim society] the military men were city men and little bound by parochial presumptions. Nowhere was mobility more drastic than among the soldiery, whose members could rise to the highest social peaks, and could campaign for distances incredible in the Occident. (Hodgson, 1974, vol. 2, p. 353.)

This whole point can be put in an alternative, simpler manner. Muslim society did *not* in fact have a multipolar state system equivalent to that of Europe in which rationalisation by the states of their societies occurred under pressure of war. Very much to the contrary, states came and went, and were of larger or smaller size at various periods, but were never long-lasting enough ever to be rationalised at all.

EUROPE: THE ORGANIC STATE IN THE STATE SYSTEM

If I had to pick out the most unique of all Europe's uniquenesses it would be that of the extraordinary 'trahison de clercs' involved in the church's spurning of the Roman Empire. St Augustine's *City of God* famously argued that God's timetable was his own, and the church in the West chose to take civilisation to the barbarians rather than to wait for them, as had the mandarins, to convert to the imperial form (Hall, 1985b). The Christian church became, to use Thomas Hobbes's phrase, the 'ghost of the Holy Roman empire', and it did much of the extensive work previously accomplished by the legions. The sense of community thereby established helped to create a consensus within which contractual relationships could work: the extensive work of the church allowed, in other words, the emergence of the European market (Mann, 1986). This dynamic twist to the European economy took place very early on, much investment being made in the years between 850 and 1100 (Duby, 1974; Postan, 1975; Cipolla, 1976). Europe had no capstone imperial government of any sort in this period and the market accordingly flourished. But we must now turn our attention to distinguishing the European state from those of Islam and India. Why was it organic rather than predatory? And in what way did the type of warfare that characterised its activities actually *help* economic progress?

The argument to be made has three parts: a counter-factual proposition, a characterisation of the organic state and an appreciation of the role of state competition. All of these parts are mutually supporting, and all centre on the undoubted fact that European society did not, despite the attempts of Charlemagne, Frederick Barbarossa, Napoleon and Hitler, develop an imperial structure after the collapse of Rome.

At first sight some of the statements in the preceding paragraph may seem slightly overblown. Surely, it might be objected, the church did seek to establish a real imperial papacy? But did it establish a theocratic status? The answer to this question must be a definite negative. The papacy never possessed its own army, whilst the various kings of Europe very plainly did. But what about the other side of the coin? If the drive to an imperial papacy was defeated as much by the presence of diverse states as by anything else, how did those states come into being in the first place? The fact that *several* sets of barbarians came into Europe at the end of the Roman empire doubtless was an initial condition in favour of a multipolar system. But we can add to this that the church played a very notable role in making a secular empire impossible. Most obviously, it welcomed the rise of states which were able to give more secure protection to its own property. But there is a more important point to be made: the church refused to serve as second fiddle in an empire equivalent to those of China and Byzantium, and thus did not create a Caesaropapist doctrine in which a single emperor was elevated to semi-divine status. Indeed, very much the opposite is the case. The church's habitual playing of power politics encouraged the formation of separate states whose autonomy eventually led to the failure of its own imperial drive. And this was not the only way in which Christianity provided the best shell for the emergence of states. The church provided the numinous aspects of kingship – most notably, the coronation and the singing of the *Laudes Irae* – that made a king more than one amongst equals. Even more importantly, the church's attack on extended kinship systems was vital (Goody, 1983). In the other world civilisations the lower classes could often rely upon kinship systems as a means of protection and mutual aid. The removal of this weapon of the lower classes made the European peasant that much better fodder for state formation.

With these background comments in mind, the first argument can be presented. Imagine what European history might have been like had the Roman empire somehow been reconstituted, or had any empire taken its place! We have seen that empires are too centralised for their logistical capacity, and thus tend to produce capstone government based on their accurate perception that secondary organisations are dangerous. Empires usually sought to encourage the economy, but this form of government historically never ultimately allowed it sufficient leeway to gather self-sustaining momentum. Why should an imperial Europe have been any different?

This counterfactual can be put in a rather different manner. All historians agree that Max Weber was indeed correct in the more materialist part of his theory concerning the rise of the West, namely in his contention that only in Europe did cities gain full autonomy, possessing their own governments and armies rather than being controlled by the arbitrary rule of others. Consequently it provided a space in which the merchant was king, and in which bourgeois values could gell and solidify (Baechler, 1975). We live in the world created by this civilisation. *Why* was there such autonomy? The North Italian cities gained autonomy because there was no single centre of power in Europe. Specifically, they benefited from being in a power vacuum between pope and emperor, such that they were able, as is often the case in Third World countries today, to get the best for themselves by opportunistically chopping and changing their allegiance (Burke,

1986). How much they owed to their freedom from interference and freedom to experiment is simply seen: once they became part of the Spanish mini-empire they contributed virtually nothing new to European civilisation.

This first point amounts to reiterating that political fragmentation was a necessary condition for the autonomy of the market. But the Indian and Islamic cases have demonstrated that such fragmentation is not sufficient by itself to encourage economic dynamism. What else was involved? It might at first sight seem contradictory to say that the organic state helped economic development after the largely negative comments made about capstone and predatory rule. But no simple view of 'the state' is of much use in social theory: for there are *different* types of state in different historical and social circumstances. For what it is worth, two general principles about the relations of government to the economy can be maintained. First, the absence of all government is disastrous since it encourages localism, and thus prevents trade: and the argument made already about the service provided by religion in integrating large spaces shows that no anarchist vision is encouraged here. Secondly, however, capstone and predatory governments were indeed hostile to endogenous economic development. In one sense it is a mistake to call such governments strong since they were based on weak infrastructural penetration of society; indeed their very arbitrariness in part resulted from that weakness. This gives us the clue to the distinctiveness of the European state: a limit to arbitrariness combined with, indeed in part caused, considerable and ever-increasing infrastructural penetration. Two such limits are important.

The first limit is straightforward. The European state evolved slowly and doggedly in the midst of a pre-existent civil society. It was no capstone or predatory organisation in large part because it was not a conquest state. One uniqueness of the West is the role that Parliaments played in its history: indeed so unique has this role been that German historians have considered the *Standestaat*, the representation of the three functional estates, Church, Noble and Burgher, a distinctive stage in world history (Myers, 1975). As civil society pre-existed the monarch, his only way of gaining money was to co-operate with this society. European pluralism, in other words, has an extremely long history.

The paradox of this situation is that restraint on government in the end generated a larger 'sum of power'. Perhaps the most important mechanism in this process was the making of money by the creation of a certain infrastructure for the society. This is most clearly seen in the provision of justice. The lawyer has a very central place in European society, and this results from the king's desire to gain the profits from justice. Fees were charged for every legal transaction, and these came to provide an important part of the revenue of most monarchs after about 1200. This is not of course to say that the law was equally open for all to use; but it was available. And increasingly European states provided other sorts of infrastructural help. They became good at managing disasters of various sorts; by the eighteenth century, for example, considerable help was available to the victims of earthquakes, whilst disease was quite rigidly controlled by quarantine laws (Jones, 1981, ch. 7). Furthermore, the internal colonialism whereby Scots, Irish and Welsh were integrated into a single community – a process repeated elsewhere in Europe – created a single market. Consciously, rulers had encouraged trade for a long time. They did so because a disproportionate bulk of their revenues came from customs and excise. They did all they could to attract traders; a typical piece of legislation in this matter being Edward I's *Carta Mercatoria* of 1297. It is worth trying to summarise the general spirit at work here. It is not being claimed that 'society' had suddenly come to include everybody, although the degree of literacy and the eventual creation of a national tongue do witness the emergence of what is properly called the *nation* state. But what is apparent is that large sections of the powerful in society proved prepared in the long run to give quite high taxation revenues to the crown because they realised that their own interests were usually being served. Conflicts of course occurred, and they make up much of European history. But the more important fact remains the organic quality of the system. It can be summed up in the matter that so impressed Tocqueville on his visit to England. Where many aristocracies – Chinese, Roman and, until 1789, French – hid their wealth from the state and refused to do its bidding, the English aristocracy and gentry manned local government and taxed itself. The level of infrastructural support and penetration was correspondingly high. A Confucian bureaucrat moved every three years simply could not know enough about local conditions to serve a particular area well, representation to a central assembly by local aristocrats from the area created a different result.

The second general restraint on the arbitrariness is also the third general point to be made about the European polity. The complete 'formula' of the European dynamic is that competition between strong states inside a larger culture encouraged the triumph of capitalism. Individual states did not exist in a vacuum. They were rather part of a competing state system, and it was that system, particularly the military organisation it engendered, that played a considerable part in determining the character of individual states. Political competition proved beneficial to economic progress. Why was this?

A state system encourages emulation. This can be seen in artistic matters, but it extended to the establishment of various scientific clubs in eighteenth-century France in conscious imitation of their English rivals. Such emulation is ultimately only possible between states which recognised each other as of more or less similar standing; empires do not tend to copy the culture of small neighbours whom they see as mere barbarians. And the reference to empires brings out other facts about a state system that proved beneficial for economic growth. A state system always had an inbuilt escape system. This is most obviously true in human matters. The expulsion of the Jews from Spain and the Huguenots from France benefited, and was seen to benefit, other countries and this served in the long run as a limitation on arbitrary government. Very importantly, capital was equally mobile. Thus Philip's abuse of Antwerp led, within a matter of years rather than decades, to the rise of Amsterdam. In a brilliant passage making this point, W. H. McNeill has shown that time and again Philip II *wanted* to behave like an autocrat but the mobility of capital defeated him (1982, ch. 1). This was particularly true of his relationship with Liège, the foremost cannon producer of late sixteenth-century Europe. When Philip pressurised them too hard, artisans and capitalists simply went elsewhere. A certain measure of decent and regularised behaviour was ensured by these means.

However, perhaps the fundamental mechanism at work in the relationship between state competition, the organic nature of the state and economic progress was that of military competition. The revelation of German industry applied to war in 1870 sent a ripple of anxiety throughout European capitals; states were forced to rationalise their societies to survive. Yet state competition was responsible for rationalising European societies *prior* to the age of industry. Consider again the German case. Dramatic defeat by Napoleon was not ascribed to greater industrial development, but to the impact of an ideologically motivated citizen army. The reform group around Hardenberg realised that serfs could no longer provide an effective army; the reforms of 1807, 1811 and 1818 changed the Prussian social structure at a stroke. The purpose of such changes was military but the commercialisation of agriculture that resulted was economically beneficial. This mechanism was at work in Europe roughly from 1100 when the multi-state character of Europe finally crystallised. Throughout the Middle Ages there was a breeding race to provide heavier, more effective cavalry, and other great changes were associated with the rise of bowmen and pikemen, the adoption of gunpowder and the consequent need for new Italian defences, the vast increase in army size in the seventeenth century, and the creation of a citizen army during the French Revolution, and so on. Each of these changes necessitated money, and it was the search for funds that necessitated the king calling his estates, and raising funds by providing the infrastructural services mentioned.

As noted, the European state became able to generate great power. The organic quality of the European state arose from its having to accept and co-operate with other elements in civil society if it was to survive in a social society of state competition. Why was it, however, that the more powerful European state did not turn inwards in order to establish something more like an imperial system? Roughly speaking, European absolutism represents just such a move, and it is important to stress how unsuccessful it was. It is convential to compare absolutist France with England in order to give the impression of greater strength in the former case. This is mistaken, since English society generated more power *without* an absolutist façade; it proved this in defeating France in war on every occasion bar one in which they met in the eighteenth century. This returns us to the question of competition. No state could afford to go it alone without risking defeat. It is hugely significant that by the middle of the eighteenth century France was sending its intellectuals to England, and was in other ways trying to copy her secrets. All this suggests that there must be a prime mover amongst the states in order to get competition to work in the first place. In fact, there were several prime movers in European history, the torch of progress being passed from Italy, to Holland and to England. The latter played a highly significant part as such a torch bearer, and it seems no accident that this state possessed a powerful and, crucially, *centralised* estates system which insisted on the state remaining organic during the absolutist period (MacFarlane, 1987).

CONCLUSIONS

I have sought to amend Nef's thesis that war militates against human progress by showing that in one civilisation the competition of strong states within a larger cultural arena played a crucial role in the triumph of capitalism. However, when either of these two factors – a strong state and a larger cultural area – is missing, blockages to the emergence of capitalism resulted. War did help create the Chinese empire but that form proved inimical to the autonomy of the market. In contrast, war in Islam and in India was wholly destructive, although the extent of that destruction can sometimes be exaggerated. So, war helped progress in particular circumstances and at a particular time. In the previous paragraph, and there alone, I have conflated progress with the triumph of capitalism. This conflation may be defensible, presumably must be so to Marxists. In conclusion, however, reservations spring to mind. My argument has been that the instability of a state system proved energising. But 1914 showed that instability could also be destructive. Now that weapons of total destruction dominate our lives, it is impossible not to be nervous about state competition.

American hegemony after 1945 limited state competition in Europe, albeit the imperial power was involved in traditional state competition with its rival superpower. Now that this hegemony is in question, it behoves Europe to consider urgently institutions which control and limit state competition. For in the advanced area of the modern world, any sustained confrontation would, almost certainly, only bring disaster.

REFERENCES

Baechler, J. (1975) *The Origins of Capitalism*, Oxford: Basil Blackwell.

Burke, P. (1986) 'City States', in J. A. Hall (ed.), *States in History*, Oxford: Basil Blackwell.

Cahen, C. (1970) 'Economy, society, institutions', in *The Cambridge History of Islam, Vol. 2, The Farther Islamic Lands. Islam, Society and Civilisation* (eds), P. M. Holt, A. S. Lambton and B. Lewis, Cambridge: University Press.

Cipolla, C. (1976) *Before the Industrial Revolution*, London: Methuen.

Cook, M. and Crone, P. (1977) *Hagarism*, Cambridge: University Press.

Crone, P. (1980) *Slaves on Horses*, Cambridge: University Press.

Duby, G. (1974) *The Early Growth of the Medieval Economy*, London: Weidenfeld & Nicolson.

Dumont, L. (1957) *Religion/Politics and History in India*, The Hague: Mouton.

Elvin, M. (1973) *The Pattern of the Chinese Past*, Princeton: Princeton University Press.

Goody, J. (1983) *The Development of the Family and Marriage in Europe*, Cambridge: University Press.

Hall, J. A. (1985a) 'Capstones and Organisms', *Sociology*, vol. 19.
Hall, J. A. (1985b) *Powers and Liberties*, Oxford: Basil Blackwell.
Hall, J. A. (ed.) (1986) *States in History*, Oxford: Basil Blackwell.
Hodgson, M. (1974) *The Venture of Islam*, Chicago: Chicago University Press.
Hopkins, K. (1976) 'Economic Growth and Towns in Classical Antiquity', in P. Abrams and E. A. Wrigley (eds), *Towns in Societies*, Cambridge: University Press.
Huang, R. (1974) *Taxation and Governmental Finance in Sixteenth-century Ming China*, Cambridge: University Press.
Hutton, J. H. (1963) *Caste in India*, 4th ed., Oxford: University Press.
Jones, E. L. (1981) *The European Miracle*, Cambridge: University Press.
Karve, I. (1961) *Hindu Society*, Poona: Dacca College.
Lapidus, I. (1967) *Muslim Cities in the Later Middle Ages*, Harvard: Harvard University Press.
MacFarlane, A. (1987) 'The Cradle of Capitalism', in J. Baechler, J. A. Hall and J. M. Mann (eds), *Europe and the Development of Capitalism*, Oxford: Basil Blackwell.
Mann, M. (1977) 'States, Ancient and Modern', *European Journal of Sociology*, vol. 18, pp. 263–98.
Mann, M. (1986) *The Sources of Social Power. Vol. I. A History of Power from the Beginning to AD1760*, Cambridge: University Press.
McNeill, W. (1982) *The Pursuit of Power*, Oxford: Basil Blackwell.
Myers, A. R. (1975) *Parliaments and Estates in Europe to 1789*, London: Thames & Hudson.
Nef, J. U. (1950) *War and Human Progress*, Cambridge, Mass: Harvard University Press.
Postan, M. M. (1975) *Medieval Economy and Society*, London: Penguin.
Stein, B. (1960) 'The Economic Function of a Medieval South Indian Temple', *Journal of Asian Studies*, vol. 19.

3 War and Social Theory: Into Battle with Classes, Nations and States

Michael Mann

It would be easy to polemicise against 'orthodox sociology's' shameful neglect of war; to lament the paucity of sociology's contribution to the most urgent social problem of our time – peace; and to deride the naive, pacific optimism of the 'classic theorists' whose writings form the theoretical core of our own education and that of our students. But the neglect may now be over. Recently sociology has been paying more attention to war and peace; while the surrounding political and cultural climate has changed more radically. In the 'Star Wars' programmes – I do not mean the fantasy version by Ronald Reagan, but the real one by George Lucas – whole planets can be destroyed by a single weapons system. Today both adults and children recognise that as contemporary reality. This is paralleled by the more surreptitious growth of chemical weapons, persuading many commentators that the world may soon end, not with a bang but with a blister. If sociology has anything useful to say, it will have a large and receptive audience.

Thus I will not polemicise, but attempt to be constructive. First, I distinguish two relevant schools of nineteenth-century sociological theory: the liberal/Marxian and the militarist. Second, I draw out from each a core concept – respectively 'class' and 'nation' – and one shared concept – 'the state' – and revise them in the light of the twentieth century. Third, I chronicle the interrelations between these three major social actors in the recent history of war. I argue that much of our present danger stems from the way in which classes, nations and states have become closely entwined in the nineteenth and twentieth centuries. Finally, I conclude that the world might be a safer place if we could take class out of geo-politics.

TWO SCHOOLS OF THEORY: LIBERAL/MARXIAN AND MILITARIST

From the Enlightenment to Durkheim most major sociologists omitted war from their central problematic. This was not neglect; it was quite deliberate. They believed the future society would be pacific and transnational. Industrial, or capitalist, or 'modern' society would be unlike the preceding feudal, or theocratic, or militant societies. Power could now operate pacifically, without physical force. In their various theories rational, technocratic 'industrials' might now rule; 'profit' might replace 'plunder'; the surplus might be extractable by purely 'economic means'; or the market or the division of labour, once underway, might be self-regulating. Power would also operate transnationally. The state would remain puny, or even wither away, in the face of the massive global impact of industrialism, capitalism and science. Social classes would also become transnational. Whether classes were defined according to property, the market, or occupation, they could be found interchangeably at both the global level and the level of the individual national state. These notions dominate the theories of Smith, St-Simon, Comte, Spencer, Marx and Durkheim – our liberal and Marxian founding fathers.

This was an understandable view of the nineteenth century, as seen from an Anglo-French perspective. It is often said that there was a century of peace from 1815 to 1914. This is approximately true for the experience of Great Britain, and up to 1870 of France. It is not so true of the other Great Powers, Russia, Austria, Germany and the United States. But pacific transnationalism suited the interests of the two greatest Powers of the early nineteenth century. Global penetration by industrialism, capitalism and science would enhance British, and to a lesser extent French, hegemony.

The view from central Europe, and for a time from America, differed. Friedrich List, supported by American economists, challenged the *laissez-faire* theories of Manchester. Germany and the US overthrew British economic hegemony from the 1880s. Germany and Austria also harnessed economic growth more explicitly to military might from mid-century. Theorists there drew upon Social Darwinism to develop a more militarist approach. Gumplowicz, like Marx, was a materialist: society was driven forward by desires for economic gain and possibilities for the exploitation of labour. But militarism was the way to achieve both.

Class structure resulted from wars between 'peoples' and from the expropriation by the victors of the vanquished. Rustow transformed this into a theory of 'superstratification'. 'Peoples' became ethnically-homogeneous units, nations and even *races*, struggling for survival, in the work of Ratzenhofer (an Austrian general) and others. The political climate affected liberals like Hintze and Weber, and some Marxists wavered, developing theories of imperialism in which national classes perpetrated wars. In the United States, writers like Sumner explored 'folkways', 'in-groups' and 'outgroups' and ethnocentrism. Few of these sociologists believed the future lay securely with transnational pacifism – unless the world was first conquered by a single nation.

Who won this struggle over sociological theory? The result was deeply ironic. The appalling slaughter of 1914–1918 and 1939–1945, together with Fascism, would seem to support militarist theory. Peoples solidified under slogans of extreme, often racist, nationalism. Class struggle withered away at the onset of war, was often institutionalised faster as a result of victories, and intensified most in defeat. Geo-politically, Europe exhausted itself and suffered 'superstratification' imposed by American and Russian imperialism.

But unfortunately for the militarists, *their* armies lost. The Austrian Empire disintegrated; Russia was conquered by Marxism; Germany lost two wars and its militarist theories were outlawed from civilisation. Finally, the United States became a superpower and re-discovered the usefulness of British transnational *laissez-faire* for its own global hegemony. As liberalism and Marxism divide up the geo-political and geo-economic world, they naturally dominate its sociology. Since 1945 the militarists have been forgotten, the waverers purged of their more violent side (e.g. Weber's *Herrschaft* became not 'domination' but 'authority' in English translation), and the 'classic tradition' of liberal/Marxist pacific transnational sociology has been enshrined in pedagogy.

In fact neither school's theories can be accepted today. Liberals and Marxists exaggerated the peaceful transnational powers of industrial capitalism, militarists exaggerated the power and cohesion of the nation and the race. We can appreciate the contemporary circumstances which led them to their conclusions, but place them in a broader historical perspective. We have to start this from scratch, however, because the liberal/Marxist conspiracy has suppressed much of the history of the relationship between war, classes, nations and states.

AMENDING THE MASTER-CONCEPTS: CLASS, NATION AND STATE

Class

The liberal/Marxian school stressed the power of classes in modern society. In agrarian societies classes had been particularistic aggregations of households and lineages; now, however, classes would act as universal collectivities over the whole space of a society. In particular, they would have a profound collective impact upon the state. I will not quarrel with this. In the rest of what I say, collectivities like 'the capitalist class', 'the working class' etc. will stride about modern history. I hope I can be allowed this crudity without having to either define or qualify these classes at length.

But the liberal/Marxian school also saw classes as transnational. This I wish to question. In fact, we can hypothesise three possible types of class structure: transnational, inter-national and national.

(a) *Transnational*: class organisation and struggle proceeds right across state boundaries, without significant reference to them, occurring throughout the global reach of industrial or capitalist (or whatever) society. States and nations are irrelevant to class struggle, and are weakened as power actors by the global reach of classes. The material 'praxis' of classes can thus supervise and correct the state's conduct of geo-politics. There can be no autonomy of the state here. This was the liberal/Marxian view.

(b) *Inter-national*: all or some of the inhabitants of one state form a 'class' in relation to all or some of the inhabitants of another. Nations can struggle with one another, exploit one another, and so become classes with their own distinctive class praxis. This was the 'superstratification' theory of the militarist school, and it has also influenced Marxism in the shape of theories of imperialism and dependency. Inter-national class relations will often turn warlike because such classes control armies.

(c) *National*: class organisation and struggle occurs within the confines of state boundaries, without significant reference to the world outside or to class struggles occurring in other states. In this case class praxis is not 'anchored' in international space. Though classes might get caught up in domestic struggles over the identity of 'the nation', they are inward-looking, divorced from, and incompetent in geo-politics. This possibility was neglected by both schools.

From the perspective of the late twentieth century we can see the role of all three in recent historical reality. I will stress *national* classes, which will support neither school of theory but lead to a more complex view of modern war.

Nations

Here we must amend militarist theory. We cannot define nations ethnically or racially. Nations do not derive from the same 'blood' or 'ethnic stock'; their genealogical histories are myths; they have no 'natural' existence or rights to their own states; warfare, no matter how ferocious, is not conducted between gene groups. The closest real approximation to the nationalist myth is when societies differ by physical phenotype, but their conflict still needs further explanation (and this type of warfare has not dominated Western history). The furthest away is the present superpower confrontation, for the United States is a nation-state created recently out of polyglot immigrants from several continents; while in the Soviet Union nationality provides only a regional and not a state-wide identity. Indeed, before the nineteenth century, there were very few 'nations'. Community identities were far more often provided by locality, class and religion, than by ethnicity or state membership. Yet in the nineteenth and twentieth centuries nations were indeed created, and almost all states came to legitimise themselves as 'nation-states'. Wars were fought between these states, often with the enthusiastic support of the 'nation'.

So what are nation-states, if they are not ethnic groups? They are *citizen* states, states of mass political membership, the first states in history in which all adult inhabitants have been active participants. At first citizenship was restricted by class and to men. But the meaning of 'nation' became clear right at the start. In the French Revolution, as Hans Kohn (1967) has noted, 'nation' changed its meaning – from the inhabitants of a territory or an aristocracy linked to their monarch by blood, to a political community of free, participating citizens. It kept this predominantly political meaning for almost 100 years, until Social Darwinism pushed blood and territory back into the definition. Thus the forward surge of nationalism and the continued relevance of war and militarism was connected to mass citizenship. The connection was made obvious with the emergence of mass mobilisation warfare. Citizens did more than wave banners. Men fought in the front-line, and men and women accepted additional labour burdens in the 'rear'.

States

The two schools had different views of the modern state. The liberal/Marxian school saw it in domestic and primarily economic terms; the militarist school in geo-political and military terms. Nevertheless, both saw the state as a single cohesive institution, reducible to the dominant groups in its civil society. Thus the state élite represented the interests of the dominant class(es) – the Marxian view; or it mediated systematically between classes – the liberal view; or it represented the interests of the dominant military caste or of the nation or race – the militarist view. In these theories the state has little autonomy or 'privacy': the praxis of classes or nations supervises its activities.

I shall challenge this. The modern (Western) state is not single but dual, its domestic life separable from its geo-political. Moreover, the state élite has retained, even increased, its autonomy in the sphere of geo-politics. Geo-political privacy, even extending to war-making, has been much greater than in the domestic sphere. This is for two reasons.

The first reason concerns the general nature of geo-politics. Diplomacy is far less regulated, routinised and predictable than are major domestic politics. Diplomacy involves a number of autonomous states among whom there are few normative ties, yet continuous re-calculation of the main chance. The actions of one set up ripple reactions among the others, amounting to an unpredictable whole. Thus all states find, from time to time, that they are suddenly boxed into a corner, faced with unwelcome enemies or allies, or with a Hobson's choice between 'backing down' or actions that will be defined as highly aggressive. The *crisis* is essential to geo-politics, and, if serious, may suddenly confront nations or dominant classes with wholly unexpected, potentially devastating, but restricted policy choices. Secret diplomacy is set up to counteract some of the 'ripple effects' of geo-politics, and this further increases the privacy of the state. Indeed the state rulers may find that their diplomats and soldiers have developed their own secret procedures.

There were some spectacular examples of all these processes in the run-up to 1914: the Agadir crisis, the exposure of the secret Anglo-Russian naval treaty, the Russian choice in July 1914 between backing down before Austrian aggression in Serbia or having to mobilise against both Austria and Germany (the Russian High Command suddenly assured the Tsar that mobilisation only against Austria was technically impossible). Thus states, and even state departments, in all historical periods have dragged even the most powerful of domestic classes into geo-political strategies and even into wars that were not of their choosing.

Second, the state's autonomy and privacy varies according to the dominant type of class organisation. *Transnational* classes are anchored in geo-political space. They can supervise their state's diplomacy. *Inter-national* classes have a clear geo-political strategy of their own. They can supervise the state's diplomacy and steer it against their enemies abroad. But *national* classes have no geo-political anchorage or strategy; they are inward-looking and lack expertise or interest to supervise their state. I will argue that the importance of *national* classes in the modern world has increased the autonomy and privacy of the state, even to war-making.

For these two reasons, modern *states*, as well as classes and nations, have made war – as my title suggests.

So classes may be transnational, national or inter-national. Nations must be defined by political citizenship, not ethnicity. States have an autonomy and a privacy in geo-politics. Let us now consider these actors in three phases of Western history.[1]

HISTORICAL PHASE 1: PRE-1780

Making war and peace was formally the private prerogative of the medieval prince. However, in reality war also required the feudal levies of the nobility or their consent to taxation. The nobility was additionally a *transnational* class, linked by genealogy and culture across Europe as a whole. So geo-politics and war were anchored in its rivalry for land, heiresses and honour. Moreover, wars were not devastating, did not involve the mass of the population, and were profitable to most surviving states.

However, the expansion and commercialisation of agriculture then created quasi-national markets at home; while abroad it thrust merchants into a closer relationship with their own state. The nobility lost much of its transnational solidarity, and its military levies lost effectiveness. Nobles became military and civil office-holders of the state. Mercantilism increased the *inter-national* class rivalry of merchants and nobilities. Stronger national markets and states also turned them inwards into *national* class organisation. The prince retained his formal geo-political prerogatives. The masses were still uninvolved in geo-politics and war (except in religious wars). War remained profitable because of spectacular European expansion, and because it was not particularly devastating. Between 1500 and 1780 there was also a massive reduction in the number of states, from about 500 to just under 100 (Tilly, 1984), largely as a result of war. In a strict sense there were more losers than winners. But history is written by winners. Progress was seen as coming, among other things, from war.

Three legacies were thus handed down to industrial society. First, states' geo-politics and war-making was formally private. That remained their prerogative even in countries where their domestic prerogatives had been severely curtailed. Second, though they usually pursued foreign policies that were in the broad interests of the dominant domestic classes, the transnational anchorage of these classes had declined. Thus the state's geo-political privacy increased. Third, war was a normal and rational part of geo-political strategy for the relatively advanced state: it brought territories, markets and geo-political dominance, and it did not cost much in social resources.

I have a quotation that will illustrate the legacies. In 1740 Frederick II of Prussia invaded Silesia and eventually wrested it from Austria. Silesia became central to the Prussian economy, and so to Germany's rise as a Great Power. This is how Frederick himself described what turned out to be a world-historical act:

> At my father's death, I found all Europe at peace . . . The minority of the youthful Tsar Ivan made me hope Russia would be more concerned with her internal affairs than with guaranteeing the Pragmatic Sanction [the treaty allowing a woman, Maria Theresa, to succeed as Austrian Empress]. Besides, I found myself with highly trained forces at my disposal, together with a well-filled exchequer, and I myself was possessed of a lively temperament. These were the reasons that prevailed upon me to wage war against Theresa of Austria . . . Ambition, advantage, my desire to make a name for myself – these swayed me, and war was resolved upon. (Quoted by Ritter, 1969: I, 19.)

Note also how the rival states are personally named – another indication of the geo-political privacy of these dynasts.

I will now pursue these three legacies – the privacy of geo-politics, the decline of class supervision, and the rationality of war – into modern times.

HISTORICAL PHASE 2: 1780–1945

The Industrial Revolution had contradictory implications for class organisation. On the one hand it converted the territories of the major states into fully-fledged 'civil societies' in which universal, extensive classes co-operated and conflicted with one another. Regulating their relationships involved politics, focusing class organisation inward, onto the national terrain, away from both local and transnational arenas. On the other hand, industrial capitalism became global, involving classes in transnational and international praxis. The situation of classes became more complex, and we must distinguish carefully between the organisation of different classes in different periods and different states.

First, I discuss the capitalist class up to about the First World War. After 1815 industrialisation went through a transnational phase. Capital and commodities flowed straight through state boundaries. In continental Europe most of the first industrialising areas were cross-border regions, like northern France and the Low Countries, the Saar and Rhineland, and Silesia and Bohemia. Capital was organised transnationally and it favoured conciliatory geo-politics. This was the breeding ground of liberal and Marxian theory.

But after mid-century the rise of Germany, of protectionism, and of greater state participation in the economy created national and sectoral divergencies among capital. In Germany heavy industry became more closely enmeshed with the state, and favoured more aggressive geo-politics than light industry or finance capital. In France the opposite was true: the closest geo-political connection was between finance capital and the Quai d'Orsay. In Britain no major section of capital favoured aggression – the hope was that Germany would either go away or learn proper geo-political behaviour. But as international competition intensified, industries like steel and metal manufacture could grow by building warships and heavy guns. The growth of mass consumption markets within each country also expanded inward-looking national organisation among many other capitalists. Capital became divided.

There were different resolutions in different countries. In Britain capital's divisions were partly responsible for the weakness of British foreign policy, especially its inability after 1900 to give unambiguous signals to Germany as to how far British treaty commitments would be backed up by force. German capital became more united behind the aggressive geo-politics of the Alliance of Rye and Iron – the Junker class and heavy industrial capital. This was the breeding-ground of militarist theory. But the unevenness of capital's influence – ambiguous in Britain, more militarist in Germany – made diplomacy more difficult and Europe more dangerous. It lessened the chances for the transnational predictions of liberalism and Marxism.

Thus no single form of capitalist class organisation predominated. Capital's disunity consequently prevented this 'ruling class' from supervising state diplomacy to anything like the same extent as had the medieval nobility. The capitalist class might rule domestically – but not geo-politically.

Other classes were even less anchored transnationally. The middle class was mainly concerned with obtaining citizenship – the franchise, legal and religious equality and educational opportunity. It demanded meritocratic reforms of institutions, a fair taxation system, and protection from the 'dangerous classes' below. All these demands were addressed to the national state. When they were granted, political success 'naturalised' the middle class (leaving on one side the special situation of multi-national states like Austria). Without transnational anchorage, and without direct experience of international competition, the middle class became overwhelmingly *nationally* organised.

But the middle class went further. It correctly identified its own economic, political and cultural progress with the achievement of national citizenship. It became intensely proud of being 'British', 'French', 'German' etc. Its nationalism is often portrayed as paranoid, the projection of personal anxiety and repression onto the world. But its nationalism was joyous, celebratory, the expression of its sense of participatory citizenship. In Germany, Britain and France, the middle class dominated jingoist, chauvinist, militarist and even racist pressure groups. In the last decades before 1914 states found themselves confronted by a new problem. When boxed into geo-political crises, they were urged on to further aggression by this middle class 'public opinion'. Middle-class supervision of geo-politics was unstable, however, because it was not anchored in international praxis.

The working class was not so chauvinist. It had not achieved full citizenship by 1914, so the state was not 'its' state. Nevertheless, its most organised class struggles – for Factory Acts, legalisation of trade unions, the franchise, reform of Poor Laws, etc. – were directed at the state. Despite the transnational rhetoric of socialism, workers were not transnationally anchored. Their praxis and their organisation was becoming steadily more *national*, leaving them without great interest or expertise in geo-politics. Radical workers followed the leadership of pacific, transnational liberals who were their allies in their domestic class struggles. On occasion the mass of workers could be rallied round the flag, and in 1914 they went loyally to war, though with far less enthusiasm than the middle class.

So the rise of extensive, universal classes had made states more accountable for their domestic actions, but not for their geo-politics. Before 1914 capital pushed in contradictory directions, the middle class shoved erratically towards an uninformed militarism, the working class had other priorities.

Thus the second historical legacy, the conduct of geo-politics, changed little in the nineteenth century. In semi-parliamentary regimes like Austria or Germany, the constitution reserved foreign policy – sometimes excluding trade treaties, but including military budgets – as the monarch's prerogative, not to be scrutinised by parliament. Even in Britain scrutiny was limited. Foreign policy was supposedly initiated by Parliament. But discussion of policy was kept private. The Foreign Secretary normally sat in the Lords, not the Commons. He brought policy matters not to full Cabinet but to informal meetings of a few senior statesmen. Parliamentary requests for information were regularly repulsed with the phrase 'not in the public interest' (Cromwell and Steiner, 1972). The British state kept its geo-political privacy even while miners' MPs were crowding into the House of Commons.

But would geo-politics still routinely involve war? Was not the third historic legacy, the rationality and cheapness of war, now ended? With hindsight, obviously yes. In the twentieth century it became rational only to enter wars towards the end, as the early combatants exhausted themselves, and on terms, as the United States did. The costs of 'success' also rose phenomenally. Perceptive observers could see the escalation of the costs and casualties of war, from the Napoleonic

Wars, through the American Civil War, to the arms race around 1900.

But the states, the diplomats and the General Staffs did not pay much attention to the American Civil War. The General Staffs believed that the Prussian victories in 1867 and 1870 over Austria and France had demonstrated that speed of mobilisation, advance and reinforcement could bring a decisive result. That is why in the run-up to 1914, when the geo-political situation became really dangerous, the generals stopped restraining the militarists and added their weight to them. 'Get your retaliation in first' was the advice of the Austrian generals over Serbia, of the Russians in mobilising, and of the Germans in their pre-emptive strike into Belgium and France. The escalation of the horrors of war only happened in Europe because the French armies held their ground in 1914 and 1915 despite enormous losses. Until then the place of war in geo-political strategy was unchanged.

So was everything changed in the mud of the Somme and the Marne? Did the full devastation of war between equally matched opponents now bring a more pacific tone to geo-politics? With hindsight we know this did not happen, and for a variety of reasons. But one reason is germane to my theme. The war became a 'people's war' and the people wanted victory even at the cost of slaughter. The people were somewhat isolated from the front (except in France) and did not appreciate its full devastation. But also, the experience of the middle class before the War – progress through the nation – now became more generalised to the people as a whole. The people sacrificed but not for nothing. A bargain was struck, fairly explicitly: at the end of the war there would be extension of the franchise (probably including women) and welfare reforms. The downpayment was made already: full employment and greater trade union rights. The entry of the working class, and of women, into citizenship was accelerated by mass mobilisation warfare. This had occurred already in the North during the American Civil War; it was to happen again in Europe in the Second World War.[2]

So in the first half of the twentieth century the middle and working classes became national citizens, and were prepared to fight and toil to defend the symbols of their citizenship – monarch, flag, homeland and kith and kin. As modern classes emerged, they became predominantly *nationally* organised. As class struggles were regulated and institutionalised, nations emerged and classes developed a certain loyalty to the nation. But, contrary to militarist theory, this was not anchored in inter-national praxis. Nations were not interested or competent in geo-politics. Peoples were still plunged into wars through the private machinations of state élites. True, when tensions were high and policy options began closing down, or when war was actually underway, 'public opinion' could become bellicose and make it difficult for the diplomats to back down. But mass militarism was not anchored in praxis and so was volatile. If the leaders of the nation could not deliver victory, then the cry of 'treason' went up against them. Sections of the middle, and especially the working class escalated citizen demands, supported revolutionaries, and appeared sudden converts to transnationalism. This happened in all the defeated Powers (Russia, Austria, Germany and Hungary) in the years following 1917.

We can draw three conclusions about this phase. First, war remained a rational, accepted part of a geo-political strategy that in turn remained largely the private responsibility of the state. Second, class organisation took a largely *national* form, and not either the transnational form predicted by liberalism and Marxism or the inter-national form predicted by militarist theory. This meant that class praxis could not supervise geo-politics. Third, when the rationality of war weakened, in the twentieth century, a shallow, volatile chauvinism emerged to disguise this, at first among the middle class, then among the working class (and probably among women) too. Our present predicament stems from this 'negative reinforcement' which classes have added to the willingness of state élites to use war as a rational instrument of geo-politics. The way that class struggle was resolved in citizenship had made the world a more dangerous place.

HISTORICAL PHASE 3: POST-1945

Since 1945 the most obvious change has been in the devastation of war. The 'kill ratio' of weapons has been estimated to have increased half-a-million times from the V-2 warhead of the Second World War to even a 25-megaton nuclear warhead today (Robinson, 1977). If the two superpowers went to war against each other, Armageddon would result. One of the historic legacies, war as profitable and rational, has ended. This may not yet be true of the confrontation of minor states, but militarism between the superpowers has changed fundamentally.

It might seem, therefore, that geo-politics is now too important to be left to the state. But it still is. Despite looming Armageddon, the combination of private geo-politics and volatile, shallow popular chauvinism continues. In another paper (Mann, 1985) I have identified two types of contemporary militarism in Western and Soviet societies: 'deterrence science militarism' and 'spectator sport militarism'. The former is shared by diplomatic, military and political élites of both superpowers and their allies. Regarding deterrence as workable, they have evolved a complicated set of geo-political strategies, rules of behaviour and signals to each other, in which public opinion has little knowledge or interest. Indeed, contemporary weaponry has intensified the state's privacy, as military secrets are jealously protected and as abstruse computer-simulated war-games dominate the training of élites. Though the superpowers publicly rant and rave at one another almost continuously, peace is preserved by their real adherence to rules governing legitimate spheres of interest, the behaviour of client states, the difference between fighting soldiers and 'advisers' etc. In recent years the public has only become aware of these geo-political complexities at exactly the same point as in the previous historical phase: when the rules falter, usually because of the independent action of supposed clients, and the superpowers become boxed into crises, with options narrowed to 'backing down' or aggression. America's adventures in Iran, the Lebanon and central America are all recent examples. That is where mass public opinion begins to show an interest. Its 'spectator sport militarism', which shouts xenophobic encouragement from the sidelines to 'our boys', the professional soldiers, then becomes dangerously destabilising.

So why has so little changed? If my model is correct, the answer lies in the stability of the historic relations between transnational, inter-national and national class organisation. Yet there has been one major change in the relationship between class praxis and geo-political struggle. The latter is not now between capitalist states, but between them and a self-styled socialist bloc of states. Moreover, since 1945 the economies of both blocs have become internally integrated. Within the West capital has enormously increased organisation of a kind we normally call '*transnational*'. These co-exist with peaceful '*inter-national*' rivalry between capitalist nation-states. Various global institutions embody this duality of class praxis: the IMF, the World Bank, GATT, multi-national corporations, Euro-dollars etc. Yet in relation to the superpower confrontation, this class praxis is really '*national*' – confined within the sphere of interest of the US, the capitalist superpower state. No capitalist organisations significantly penetrate across the Iron Curtain, though there are state-supervised trading links between the two blocs. Thus class struggles in the West do not directly affect the economic interests of Soviet or East European citizens. Nor do class struggles in the Soviet bloc greatly affect the economic interests of Western citizens. Thus social classes have neither transnational nor inter-national praxis which would give them genuine interest or competence in geo-political rivalry between the superpowers. This is in marked contrast to their interest and competence in geo-politics internal to world capitalism, where classes lobby constantly on issues such as free trade versus protectionism. The geo-politics of economic and military power have become largely separated.

But there is another, novel linkage between class struggles and superpower conflict. The external geo-political enemy can be plausibly associated with an internal class enemy, and the combined struggle is then presented as a struggle for world civilisation itself. This is not unique to the contemporary world – for example, classical Greece and Persia struggled in this way – but it means that geo-politics becomes peculiarly ideological. In its official ideology the Soviet Union represents the vanguard of the global proletarian revolution, while the West and internal opposition both represent the capitalist enemy. Western hawkish ideology argues the converse: Western socialism is a covert agent for state dictatorship on the Soviet model. Both superpowers assert that their struggle is rooted in class praxis, of a novel, mixed transnational/inter-national type.

Indeed, this was plausible in the years after 1917. A large part of the Western working-class movement looked to Moscow for inspiration; the Bolsheviks led the Comintern against global capitalism; and Western capital sought to snuff out Bolshevism in its homeland. But ever since its plausibility has declined. The Comintern was wound up in 1942 in the interests of the geo-political alliance against Fascism. Since 1945 the superpowers have learned the rules of 'deterrence science militarism', refraining from encouraging 'class allies' in each other's territories. In any case, Western socialists now distance themselves from Soviet-style 'socialism'. Eurocommunism and the decline of Communist parties still loyal to Moscow have been the last, decisive nails in the Comintern's coffin. There is an additional conspiracy theory that ruling classes in both West and East deliberately use the threat of the enemy to keep down their subordinate classes. Maybe they do in the East; but in the West, outside of the paranoid Right, capital does not feel itself in imminent danger of class revolution even if the Soviet bogy was withdrawn. Capitalists are not sufficiently threatened by the working class movement in any advanced country to rationally continue risking nuclear war. So there has been a historical lag between reality and ideology. Today no genuine, deeply-rooted transnational/international class praxis directly divides the superpowers.

However, we must also consider more indirect links between class praxis and the superpowers. The first is routed through developing countries, whose reformers sometimes turn to the Soviets for help against Western capital. The West often also pre-empts this possibility by precipitously repressing the reformers. There is an element of inter-national class rivalry in this, both blocs seeking economic as well as military dominance over developing countries. For these reasons the capitalist class has maintained its aggressive geo-politics against 'world-wide communism'. This also applies, for slightly different reasons, to the Soviet ruling class.

But the economic part of this rivalry is asymmetric. Western capitalism offers developing countries far greater investment capital and markets than can the Soviets. Countries have turned to the Soviets primarily for arms, and because they have been spurned first by the West. Only the terms of interdependence with the West have raised stumbling-blocks, but these have been either geo-political or Western opposition to local reform, not local preference for economic and political interdependence with the Soviets. For example, Western support for Israel has been the key factor in the pro-Soviet phases of Egypt, Syria and Iraq; local geo-political complexities brought the Soviets into the Horn of Africa; while Western resistance to local reform was decisive in Cuba and Vietnam and has changed the outcomes of class struggles throughout central and Latin America. Again the genuine linkages of class praxis are weaker than the ideology of geo-politics suggests – a point to which I return in my conclusion.

The second indirect link between class praxis and geo-politics is provided by the historic legacy of nationalist citizenship. Are Western middle and working classes still trapped within predominantly *national* organisations, spouting superficial chauvinism? The answer is yes, but perhaps in Europe (and Japan), if not in America or the Soviet Union, we are coming to the end of an era. The popular equation of citizenship with war mobilisation ended around 1950. It is not likely to be revived, given the nature of war today. The equation of prosperity with economic-military hegemony is still real in the United States, but it has faded in Europe and Japan. A sense of social progress and citizenship may still be associated in the US and the USSR with national military greatness. But it is becoming anachronistic in Europe and Japan.

So in this third phase two historic legacies have remained unscathed: the state's geo-political privacy and its willingness to use the threat of war as a rational instrument of diplomacy. Classes have still not emerged fully from the second historical phase, in which citizenship in the nation-state turned them inward into *national* rather than outward to *transnational* organisation, yet also encouraged them to embrace the politics of *inter-national* aggression. The latter received a peculiarly dangerous twist when the Bolshevik Revolution gave geo-politics an ideology of direct *transnational* class struggle. Thus all three of my collective actors – classes, nations and states – share responsibility for our present danger. Indeed it is their interconnections that make us fear the end of the world. The mass enthusiasm of class struggle and national citizenship has been added to the private geo-political strategies of state élites, now armed with nuclear and chemical weapons.

HOPE FOR THE FUTURE: TAKING CLASS OUT OF GEO-POLITICS

So to see how the situation might improve we must centre on whether class and geo-politics can be further separated. Perhaps mild optimism might be in order. In the late twentieth century the destabilising role of class in geo-politics is declining, and its decline can be further assisted.

First, the Western working-class movement might finally sever the last link with the vision of 'socialism' as represented by the Soviet Union. A few intellectuals and trade unionists still retain the sentimental attachments of their youth. What especially lingers is an anachronistic appraisal of Soviet foreign policy, based on events in the Soviet civil war period (Soviet realistic fear of encirclement, purely defensive mentality etc.), supposedly still dominating Soviet geo-politics. Yet Soviet *realpolitik* is not greatly influenced by the nature of its domestic regime (whether we see that as socialist or as totalitarian). It is the *realpolitik* of a Great Power, little different from those of any Great Power in history, including Great Britain in the nineteenth century. Socialists could perhaps send an even clearer message to capitalists: yes, we are engaged in class struggle against you, but this is not remotely connected to the superpower confrontation. Similarly, Western capital might perhaps be encouraged toward greater realism: Western socialist movements have nothing in common with the interests of the Soviet Union; the Soviet Union is neither particularly socialist nor particularly evil in its geo-political intent but just a foreign Great Power; and nuclear brinkmanship is not in anyone's class interests. The recent alliance in the West between capitalism and militarism is obsolete. Class politics and geo-politics are separable.

Thus could be rendered obsolete some of the historic linkage between *national* and *transnational* class struggles, and *inter-national* geo-political confrontation. The only remaining linkage would be Western capital's fear of Third World reform movements backed by the Soviet Union. But on this point my analysis renders pertinent a strategy long advocated by Western liberals. President Carter's Angolan policy provides the model. Angola needed the West; it could get little objective benefit from the Soviet Union; therefore the West could negotiate amicably with whatever regime arose there, no matter what it called itself. The Western oil companies might receive lower profits from a self-styled 'Marxist' regime than from a South African-backed one. But this was worth sacrificing for (a) keeping Western influence and profits for other companies in Angola (the Carter argument) and (b) defusing the last remaining linkage between Western class politics and the superpower confrontation (my argument). The geo-political benefits for the West, and the boost to world peace, would be considerable. Such a strategy might increase tension by isolating the Soviet Union in her own bloc. But if the Soviet Union wishes to compete with a more enlightened West over the developing countries, then it could do so, with butter rather than guns, and by encouraging real socialist democracy there. And if propaganda of all hues were confined to geo-political issues, then it would at least be dealing more with the reality of the situation.

To take class out of geo-politics would not in itself bring peace. But it would concentrate our minds on a simpler, less emotionally-laden choice: is the game of geo-political rivalry alone worth the risk of Armageddon?

NOTES

1. Because of the lack of space I will not proliferate empirical detail or literature references in this essay. In consequence my arguments may seem bald and assertive. Full support for them can be found in my *The Sources of Social Power*. Details of the first historical phase are in Volume I (Mann, 1986) and of the second and third in Volume II (Mann, forthcoming).
2. These generalisations apply best to Britain; they apply largely to Austria-Hungary and Germany in the First World War, and partially to the US in

both wars and to Italy in the First World War; they apply least to Russia in both wars and France in the First World War. The complex relations between war, reform and revolution will be treated at length in Mann (forthcoming); see also Martin Shaw's contribution to this volume.

REFERENCES

Cromwell, V. and Steiner, Z. (1972) 'The Foreign Office before 1914: a Study in Resistance' in G. Sutherland (ed.), *Studies in the Growth of Nineteenth-Century Government*, London: Routledge.

Kohn, H. (1967) *Prelude to Nation-States: the French and German Experience 1789–1815*, Princeton, N.J.: van Nostrand.

Mann, M. (1985) 'The Roots of Modern Militarism', unpublished paper.

Mann, M. (1986) *The Sources of Social Power. Vol. I: A History of Power from the Beginning to AD 1760*, Cambridge: University Press.

Mann, M. (forthcoming) *The Sources of Social Power. Vol. II: A History of Power in Industrial Societies*, Cambridge: University Press.

Ritter, G. (1969) *The Sword and the Sceptre. Vol. I: The Prussian Tradition, 1740–1890*. Coral Gables, Florida: University of Miami Press.

Robinson, J. P. (1977) 'The Neutron Bomb and Mass-destruction Conventional Weapons', *Bulletin of Peace Proposals*, Vol. 4.

Tilly, C. (1984) 'The Geography of European Statemaking and Capitalism since 1500', *Center for Studies of Social Change, New School for Social Research, New York, Working Papers*, No. 4.

4 Hi-Tech Armaments, Space Militarisation and the Third World

Paul W. Hoag[1]

INTRODUCTION

Space militarisation is an outgrowth or extension of the general technical revolution in armaments and should be analysed as one category of high technology weaponry. I argue below that modern warfare upon the earth's surface in fact depends, in its most technologically robust form, upon military space systems; I will suggest that modern warfare cannot be fought without space systems. Three main sections follow: (1) earth-based high technology weaponry; (2) space militarisation; and (3) effects upon the Third World. Certainly these three subtopics overlap and interweave with each other. A specific historical example might well illustrate or involve two or more of the subtopics; so too might a particular technology, such as microelectronics.

HIGH TECHNOLOGY WEAPONRY

Tremendous technological forces are rapidly altering the techniques and equipment of war. To impart a sense of the quality of change without exhaustively cataloguing all innovations, I will focus on land force weaponry and, in particular, the high technology weaponry of the US Army; but other examples can be found in all the military services of all industrialised nations and in many less developed countries as well.

Superior technology has been the goal of military planners throughout the history of warfare, but the developmental intensity and dominance of high technology in modern weapons systems is unprecedented. Also unprecedented is the current and planned military expenditures of the US government. An enormous national commitment to arms and especially to expensive, state-of-the-art weapons technology is burdening the American economy and is changing international political and economic circumstances (though not necessarily as intended). While not documenting all important changes, this section will describe a sample set of tactical, non-strategic, non-nuclear research, development, evaluation and acquisition programmes currently administered by the US Army. Readers are asked to remember that only part of the Army budget is described and that analogous high technology programmes can be found throughout the US national security structure and in all modern armed forces.

The consequences of the changing nature of modern war can be seen in the tactical history of the last three wars fought by Israel. Before 1973, Israeli armour and infantry manoeuvred under extremely strong air cover, because Israeli pilots flying American-made warplanes were superior to Soviet-supplied Arab air forces. In 1973, Israeli aircraft (mostly F-4 Phantoms) suffered greatly from attacks by Soviet-made SA-6 surface-to-air missiles. During the June 1982 war, and particularly during the air battle of 9 June, the Israeli air force decimated the Syrian air force and took out the SA-6 sites in Lebanon's Bekaa Valley. The difference between 1973 and 1982 was American-made F-15 and F-16 warplanes, electronic countermeasures and counter-countermeasures systems (some American-made), and radar-seeking missiles.[2]

How did the Israelis achieve this feat of arms? It was mostly by the adroit application of high technology battle systems. The attack was coordinated by air controllers and electronic warfare specialists aboard an airborne warning and control aircraft (AWAC) circling Lebanon. An AWAC aircraft carries extremely sophisticated radars, computers, communications, and electronic warfare devices. When the AWAC was on station, the Israelis launched remotely piloted vehicles into the Bekaa Valley.

Remotely piloted vehicles (RPVs) are drones only six to eight feet long, yet carrying a great deal of electronics. The remotely piloted vehicles appeared to Syrian radar operators as airplanes; that is, the RPVs gave off signals and electronic signatures consistent with signals from real attack aircraft. The Syrians, fooled into believing that they were under attack, turned on their target acquisition radars in preparation for launch of surface-to-air missiles. Israeli controllers aboard the AWAC aircraft detected the radar signals and launched missiles, which followed the radar signals back to their source and thus destroyed the radars. Consequently, the Syrian missiles were useless for defence because they were blind; in addition, the Israelis now knew the exact location of all Syrian missile sites and could order follow-up attacks upon the sites.

Meanwhile, the Israeli air force was assembling out over the sea. The Syrians scrambled fighter aircraft to intercept and defend against what they falsely believed was a first wave of aircraft. As soon as the Syrian aircraft reached a speed of about eighty knots, AWAC controllers knew the position and type of each Syrian fighter. The Syrian pilots depended strongly upon vectoring instructions from ground controllers whose communication systems were being jammed by Israeli electronics. The airborne Israeli controllers had only to touch their computer screens with light wands, and the AWAC's computer told each Israeli plane's computer which Syrian aircraft to attack. The Israeli air force swarmed down upon the Syrian planes, whose pilots were still uncertain of their targets. The Israelis destroyed at least 17 out of 19 SAM-6 batteries and 80 Syrian planes at the cost of one Israeli aircraft. The 9 June 1982 attack is a specific historical example of the application of high technology weaponry;[3] let us now examine US Army weaponry.

The American Army is preparing to fight on an electronic battlefield where night is little protection and where friend and foe use radar, lasers, computers, and extremely accurate fire. New generations of munitions and delivery systems increasingly imply that 'something quite remarkable has been added to modern military forces: weapons in large number, each having a high probability of hitting its target with a single shot'.[4] One indication of intense change is the scheduled introduction of more than 100 new equipment items into Army units stationed in Europe.[5]

The modern American air cavalryman is carried into battle by a Sikorsky Black Hawk transport helicopter, which can carry an entire combat-equipped infantry squad or a 105-mm howitzer with its six crew-men and 30 rounds of ammunition. Black Hawks can fly at about 150 m.p.h. for over two hours and were used in the 1983 Grenada invasion. The twin-engined Black Hawks can self-deploy over significant distances, including sea routes, and can apparently carry as many as 20 soldiers. The cost of fielding 1107 Black Hawks is estimated at $6.63 billion ($5.98 million apiece). The Black Hawk will also dispense mines and aerial ordnance and will carry electronic artillery targeting equipment.[6]

Before a manned aircraft is committed, a Remotely Piloted

Vehicle (RPV) such as was used in the Bekaa Valley attack can be dispatched. A US RPV is a 6½-ft long, remote-controlled aircraft with a 13-ft wingspan and carries a surveillance television camera, a target tracker, a laser range-finder and target designator, and will eventually carry a forward-looking infrared device for night observation. RPVs are difficult to hit and excellent for scouting. It is reported that by using Israeli-made RPVs, combat commanders and 'the Israeli minister of defence [were] able to watch on [their] television monitor[s] and see the [1982] battle in Lebanon unfold, including attacks on SAM sites'.[7] The contract for an RPV to support artillery targeting has been won by the Lockheed Aquila, for which the US Army requested $134.6 million in Fiscal Year 1986 (FY 86).[8] The US Southern Command uses the Sky Eye RPV, in support of the El Salvadoran military's war against rebel forces.[9]

The Army's standard heavy anti-tank missile is the tube-launched, optically tracked, wire-guided (TOW) missile. This two-stage, solid-fuel missile is tracked by an optical device which follows an infra-red source in the missile's tail. The electronic guidance unit measures the course and issues corrections over a pair of fibre-optic wires that unreel as the missile flies; the gunner need only keep a crosshair sight on the target. A heavier warhead with a new microprocessor (TOW2) is now available, and the Army sought to buy 20 100 of the new and improved missiles in FY 86, for something less than $16 000 per missile. The TOW

> is deployed, or is planned to be deployed in infantry, light infantry, mechanized infantry, antitank, air assault, airborne, armoured cavalry, the Bradley [armoured personnel carrier], and COBRA/TOW [helicopter] units.[10]

TOW missiles were used in the attack on Fort Frederick during the Grenada invasion.[11]

Close above the battlefield, seeking tanks, or serving as close air support, will fly Apache Advanced Attack Helicopters. The Apache is a new generation helicopter gun-ship and can carry 16 TOW missiles or 16 Hellfire laser-seeking anti-tank missiles, along with two 2.75-inch rocket pods and a 30-mm chain gun with 1200 rounds of ammunition. Designed for the electronic battlefield, the Apache is equipped with an advanced infra-red suppression system, which reduces engine heat and hence vulnerability to enemy infra-red detectors and missiles. Fire accuracy is greatly enhanced over Vietnam-era Cobra gun-ships by use of a fire control computer, a

Pilot's Night Vision System (PNVS), and a Target Acquisition and Designation System which includes Forward Looking Infra Red (FLIR) sensors, a visible-light sight, and a laser ranging and target designation unit. The pilot-gunner wears a helmet, to which is attached a monocle imbedded with electronics. Through his electronic monocle, the pilot-gunner places crosshairs on a target as the plane and target move; sensors follow head and eyeball movement to track the target; the pilot-gunner fires a laser-guided missile to the target, which has by now been marked with a laser designator. The target can hardly escape, unless employing extremely sophisticated radar, laser, infrared, and other electronic countermeasures. The Apache is itself a prime target and must, for safety, employ state-of-the-art electronic countermeasures; thus, force superiority becomes a struggle for technological supremacy. The first Apache battalion is to be fielded in 1986, and the Army plans to buy 675 Apaches by the end of this decade, for a total programme cost of about $13.5 million per aircraft.[12]

Improved Conventional Munitions (ICM) are munitions fired by conventional artillery pieces but which incorporate technologies permitting terminal guidance and cargo-carrying. Terminal guidance means that the shell's warhead no longer falls only where its trajectory dictates, but is instead guided by a sensor and fins to a target. Cargo-carrying means that instead of delivering a single load of high explosive, the round carries a cargo of smaller submunitions, scatterable mines, or reconnaissance devices. The basic 155-mm carrying shell contains 88 submunitions; the cargo shell opens over the target area and the 88 dual-purpose submunition canisters are ejected. The canisters spew, over a wide area, shaped armour-penetrating charges as well as fragmentation grenades designed to kill exposed or only lightly protected people. Shaped charges are partially hollow; upon impact shaped charges form an explosive gas which cuts through the metal and disperses hot gas and fragments. If the canisters do not find targets upon landing, they wait. Presumably, this is why curious children have been hurt by 'unexploded American-made anti-personnel "bomblets"' in Beirut.[13]

Many of the improved munitions will be used in a powerful rocket system currently being deployed; the Multiple-Launch Rocket System (MLRS) is a free-flight, high volume of fire, NATO artillery rocket weapon. The MLRS is meant to perform in all weather, day or night, and be effective (devastating really) against artillery units, rocket counter-batteries, supply areas, air defence systems, trucks and lightly armoured vehicles, and people massed in the open. The MLRS has tank treads and two self-contained pods, each with six 13-ft rockets. All 12 rockets can be fired simultaneously at a single target, or two to 12 rockets can be 'ripple fired' at a number of targets. During a 'ripple fire' sequence, a control system re-aims between rocket firings, yet the sequence can fire all 12 rockets in a minute. Each rocket's warhead holds 644 submunition canisters, so that a full MLRS load delivers 7728 little dual-purpose bomblets and can saturate an area of about 30 000 square yards in a minute. After firing, the MLRS can (and should) quickly depart and quickly reload.

The MLRS is directed by a computer which can position, aim, set fuses, fire, prompt the crew in plain English, German, or French, maintain digital communication with other units, and make all calculations. The vehicle has a position determining system hooked into a north-seeking gyro-compass. Remembering its original position, this device calculates present location by measuring the distance and direction of movement. The expected cost per vehicle, each with 174 rocket pods, is $1.6 million.[14]

The Firefinder Artillery/Mortar Locating System is composed of two phased-array radars, one for artillery and the other for mortars; both are advanced, pulse Doppler radars with electronically steered beams to provide virtually continuous coverage. Both use advanced signal-processing and computer-aided analysis to help pick out objects as small as a mortar shell out of background clutter at 10 000 metres; Firefinder detects shells, automatically analyses the trajectories, and plots the trajectories back to their origin. Firefinder can request return fire before the first incoming shell has landed, and 'proved highly successful in locating hostile artillery positions for Marine Corps forces in Lebanon in 1983'. The entire Firefinder programme cost is estimated at $815 million.[15]

As the preceding examples show, a technological revolution has transformed armaments, and an expensive revolution it is. What may be less clear, but is no less certain, is that the power and accuracy of modern armaments have blurred the distinction between conventional and strategic weapons. There used to be a clear distinction between the two types: strategic weapons usually meant nuclear weapons, as in 'strategic deterrent'; non-nuclear weapons were called conventional or tactical arms. But at the upper limits of destructiveness of modern so-called conventional weaponry, it is hard to tell the difference, save for radiation, between conventional weapons and small nuclear weapons. At least one expert has suggested that if a full scale conventional war broke out in Europe, then flying over the battlefield two weeks later the scene would be, in visual terms, little different from an attack by Hiroshima class nuclear weapons.

SPACE MILITARISATION

Why are all the above details of high technology weaponry relevant to space militarisation? The answer is that modern warfare, including conventional warfare, is what I have termed 'space-dependent'. That is, many modern weapon systems cannot be used as designed or cannot be used at all, without using space-borne military systems. Even the effectiveness of weapons which do not use information from satellites is intertwined with space systems, because weapon deployment depends upon space-based communications systems. Consider as an example the Multiple Launch Rocket System (MLRS) described above. The MLRS keeps highly accurate track of its own position and thereby knows accurately the distance and direction of assigned targets, once it is told its starting point – the more precise the original fix is, then the more accurate is the fire. This implies a need for quick and precise navigation, which in turn implies the use of a satellite navigation system. The full effectiveness of MLRS is best guaranteed by a space asset, and this is true for locating both the MLRS vehicle and its target.

Some readers may think that the militarisation of space is something for the future, something that is presently being developed, but space has already been militarised to the point that modern war cannot be waged without the use of military space systems. Military space systems are essential for geodesy, meteorology, command, control, communication, intelligence, early warning, surveillance, reconnaissance and navigation.

Satellite geodesy provides highly accurate information about the shape of the earth and the values of the earth's gravitational field. Such information is essential for increasing the accuracy of ICBMs and cruise missiles. Military meteorology satellites can forecast weather conditions for battle, as well as atmospheric conditions which affect missile performance.

Command, control, communications and intelligence (C^3I) are a high priority among new military systems; for without these functions, other military functions are useless. Therefore, a great effort is being made to guarantee secure and survivable C^3I systems. MILSTAR satellites will provide the US with C^3I capabilities even after a nuclear exchange; it is therefore possible to consider MILSTAR as a nuclear war-fighting system.

The credibility of the nuclear capabilities of the superpowers rests upon early warning. Without early warning, it might be possible to destroy an opponent's retaliatory capability before a so-called deterrent response could be launched. Both superpowers rely upon satellite sensors for early warning.

Accurate navigation is obviously desirable for military manoeuvre, but beyond this obvious need is the fact that without precise navigation many modern hi-tech weapons lose their devastating accuracy. By late 1986, the US intends to have in place 18 Global Positioning Satellites. Also called Navstar, these satellites will give any observer with the proper receiver the receiver's surface position and altitude within 50 feet or less.

The past few years have revealed several instances of the use and value of space systems for military missions. These examples are from Iran, Grenada, the South Atlantic, and Chad.

Readers will recall that the US tried and failed to rescue hostages from its embassy in Tehran. Before the mission was cancelled, President Carter spoke with Colonel Beckwith at Desert One over a satellite communication system. For the supreme commander of the world's most formidable military power to speak directly with a colonel in the field is something quite remarkable. On the other hand, the Marine Corps has implied that certain communication defects which undermined the command and control of landing forces during the Grenada invasion are being solved by the acquisition during 1986 of satellite terminals; the manpack satellite terminals are now being introduced, and each Marine Amphibious Force will receive 16 terminals.[16] The value of satellite reconnaissance is underlined by hints in the open military literature that some of the 82nd Airborne's support helicopters, which happened to be in a training exercise, were not recalled to prepare for action in Grenada, but continued the exercise because of the fear that Soviet satellites would alert Cuban forces.[17]

Once the United States decided to abandon neutrality in the Falklands/Malvinas war, the British fleet gained access to US military communications, reconnaissance and meteorological satellites. The value of reconnaissance and the value of communications with the British fleet along its 8000 mile journey to the South Atlantic are surely obvious, but the political consequences are not; consider the fierce debate aroused by widespread suspicion that before the British submarine *Conqueror* sank the Argentine warship *Belgrano*, a very high official in England was consulted. The need for meteorological satellites may not be obvious, but the South Atlantic weather was violent and changeable and included snow, rain, cold and high seas and winds. Such circumstances are militarily appalling and strongly affect air operations and the electronic environment. Ordinarily, weather patterns in the South Atlantic are revealed by frequent individual weather reports from the many ships at sea; but when a war zone was declared, civilian ships left the area and the weather reports ceased. Therefore, US satellites were needed.[18]

After France sent the French Foreign Legion to Chad, the Legion established an East–West line in order to block the southerly advance of a Khadafy-supported rebel army. When Libyan-backed forces made what was apparently a major excursion out of their stronghold in eastern Chad, an excursion which seemed to ground observers likely to turn the legionnaires' right flank, the French did not rush reinforcements east. This was because legionnaire commanders had access to intelligence from US reconnaissance satellites and knew that the Libyan manoeuvre was not a serious threat.

Notice that even Britain and France, which are, after all, major industrial powers with well equipped armed forces needed US military space systems to wage war. Imagine how much more difficult is the dilemma of a Third World nation.

Since President Reagan's speech of 23 March 1983, which has been labelled his 'Star Wars' speech, there has been a great deal of attention to futuristic space weapons. This sudden attention has misled many people to believe that space militarisation is something that is yet to come. Though space militarisation is already a fact, it is true that an immense and expensive effort is under way to develop an entirely new order of space weapons. Collectively, these weapons are termed ballistic missile defence or the strategic defence initiative (SDI).

SDI can be presented in a way which is compellingly persuasive – as the President did; SDI can be offered as a defence against nuclear attack in which machines fight machines above the surface of the earth, thus removing the terror of massive nuclear attack. Because the SDI proposal plays to the great fear that all rational people have of a nuclear exchange, it can be expected that these types of space weapons will be intensely funded. President Reagan told Americans that their technological prowess offered hope for strategic security without mutual destruction. With his 'Star Wars' speech, President Reagan did at least two things: first, the President aroused hope for a high technology fix for the horrifying possibility of nuclear holocaust; and, second, he brought the militarisation of space to wide public attention. What is this high-technology optimism? At a minimum it is that: strategic security becomes a matter of defensive, not offensive, strategic systems; world war is removed from the human habitat and is instead fought in space; wars no longer attack people, rather war is fought between machines. Such a scheme has immense popular appeal.

Until SDI, relatively scant attention was paid to military space projects, though both the US and the USSR have flown military space missions for at least 20 years. The SDI concept is to use particle beams, lasers, and/or kinetic energy vehicles, sometimes called 'smart rocks', to strike the missiles in near-space and space. One type of smart rock is known as the rail-gun proposal; a projectile (perhaps one kilogram) is accelerated (more than 10 km/s) along a space-based rail by induced magnetic force. In the near term, rail-guns in space and hypervelocity rockets on the ground defending missile sites may be the closest thing to an almost off-the-shelf deployable system. But the real 'Star Wars' scenario is with laser and particle beam weapons.

The Reagan administration has committed itself to well funded laser and beam research, but there is considerable controversy over whether such systems could ever be effective. Numerous scientists contend that the SDI technologies are not feasible.[19] In the short term, simple defences such as spinning a missile to diffuse energy can defeat lasers, but in the long term it is risky to predict that no effective technology can be developed. What is clear is that the effort will be extremely expensive. Even so, as long as Ronald Reagan has a strong influence on the US budget (which is likely to be longer than Reagan is President), then very large amounts of money will be spent on SDI research.[20] Indeed, the President has moved to protect the SDI programme from the general budget reductions mandated by the Deficit Reduction Act of 1985, more commonly known as Gramm-Rudman-Hollings.[21] During the last half of this decade, the US plans to spend $27 billion on research for space-based anti-ballistic missile systems.[22]

A serious problem for the SDI plan is the very short response time permitted, since it is necessary to attack the missile as it enters space or even earlier. The time from launch to space is so short that humans cannot be relied upon to process the massive amounts of information from sensors and to make the correct and timely decision. It is therefore necessary to rely upon computerised machines; essential for these extremely high speeds are large memories, robotics, and artificial intelligence. This explains why in the US artificial intelligence is a military project and, in part, why the very high speed integrated circuit (VHSIC) development programme was funded directly by the Department of Defense. Artificial intelligence, robotics, and the fifth generation computer currently under development in both the US and Japan are essential for SDI deployment.

EFFECTS UPON THE THIRD WORLD

The evolution of high technology armaments and the militarisation of space has profound and disquieting implications for the Third World. The effects upon the Third World are likely to be varied, but ominous. I would suggest that there are at least five serious effects: (1) undermining of non-alignment and independence from superpowers; (2) limited access to useful technologies; (3) destabilisation; (4) increased neo-colonial pressure; and, (5) increased suffering during indigenous revolts.

To illustrate the argument and advance the discussion, let us assume a hypothetical Third World nation, and let us cast ourselves in the role of national planners. Assume further that this particular nation is perfectly benign, has no ambitions upon its neighbours, and wishes nothing more than to be left in peace to follow its own destiny. Now try to think of a place to locate this country – a place where this small country will have no reason whatsoever to fear its neighbours.

Real nations do not choose their location nor are they free to move to a safer locale, few nations are perfectly benign, and few regions are devoid of obvious threats. Where there is not an Idi Amin or Pol Pot who cannot be trusted, there are traditional ethnic or religious foes, or ambitious leaders dreaming glorious dreams of 'Greater X'. There may be resources near borders only loosely defined, or there may be fishing rights to defend. Alternatively, a neutral country may need to seal its borders against rebel or government forces in order to avoid involvement in a neighbouring civil war. For many reasons, even a peaceful Third World nation may have a legitimate need for self-defence armaments. If we concede this point, we are then faced with the task of choosing armaments for this small nation caught in unfortunate circumstances; here we encounter a very serious problem.

Because of the massive introduction of high technology weaponry, simple arms are insufficient for self-defence. Simple arms of even one decade ago are no match for contemporary weaponry, particularly if our potential enemy has acquired or is likely to acquire higher quality arms. If we assume the best of financial circumstances, then our hypothetical nation can afford to purchase first-rate modern armaments. Since we do not have the technology to manufacture the needed military equipment, we must import. But since we have assumed good finances, it should not be a problem to buy good weapons; indeed, with cash, we might advantageously play one manufacturer against another. Though arms may be purchased from a private enterprise, arms shipments always involve governmental permission; but with lots of money, this is not a problem – if a superpower will not sell to us for political reasons, France or another supplier will. So we are able to purchase adequate amounts of good military equipment and our problem is solved, but two new problems now arise.

The first new difficulty is training and spare parts. Not only must soldiers, sailors, and pilots be taught how to use our new equipment, technicians must be trained to maintain and repair the equipment, and to repair the equipment, the technicians must have replacement parts. Perhaps we were clever enough to arrange for all this when the equipment was purchased, but probably not. Typically, 'the finance minister is under the delusion that when he buys the airplane his problems are over, when in fact he's only made a 20 per cent down payment on the lifetime cost of the plane.'[23] But in our case, this should not be a large problem, because we still have plenty of money.

The second problem is that our solution does not last. Our defence minister informs us that our equally well funded, unfriendly neighbours have begun to buy equipment specifically designed to defeat ours on the basis of technological superiority. They have bought new jammers which render our previously impenetrable radars into useless noise makers or, worse yet, falsely reassuring sentries. To our dismay, we realise that our still relatively new equipment is not sufficient for our self-defence; the relative advantage of new weaponry degrades faster and faster as technology accelerates. So we are again faced with the need to purchase modern arms; but we now understand that since the pace of technology is quickening, this solution is increasingly a short-term solution.

The treasury has more bad news; the price of all manufactured goods, including arms, has risen significantly since our last purchase. But world prices for commodities, including the two we export, have dropped. We cannot pay for the new round of arms purchases, unless we can arrange some combination of loans and special, concessionary pricing. Not surprisingly, without cash, some formerly eager sellers are no longer eager. On the other hand, some sellers are most anxious to be helpful; they inform us that their government is prepared to make loans and to provide military training teams. This is not the best situation for our independent and non-aligned status, but it is the best available solution – and our neighbours are making us very nervous. We decide to accept the loan and the trainers.

Three years have passed, and our defence minister has just informed us that we again need improved radars, particularly for our aircraft. Recently, there have been a number of armed border clashes as we have insisted upon defending our national sovereignty against our neighbour's attempted land grab. However, our neighbour has just acquired a new type of missile; our aircraft can handle these missiles, but only with the improved radars.

Unfortunately, we still owe most of the principal upon the loan we obtained to finance our second major arms purchase. Our ambassador explains our most recent problem to our supplier's government. We learn that the new radars can be purchased with a new loan, it is just a matter of negotiating the details; during negotiations, the other government makes a suggestion. Why not accept an electronic listening station somewhere on our soil – small and inconspicuous, only a few acres at a remote site. The station would put several million units of hard currency into our local economy and would make it much easier for their State Department to explain to their legislature why it was important to extend another loan to us; the negotiators also let us know that since our neighbours have been buying arms with loans from an antagonist of their government, other direct military assistance is available, if the details can be arranged. As national planners, what should we do; should we start down this slippery slope, away from non-alignment? Can we afford not to?

In reality, few small nations can afford high quality armaments. To obtain such weapons they must have credits and military assistance which comes only at a political price, or at least, only for a political purpose. Even if a nation could somehow afford the highest quality weaponry, it might well have to strike a deal with a superpower, because certainly no small LDC has the capability to manufacture the highest technological level of weaponry. Saudi Arabia, which could pay for the arms it desired, bought American F-16s. But F-16s sold to the Saudis were export models without all the avionics and electronics found on US Air Force F-16s. Even when the Reagan administration has proposed the sale of sophisticated high-technology weaponry to Arab nations, the US Congress has blocked such sales for political and strategic reasons – it is not just a matter of money.

Though many Third World nations seeking arms cannot pay for them, high volume arms transfers continue from both East and West. Measured in current dollars, arms transfer agreements to the Third World totalled over $257 billion between 1974 and 1982. On an annual basis, arms transfers doubled during this period, though growth did vary year to year.[24] In just the years 1975–9, arms transfers by region totalled $17.2 billion to Africa, $9.5 billion to East Asia, $5.5 billion to Latin America, $32.9 billion to the Middle East, and $3.6 billion to South Asia.[25]

How is it that impoverished countries can buy arms? Countries which qualify, in policy terms, for US arms transfers might use one or more of three available methods: grants under the Military Assistance Program, direct US government loans with maturities up to 12 years, and federally guaranteed loans. Direct loans can be low interest and could be forgiven; guaranteed loans may have maturities up to 30 years.[26]

Why is the conservative Reagan administration willing to help escalate the US deficit by granting concessions and give-aways for arms sales? Primarily for two reasons:

> First, the administration concluded that due to the worldwide economic downturn, few countries could afford to finance the procurement of defence equipment at commercial . . . interest rates; second, the administration wanted to be able to offer some form of compensation during negotiations for base rights and facility access agreements in areas strategically critical to US defence needs.[27]

Between 1976 and 1983, the US Foreign Military Sales (FMS) programme made guaranteed loans to a dozen countries which were already in default (or at least arrears) on prior guaranteed FMS loans: Bolivia, Costa Rica, El Salvador, Lebanon, Liberia, Morocco, Nicaragua, Senegal, Sudan, Tunisia, Turkey and Zaire. The Reagan administration proposed in FY 83 that Sudan's FMS $100 million programme 'change to $100 million indirect loans with half forgiven.'[28]

' "The Sudans and the Moroccos just don't have the cash," [said] William Schneider Jr., [U.S.] undersecretary of State for security assistance.'[29] For FY 87, the administration has planned a 45 per cent increase in foreign aid (economic and military) for Sudan, which has Libya for a neighbour.[30]

Despite the Gramm-Rudman deficit-reduction law, the Reagan administration's initial plan for FY 87 is to increase by one-third US military assistance programmes; foreign aid would increase $1.1 billion, though it is not clear how much would be arms transfers. Though these amounts are unlikely to survive Congressional scrutiny, they do show the present administration's determination to make maximum use of economic and military aid for foreign policy purposes. For example, the Philippines would reportedly receive an 85 per cent increase in military aid.[31]

Although I have used US data to document the argument (because US information is easiest to obtain), the Soviet Union has a large arms transfer programme and has had goals and experiences largely similar to those of the US.[32]

Imagine that somehow a Third World nation obtains a sufficient amount of high technology weaponry (both quantity and quality) to engage a European industrial power, or a nation supplied by such a power, on its own military terms. Still, a powerful, high technology, military force multiplier[33] is absent – military satellites. If for illustrative purposes, we make the heroic assumption that our Third World nation acquires the military equipment and trained personnel to equal a developed power, then it follows that our Third World nation has acquired a military which is space-dependent in two senses. First, we utilise specific military systems which depend upon satellites for navigation (fire accuracy) and communication. Second (remember we are assuming the ability to engage a major power) to employ our forces in the most effective manner, we need access to the force multiplying capabilities of communication, meteorology, command and control, intelligence and reconnaissance from space. Military satellites accomplish these functions more effectively than can be done from Earth; and, in addition, these satellites provide capabilities which cannot be done from Earth, no matter how good the Earth-bound technology we acquire.

Now, more realistically, consider the case of a Third World nation which obtains sufficient and adequate arms to engage powers in its own region – still missing is the advantage of space-borne sensors. If an adversary is able to obtain access to space systems, then the nation without access must either accept a disadvantage or also obtain access to military space systems. At the moment, only the two superpowers have the space capabilities to fully support space-dependent weaponry. Thus, even if a Third World nation could climb very high up the technological weaponry ladder, under some circumstances, it may be forced to strike a political deal with a superpower. It is therefore extremely difficult for a Third World nation to obtain the highest quality of weaponry and remain totally non-aligned. That is, at some point the most robust high-technology weaponry can be obtained only at a political cost. As long as the US and the Soviet Union lead the world in the relevant technologies, this problem will remain for Third World nations.

As space becomes increasingly militarised, technologies useful in space become sensitive national security assets. This is a problem for Third World nations because many of the technologies have highly useful civil applications for the Third World. Land resource management, medical care delivery, education, and communication are examples of projects which could conceivably be done more effectively and easily from space, to the enormous benefit of the developing world.

One concrete example is satellite communications. Most Third World nations will never be able to afford extensive land line systems; but small satellite receivers are cheaper and more effective anyway. Thus many Third World nations hope to leapfrog an entire chapter of technological history and go directly to satellite communication facilities. Perhaps the most ambitious example is India's programme for a national satellite communication programme. 'The government maintains that satellite broadcast television is the only practical way to reach India's 700,000 villages with information needed to overcome the poverty that has plagued the country for centuries.'[34] INSAT, the Indian national satellite, is multipurpose and has been used to beam television programmes on agriculture and teachers' training as well as broadcast children's shows. In addition, INSAT has 8000 telephone circuits which carry voice and digital communications – a critical capability in the management of government administration and government enterprises, such as first class tourist hotels. Furthermore, INSAT has a meteorological function and monitors floods and cyclones.[35]

But communications for military systems are of the utmost importance to modern high-technology weapons. Indeed, much space technology is potentially dual use; that is, the information obtained in space or relayed through space could be used for military as well as civil purposes. So an improvement in space technology, say space communications, can be seen as an improvement in military technology, in this instance military communications, command, and control. Thus, it can be expected that the latest technologies, which are likely to have military as well as civil applications, will not be shared with the Third World. Not only communication technologies, such as optical fibres and the most modern computer chips, will be guarded, but almost any new technology useful for a space system is a candidate for a security classification. It is therefore likely that obstacles to technology access will increase. It is possible that this will slow Third World development, at least to the degree that space-related high technologies are helpful to LDC development.

The need or desire to acquire modern weapons, which are high technology and space-dependent, will have a destabilising influence in the Third World for at least two reasons: (1) increasing dependence; and (2) financial strain. Realistically, the extensive acquisition of modern weapons implies at least some reliance upon a superpower, if only for spare parts and training. It seems inevitable that such reliance will undermine nationalistic aspirations and independence; remember that even industrial nations like Britain and France have needed assistance while waging high-technology war.

Modern weapons are frighteningly expensive. Consider what the price of a $200 000 Exocet missile (which soared to over $600 000 on the open market as soon as the Falklands/Malvinas war began) means to a nation whose median annual income is less than $2000. Modern arms are clearly a significant drain upon national development accounts. Since arms purchases are likely to be financed by debt, the nation becomes more vulnerable to a world financial crisis. Furthermore, debt increases dependency, and increased dependency and financial strain are destabilising factors.[36]

The global political economy is complex and interdependent, and superpowers are themselves not free from Third World effects. Increased dependency implies an increased number of client states and the higher risk of superpower confrontation in the Third World. With high-technology weapons spread in many places and these weapons ultimately dependent upon training, spares, and space systems, it will become harder and harder to avoid superpower involvement in regional conflicts. When Israel destroyed Syrian missile emplacements in the Bekaa Valley, the Soviet Union felt compelled to replace the destroyed equipment with top line missiles; but doing so entails serious risk. Michael Klare has joined Roger Pajak in pointing out that 'recent conflicts in the Middle East have taught Moscow that "a special relationship with arms recipients can lead to risks of unwarranted military involvement and possible military confrontation with the United States" '.[37] Klare adds that 'this is particularly true in Syria, where Soviet efforts to placate Assad's desire for sophisticated weaponry have placed Soviet military personnel in close proximity to Israel and U.S. naval forces in the Mediterranean.'[38]

Also, weaponry diffuses in unpredictable ways and with ironic, unforeseen consequences. For example, American M-16 rifles left behind in Vietnam are sold around the world, and Iran flies American made F-4s against American made F-16s piloted by Saudis. One of the many oddities of the eccentric 1982 South Atlantic war was the fact that Britain supplied weapons to Argentina as late as eight days before the outbreak of hostilities.[39]

No one knows what SDI will cost the US economy, nor what it will cost the Soviet Union to defend against or match SDI. No one can say the cost accurately, because the technologies do not yet exist; but allegedly educated guesses have ranged from 500 billion to one trillion dollars for a deployed SDI system. Such large expenditures will certainly have consequences for the US economy. Although the stated object of SDI is increased security and the replacement of the present strategic triad, there is reason to believe that much of the SDI expense will be in addition to, not in place of, current expenditures. Even if the SDI proposal works better than expected when deployed, it will be necessary to retain and maintain the present nuclear force at least during the transition to a space-based ballistic missile defence. This would represent a massive increase to the US defence budget – not a replacement, and certainly not a decrease. Actually, it is more likely that significant parts of the present nuclear force would not be discarded.

The costs of SDI represent a strain upon an economy which already shows some signs of crisis. While it seems unreasonable to predict that SDI expenditures will break the US economy, it does seem likely that SDI will put serious pressures upon an already strained economy. Consequently, it is reasonable to expect that the US will become more aggressive in its dealings with trading partners and client states; the 'Baker Plan' for Third World debt is an example. Therefore, it can be expected that SDI costs and other economic problems will tend to harden the US attitude in such matters as funding the World Bank and the International Monetary Fund, settling debt accounts, and in other neo-colonial relations.

A CAVEAT: FROM THE THEORETICAL TO THE EMPIRICAL

I have outlined above a logical framework for what I believe to be one technological determinant of one tendency, factor, or force in the political economy of militarism; it is one strand of the theoretical, though informed by historical example. Dialectically, it is to be expected that tendency begets counter-tendency.

As the explosive self-destruction of the space shuttle *Challenger* demonstrates, unexpected results can emerge from the most carefully tested high technology.[40] And it is most definitely true that the introduction of high technology weaponry does not guarantee the desired military or political results. Not only may specific military systems not be very effective, even if they are effective, opponents may adapt and persevere. Morocco has built an expanding wall in the Sahara desert in order to fence out Polisario guerrillas; mounted on the wall are small radars, presumably to detect men moving miles away in the desert.[41] But a recent observer reports that while the wall itself seems to be effective, the radar is 'useless or unused'.[42] Whether or not the American-supplied electronic sensors are the reason, Polisario hit-and-run raids have nearly ceased; Brahim Ghali, Polisario defence minister, has said that the Polisario may adopt terrorist tactics in response to the wall.[43]

The Vietnamese revolutionary forces destroyed and astonished the French at Dien Bien Phu; for the French confidently relied upon Western high technology: artillery and aircraft. But General Giap, unawed, organised and impressed several hundred thousand coolies who, using mostly manual labour and skilfully employing jungle foliage for camouflage, dug gun-sites and tunnelled through the valley walls, thus creating an artillery bunker out of a mountain. The Vietnamese artillery then commanded the fort and its airstrip, and the French garrison's fate was sealed.[44] General Giap's forces went on to defeat the United States – technology is not a substitute for political resolve and legitimacy. Furthermore, high technology is not necessarily the best strategy, particularly when the cost means that fewer weapons are available; there is an argument to be made for lots more of simpler, cheaper weapons.[45]

But superior military technology can make a difference, and not just in extreme cases such as when, during the Nigerian civil war, Biafrans attempted to defend themselves with cudgels and machetes against assault rifles.[46] Though the Argentines lost the Malvinas, they inflicted significant damage on the British fleet and would have inflicted more, had modern, high-technology fuses been mounted on their bombs. US forces in Grenada both suffered and benefited from modern weapons. 'A big lesson of Grenada, according to the written reports and highranking officials interviewed, is that the world's least developed nations can obtain enough modern weapons to down helicopters.' On the other hand, helicopter pilots attempting to land the first Marines encountered palm trees and scrub bush on their assigned landing zone but were able to find a flat spot to land because they were 'wearing special glasses that enhance night vision'.[47]

If the Syrians had available high-technology radars, early warning aircraft, and satellite intelligence, could the Israeli Air Force bomb Damascus without resistance? If Tunisia had available high-tech radars, early warning aircraft, and satellite intelligence, could the Israeli Air Force bomb the PLO headquarters in Tunis without resistance? Technology can matter, but its application spawns invention and adaptation: force and counterforce evoke tendency and counter-tendency.

CONCLUSION

Although proponents of advanced weapons development perpetually offer the Soviet or US threat and NATO's or the Warsaw Pact's needs as justification, the truth is that these weapons are unlikely to be used in European combat but are almost certain to be used in the Third World, against both external and internal enemies. Across the Third World these technologies will be employed against popular, indigenous revolts. Some of the high technology under discussion will become the technology of repression,[48] and a savage, bloody repression it will be. Little prescience is required to predict that especially lethal, electronically guided cannons placed aboard Black Hawk helicopters will be employed against Latin American or African peasants and tribesmen or, as is said in the jargon of the recent Guatemalan horror, against 'subversive delinquents'.[49] As Third World governments join the arms race, the ever-escalating expense of the new high technology weaponry will suck more and more scarce funds out of national development accounts. In turn, the expense will pressure Third World nations into alignments with the superpowers in return for arms.

Perhaps the gravest danger is that the astonishing sophistication and wizard-like quality of high technology tactical weaponry will beguile another Somoza, or the chief-of-staff of a superpower army, or the leadership of an industrial power into believing that the just grievances and natural aspirations of a people can be forever thwarted by superior military might – into believing that the human spirit can be crushed by machines. Especially when combined with ethnocentrism and racism, an overweening pride and confidence in technology is dangerous, even to wizards.[50]

NOTES

1. I wish to thank Rear-Admiral Gene R. La Rocque, USN (Ret.), and the other staff members of the Center for Defense Information for their advice, forbearance, and generous sharing of the Center's research facilities and files. I also thank William M. Arkin for his helpful advice on how to research military matters, delivered both personally and through his excellent book, *Research Guide to Current Military and Strategic Affairs*, published in 1981 by, and available from, the Institute for Policy Studies, 1901 Q Street, N.W., Washington, DC, 20009. Thanks also to Frances Weaver, Bernetha Gartung, and Mary Anne Brown for help at several junctures. The revision process benefited from critical discussion with Ulrich Albrect and his colleagues at the Berghof-Stifung fur Konflikforschung, Berlin. Finally, I thank Colin Creighton and Martin Shaw for their patient encouragement. Comments and dialogue are welcome and may be sent to Paul Hoag, 421 Princeton Avenue, Liberal, KS 67901, USA.
2. Clarence A. Robinson, Jr., 'Surveillance Integration Pivotal in Israeli Successes', *Aviation Week and Space Technology*, 5 July 1982, pp. 16–17.
3. W. Seth Carus and Stephen P. Glick, 'The Battle of Lebanon: the Aerial Assault', *The New Republic*, 5 July 1982, pp. 15–17; this account, though widely disseminated in the press, is dismissed as Israeli disinformation and US threat inflation by Andrew Cockburn in *The Threat: Inside the Soviet Military Machine* (New York: Random House, 1983) pp. 441–5.
4. James F. Digby, *Precision-Guided Munitions: Capabilities and Consequences* (Santa Monica, California: Rand, June 1974), p. 1, quoted by Robert Kennedy in 'Precision ATGMs and Nato Defense,' *Orbis: A Journal of World Affairs*, 22 (Winter, 1979): 898.
5. Frederick J. Kroesen, 'U.S. Army, Europe, Modernizes While Keeping the NATO Vigil', *Army 1981–82 Green Book*, October 1981, p. 49; information about weaponry described in this article was obtained from five issues of the *Army: Green Book* (October 1981–85), congressional

documents, DOD publications and information offices, manufacturers' brochures and public relations offices, other open literature, and personal interviews. I thank the officials and technicians who helped me, all of whom prefer to remain anonymous.

6. 'Ten Lessons from Grenada', *Defence Helicopter World*, June–August 1984, p. 19; also US Congress, House, Subcommittee of the Committee on Appropriations, *Department of Defense Appropriations for 1986 – Part 5*, 99th Congress, 1st Session, 1985, pp. 19, 32–35. This multivolume annual series will be referred to below as DOD Appropriations for the appropriate fiscal year, with part and page numbers given; year of publication is always the year preceding the fiscal year.
7. Robinson, 'Surveillance Integration Pivotal in Israeli Successes', p. 16.
8. *DOD Appropriations for 1986 – Part 5*, pp. 264–6; see also p. 227.
9. Ibid., p. 265, and Associated Press report in 'U.S. Spy Plane Drone Falls in El Salvador', *Wichita Eagle-Beacon*, 24 August 1985, p. 4A.
10. Ibid., pp. 245–7.
11. 'Ten Lessons from Grenada', p. 15.
12. *DOD Appropriations for 1986 – Part 5*, p. 54–5.
13. Angus Deming *et al.*, 'Beirut's War of Nerves', *Newsweek*, 12 July 1982, p. 39.
14. *DOD Appropriations for 1986 – Part 5*, p. 242; also Part 2, p. 208.
15. *Army: 1985–86 Green Book*, pp. 441–4, and Army public affairs officer.
16. *DOD Appropriations for 1986 – Part 3*, pp. 194–6.
17. 'Ten Lessons from Grenada', p. 18; of course, the real fear may have been of the American press, given the unprecedented news media policy implemented during the invasion of Grenada.
18. Early reports were that the Argentines benefited from Soviet military satellites, but this is apparently not true. See US Congress, Senate, Committee on Commerce, Science, and Transportation, *Soviet Space Programs: 1976–80 (with supplementary data through 1983), Unmanned Space Activities*, 99th Congress, 1st Session, May 1985, Senate Print 98–235, Part 3, p. 787.
19. John Tirman (ed.), *The Fallacy of Star Wars* (New York: Union of Concerned Scientists and Random House, 1983).
20. At the November 1985 Colorado Springs symposium of the US Space Foundation, SDI director, General Abrahamson explained that, unlike his colleagues, he was not really the programme manager of the project to which he was assigned – 'President Reagan is SDI program manager'. Indeed, Reagan's strong personal support for SDI is not in doubt.
21. The Congress appropriated only $297.5 billion of the $322 billion DOD request for FY 86. Then on 20 January 1986, the Comptroller General stated that another $13.6 billion must be removed to satisfy the new deficit-reduction law; but the President exempted SDI from the new reduction of 4.9 per cent. The secret DOD *Defense Guidance*, the planning document for FY 88–92, is said to give SDI 'the highest priority', equivalent to strategic force modernization. See 'DOD's FY 86 Budget Dips Below Zero Growth; FY 87 Could Be a Lot Worse', and '*Defense Guidance* Gives SDI Priority Equal to Strategic Force Modernization', both in *Armed Forces Journal International*, February 1986, pp. 16–24.

22. US Department of Defense, *Report to the Congress on the Strategic Defense Initiative: 1985*, Washington, DC, July 1985.
23. Wolfgang Demisch, an 'aerospace analyst', quoted by Rick Atkinson and Fred Hiatt in 'The Airplane Bazaar: "Export or Die" Is the Cry', *Washington Post National Weekly Edition*, 2 September 1985, p. 18.
24. Michael T. Klare, *American Arms Supermarket* (Austin, Texas: University of Texas Press, 1985), pp. 206–7; Klare's source is the Congressional Research Service, *Trends in Conventional Arms Transfers to the Third World by Major Supplier, 1975–1982* and edition for 1974–1981, published in 1983 and 1982 respectively; includes arms, ammunition, services, and construction; excludes cancelled Iranian contracts and US sales under the Commercial Sales programme.
25. Ibid., pp. 208–11; Klare's source is US Arms Control and Disarmament Agency, *World Military Expenditures and Arms Transfers, 1970–1979*, published in 1982; indicates deliveries of arms, ammunition and related equipment; excludes services and construction.
26. US Comptroller General, General Accounting Office, *Unrealistic Use of Loans to Support Foreign Military Sales*, 19 January 1983, GAO/ID–83–5, p. 1.
27. Ibid.
28. Ibid., p. 29; quote from p. 3.
29. Atkinson and Hiatt, 'The Airplane Bazaar', p. 7.
30. Associated Press report in 'Senate Panel Attacks Foreign Aid Request', *Wichita Eagle-Beacon*, 30 January 1986, p. 4A.
31. Ibid.
32. Klare, *American Arms Supermarket*, pp. 218–31.
33. A force multiplier is a technology which when applied to another military technology or system makes this second technology or system markedly more effective. A force multiplier can be thought of as a catalyst or synergistic additive. Hence, given two equal systems, the addition of a force multiplier to one of the systems makes that system superior.
34. 'The Global Village', *Nova*, transcript no. 1202, WGBH Educational Foundation, Boston, 22 January 1985, p. 3.
35. Ibid., pp. 4–6.
36. See Cheryl Payer, *The Debt Trap* (New York: Monthly Review Press, 1975).
37. Klare, *American Arms Supermarket*, p. 230, quoting Roger F. Pajak in 'Soviet Arms Transfers as an Instrument of Influence', *Survival*, Vol. 23 (July/August 1981), p. 167.
38. Ibid., citing *New York Times*, 2 March and 17 April 1983; *Boston Globe*, 29 January 1983; and *Washington Post*, 3 December 1982.
39. 'British Arms to Foe Reported', *New York Times*, 20 June 1982, p. 16.
40. Like the designers of the *Titanic*, NASA designers thought that the Shuttle's solid-fuel booster rockets were 'not susceptible to failure'; New York Times News Service quoted in 'NASA Trusted Rocket Design, Leader Says', *Wichita Eagle-Beacon*, 3 February 1986, p. 1.
41. Christopher Dickey, 'Morocco Loves Its Wall of Sand', *Washington Post National Weekly Edition*, 2 September 1985, p. 18.

42. Bernard D. Nossiter, 'Algerian–U.S. Convergence: Time to Settle the Sahara War', *The Nation*, 25 January 1986, p. 79.
43. Associated Press report in 'Morocco's Wall in Desert Changes Polisario's Tactics', *Wichita Eagle-Beacon*, 30 August 1985, p. 10A.
44. Bernard B. Fall, *Hell in a Very Small Place: The Siege of Dien Bien Phu* (New York: J. B. Lippincott, 1967).
45. To a degree, this is said to be the strategy of the Soviet Union; see Viktor Suvorov, *Inside the Soviet Army* (New York: Macmillan, 1982), pp. 181–211.
46. Michael Mok, *Biafra Journal* (New York: Time-Life, 1969), p. 38.
47. *DOD Appropriations for 1986 – Part 3*, pp. 194–5, quoting George C. Wilson, 'Flaws Seen in Grenada Invasion – Report Says Field Decisions Prevented Disasters in Nick of Time', *Washington Post*, 12 March 1985.
48. See Klare, *American Arms Supermarket*, p. 192. Klare used the Freedom of Information Act to examine export licenses granted by the Office of Munitions Control of the US State Department between 1976 and 1979. Klare reports that a third of the countries obtaining US equipment during 1976–9 have been cited repeatedly by human rights monitors for persistently abusing basic human rights. Klare found that equipment had been delivered to such fine folk as the Chilean Carabineros and the paramilitary police in Paraguay.
49. Associated Press and United Press International dispatches quoted in 'Guatemalan Troops Attack Guerrillas', *Wichita Eagle-Beacon*, 7 July 1982, p. 13A.
50. Cautionary tales can be found in David Halberstram, *The Best and the Brightest* (New York: Random House, 1972) and in Neil Sheehan and E. W. Kenworthy (eds), *The Pentagon Papers* (New York: Quadrangle Press and the New York Times, 1971).

Part II
Militarism, the State and Social Change

5 Militarisation and the South African State[1]

Mark Mitchell and Dave Russell

INTRODUCTION: STATE THEORY AND THE SOUTH AFRICAN STATE

In the last fifteen years the state has emerged from relative obscurity to occupy a position centre-stage in the social sciences. The 1970s in particular can be seen as a period in which the state came in from the cold to become an important object of theoretical and empirical investigation. A decade and a half on, it is possible to look back and attempt an assessment of the progress achieved and of the mistakes made.[2]

In brief we believe that much of the standard literature on the state is deficient in three crucial respects. First, it is based upon an 'internalist' or 'society-centred' conception of the state which fails to recognise that states are also influenced by a variety of international forces which help to shape the internal organisation of the state. Secondly most of the contributions tend to play down the significance of what have become known as the 'repressive state apparatuses', and focus instead upon the 'problem of legitimacy' or the 'manufacture of consent'. In this way state theory has tended to minimise the extent to which modern states rely upon access to the means of repression and terror to secure their political rule. Thirdly much of the literature is premised upon the assumption that states necessarily exhibit a high degree of internal organisational unity – a kind of inner structural logic – rather than a recognition that the level of institutional coherence within any state is always a highly contingent matter.

The need for this kind of reorientation of state theory and research is confirmed if we turn to a consideration of South Africa. In the first place it is obvious that the character of the South African state is shaped to a very considerable degree by both regional and global forces that lie beyond its immediate territorial boundaries. Secondly the South African state possesses a rapidly expanding set of military/security apparatuses which are utilised on a daily basis with deadly effect both inside and outside its borders. Thirdly the South African government has in recent years gone to great lengths to present its diverse policies and practices as the co-ordinated elements of a 'total strategy' for survival and this underlies the need to subject such conceptions to critical analysis.

Throughout the 1970s South Africa was confronted by an escalating set of internal and external problems that appeared to demand substantial policy reforms. Internally these problems included: an increase in the rate of inflation coupled with a deterioration in the balance of payments situation, indicating that the economic bubble of the 1960s was about to burst; a growth of militancy and illegal unionisation amongst black workers; a spiralling growth of the administrative machinery necessary for the enforcement of grand apartheid; and above all an upsurge in the levels of resistance and rebellion of black people to white rule that reached its height in the Soweto uprising of 1976. Externally the most significant change was the collapse of white colonialism in Mozambique and Angola, and the rising tide of guerrilla warfare in Namibia and Zimbabwe. In addition the climate of international opinion shifted dramatically against South Africa in the wake of the brutal repression of the Soweto riots, provoking a massive flight of capital from the Republic. Finally the election of President Carter to the White House, and the appointment of Andrew Young as US representative to the United Nations marked a period of sharp decline in relations between South Africa and its most important ally in the West.

By 1977/8 these problems had reached crisis proportions. The South African government itself began to admit that the Republic was experiencing the effects of a 'total onslaught' and had to prepare itself for 'total war'. To combat this, they embarked upon two broadly parallel and interrelated initiatives. These involved the extensive militarisation of South African society on the one hand and the development of a 'total national strategy' designed to ensure long-term survival on the other. It is these two inter-related initiatives that provide the main focus of interest in this chapter.

THE RISE OF THE MILITARY – CORPORATE STATE

It has been widely recognised that in recent years the military have come to play a pivotal role in the South African state's response to the various external and internal crises which it is facing. However, the rise of military power and influence does not in our view suggest that South Africa is on the road to a military takeover or that the National Party's long-standing hold over the state apparatus is about to be broken. Rather, we would insist that the forward march of militarism needs to be primarily understood in terms of the unique 'survival politics' practised by the new 'enlightened' rulers of South Africa (Adam, 1978; Charney, 1983). It also needs to be emphasised that the current blurring of the lines between the civil and military authorities is not an entirely new departure in Afrikaner politics. In fact there is a long-standing Afrikaner tradition of close collaborative civil–military relations, which has been emphatically renewed in the present atmosphere of crisis (Frankel, 1984).

The already important place of the military in South African political processes was greatly enhanced by the emergence of Mr P. W. Botha as Prime Minister in 1978. Botha's takeover from the previous leader, the more traditional Afrikaner ideologue Mr J. Vorster, was a decisive moment in the recent phase of militarisation. Botha, as the veteran Minister of Defence, had overseen the considerable growth of the South African Defence Force (SADF) and in office had worked closely with military strategists for over 15 years. On assuming the leadership, Botha quickly ensured that national security and military strength became the most important political priorities. Botha, following the lead of the SADF, put forward the ideal of a 'total onslaught' on the nation from outside and inside its borders. Working in terms of a new defensive ideology of survivalism, the Botha regime has attempted to mobilise white South Africa for 'total war' (Adam, 1978). Amongst other things, this militaristic world-view of South Africa's problems has not surprisingly led to a much more direct, formal involvement of senior military personnel in the upper echelons of the state.

The most significant product of this top-level civil–military collaboration has been the much-vaunted 'total strategy'. Essentially a military doctrine, the total strategy is presented in terms of the necessity for an integrated political and military response to the 'total onslaught' that is being directed against the Republic. According to its military architects the country is facing a 'total war' which can only be won through the systematic application of a carefully worked out combative strategy. The application of this strategy has so far produced an amalgamation of economic and constitutional reforms, heavy policing of internal dissent and military intervention in the neighbouring front-line territories.

What is especially distinctive about the recent militarisation processes is the extent to which the military have been given a more formal, institutionalised role in strategic planning and political decision-making. Previously, military chiefs had worked behind the scenes with the nationalist leadership in a much more informal way. The Afrikaner-dominated military leadership had a limited, indirect political role prior to 1978.[3] So although Vorster worked closely with General Van den Bergh, the head of BOSS on both security matters and the overall direction of state policy, this occurred on a largely *ad hoc*, informal basis.[4] Botha changed all this. A new streamlined bureaucratic structure has been created in which military personnel are charged with carrying out an important co-ordinating role in operationalising the 'total strategy' at all levels and in all parts of the state system.

The drive for greater administrative rationality and centralised control of the state's internal organisation is also a way of dealing with the existence of Afrikaner bureaucratic opposition to the new *verligte* policies. Such opposition comes from some of the entrenched departmental interests in the numerous 'bureaucratic empires' of the cumbersome state apparatus (Giliomee, 1979). It is also a product of the strong ideological resistance put up by the Afrikaner civil service old guard to the current government approach.

Botha's attempted restructuring of the complex, institutionally diverse state apparatus has led to the number of departments being reduced from 39 to 17 and the number of Cabinet committees cut from 40 to 6. Senior military leaders participate in all these influential committees alongside Cabinet ministers and important businessmen (Evans, 1983; Leonard, 1983, pp. 201–6). The military, in the shape of the Minister of Defence General Malan and the Chief of the SADF General Viljoen, also have a direct presence on the profoundly important State Security Council (SSC). The SSC formed in 1972 had been largely dormant under Vorster, meeting only six times during his premiership (Thompson and Prior, 1982, p. 135). The SSC now meet regularly under the chairmanship of Botha and has emerged as 'the most influential decision making institution in the country'[5] (Evans, 1983, p. 42). From being a relatively ineffectual advisory body, it has now become a powerful directive agency overseeing the work of all the government departments through its chain of 15 inter-departmental policy-planning committees. Military top-brass take part in all inter-departmental meetings regardless of subject matter, in order to carry out their strategic co-ordinating task. In effect the SSC has become the powerhouse for formulating and implementing the total strategy. This, together with the further concentration of power in the recently created office of President, has led to a decisive shift of power away from Parliament towards the executive arm of the State.[6] The restructuring has produced what appears to be a strong, militarised, political directorate that is effectively insulated from Parliamentary control and National Party decision-making.

There is considerable evidence therefore of the decay of that element of competitive pluralist politics which has existed in South Africa. We are witnessing the growth of a more authoritarian, directive corporate state.[7] What seems clear is that the ascendancy of military and business representatives into the formal political structure of the state involved some dilution of the old form of ethnically exclusive Afrikaner state corporatism. Of significance here is the Botha government's attempt to forge closer ties with both the English-speaking and Afrikaner-speaking business communities. At the important Carlton Centre Conference in 1979, Botha made his plans clear to the 'ethnically-mixed' business élite that he had specially assembled, when he declared that:

> We have our differences but we are creating reciprocal channels to plan national strategy in South Africa as a team. (Cited in Charney, 1984, p. 273.)

The relative success of this initiative can be seen in the number of business people who have been directly co-opted into the state machinery. One example is the participation of 16 business and professional men on the board of the massive parastatal corporation, Armscor, which controls the purchase and production of all armaments.[8] Another example is Botha's appointment in 1979 of 13 business executives to the Defence Advisory Board which has a watchdog role in relation to both the SADF and the arms industry (Evans, 1983, p. 43). In addition, top company directors have been invited into the new President's Council and also now serve on the Public Service Commission, which had previously been controlled entirely by the Civil Service.

Although English businessmen have been drawn into the new

corporatist forums, representatives from Afrikaner business still predominate. Afrikaners are even more to the fore of course amongst the SADF participants. Noticeably absent from the new councils of power are the trade union representatives of the shrinking white working class. On this basis, there appears to be grounds for giving qualified support to the thesis of an emerging triple alliance at the level of the state between the government, the military and big capital (*South African Review One*, 1983, p. 1). Aside from the fact that important sections of capital have remained aloof from any involvement in the state apparatus, our major qualification here concerns the continuing preponderance of Afrikaners in all the various forms of triangular collaboration. The once strong ethnic class alliance amongst the Afrikaners may now be almost in ruins but it is still a survival-minded Afrikaner élite who have directed the rise of a powerful military – corporate state in South Africa (Charney, 1983; 1984). Furthermore, despite the air being full of the language of reform, all the signs are that they will fight to the end to retain Nationalist control of the restructured apartheid state machine.

SOUTH AFRICAN MILITARY EXPANSIONISM

Since the mid-1970s there has been a heavy build up of military forces and a considerable expansion of military activities inside and outside South Africa's borders. There are a number of different indicators of South African military expansionism. Most obviously, defence spending has spiralled upwards. State expenditure on defence has leapt from a level of R904 million in 1977 to an estimated R3068 million in 1982, and in the recent Budget it has been set to rise to R4274 million.[9] Even allowing for inflation, this represents an increase in defence spending of more than 50 per cent in real terms in less than a decade.[10]

The Defence Force has greatly expanded in membership size too. Its total strength initially shot up in the late 1970s from an estimated 269 000 in 1974 to 494 000 in 1979 (Leonard, 1983, p. 108). This included a virtual fourfold increase in the number of operational troops under arms. These figures have been boosted again as a result of the 1982 Defence Amendment Act which facilitated a sizeable increase in the pool of conscripts as well as a lengthening of the required period of service for part-time servicemen and reservists. The Government now seems well on target for its declared aim of a 200 000 strong 'standing operational force' by 1990, and a total Defence Force Strength of approximately 1 000 000. This impressive increase in size has been accomplished principally by a wide-ranging, extensive military call-up system. Enlargement of the system has seen the length of national service duty doubled; the age limit for part-time military service pushed up to 60; active reserve duty stretched out to 12 years and recent white immigrants drawn into the system as well. Now, after two years full-time national service, young white males have to do extensive part-time service – two years of 'camps' of 270 days duration, and after this, periodic service totalling 720 days in either the Citizen Force or the local Commando units.[11] These two apparatuses, a core part of the intensified mobilisation for war that is now going on, are the major means through which a majority of the white male population is engaged in some kind of military activity for certain periods during the year. However, the call to arms is not solely restricted to the white population since black South Africans too have been recruited into the Defence Force, although their numbers so far are small. Significantly, these black troops have been employed in the combat areas of Northern Namibia and also in the North Eastern border regions of the Republic (Leonard, 1983, pp. 110–11). In that area four special tribally-based 'ethnic battalions' have been created.

Evidence about the military build-up and the inflated defence budget paints only a limited picture of military expansionism. There are at least three other aspects of this process which need to be considered. First, the military have been far more involved in the task of suppressing internal dissent and subversion. Troops, for example, are being used much more in a policing role. In contrast to the handling of the township riots of 1976, military units have been prominent in helping the police to restore order during the well-publicised township troubles of the past few months (Laurence, 1984). The increasing use of troops in quelling civil disorder is one dimension of the diminution of the distinction between the activities of the paramilitary South African police and the armed forces. One commentator has associated this trend with a deep historical tendency within Afrikanerdom towards the fusion of civil and military activities, whereby Defence Force functions have been fulfilled by the police and police duties have been carried out by the SADF (Frankel, 1984). Beyond such a convergence of functions and responsibilities, we would identify the most important current trend as the increasing primacy of the military over the police and the Department of National Security (DONS) in the field of political surveillance and intelligence gathering. Military Intelligence (MI) now dominates political policing in a reversal of its relationship with the former leading intelligence agency, BOSS. This only reflects the overall political superiority which the military has over the security and policing apparatuses (Leonard, 1983, p. 123, pp. 127/8).

Secondly, the military have expanded their influence in other less directly coercive ways. In an attempt to militarise white youth, they have sponsored the burgeoning school cadet system which has swollen from 57 000 cadets in 1976 to 210 000 in 1983 (Leonard, 1983, p. 117; Evans, 1983, p. 44). Many young people are offered rigorous military training at school in readiness for National Service. They are usually also subject to classroom 'Youth Preparedness' programmes aimed at steeling them for a future of conflict and war. Black youth too have been subjected to a crude 'hearts and minds' campaign through the deployment of conscripts as teachers in black schools. Under the Civil Action Programme military servicemen have been pressed into other forms of non-military service as doctors, agricultural advisers etc. in a transparent attempt to win over local black communities.

Finally, the greatest importance should be attached to the expansion of Pretoria's military operations into the front-line states elsewhere in the Southern Africa region. South African military aggression broadly takes three different, interrelated forms. First, there are the pre-emptive strikes that have been launched against the ANC in Mozambique and Lesotho and against SWAPO in Angola in order to eliminate their capacity to foment guerrilla warfare in South Africa and Namibia. Secondly there is the extensive and costly military intervention in Namibia where a protracted and intense war has been waged against the resilient SWAPO forces. This form of military intervention, absorbing as it has an increasing slice of South Africa's resources, has also been characterised by the active involvement of senior military advisers in Namibian state administration and policy-making (Cullinan, 1983). The SADF have been instrumental too in setting up an indigenous 'Namibian' army, the SWA Territory Force composed of Namibians and seconded SADF soldiers. Thirdly there is also military intervention aimed at economic subversion and political 'destabilisation'. This involves offering various kinds of military support and assistance to insurgent, anti-government forces such as UNITA in Angola and the MNR in Mozambique. Such support can then be used as a way of pressurising neighbouring states who harbour and sustain the ANC. Ultimately, it is the ANC who are seen as the paramount threat and prime military target for the SADF (Vale, 1983).

In summary, it should be emphasised that the SADF's foreign and domestic activities are part of a complex and far-reaching militarisation process. This process has involved far more than the development of an expanded role for the military itself. Rather it involves the militarisation of the entire state system and the placement of the whole South African social formation on an incipient war footing. So far, analyses of this process seem to us to have overlooked at least two important issues. First of all, there is the question of whether this militarisation process is explainable in terms of a strategic master plan. We insist that there are problems with giving the growth of militarism and the onset of war a political rationale. The next section of this chapter will challenge the uncritical adoption of the idea of a 'total strategy' in some accounts of recent developments. Following on from this, we also want to raise the issue of whether this militarisation process is under control. Rationalistic 'top-down' interpretations of South African policy processes tend to imply an omniscient power élite who are in control of both the state system and the enveloping militarisation process. In our view this sort of approach totally fails to consider whether or not the militarisation process has got its own self-generating momentum, or the degree to which it is racked by internal contradictions that even the most 'enlightened' South African technocrats would find difficult to resolve.

SOUTH AFRICA AT WAR: A TOTAL STRATEGY

A range of disparate problems, both internal and external, are normally identified as comprising the pieces of a jigsaw puzzle which collectively contribute to a 'total onslaught' upon South Africa. According to General Malan, one of the key architects of the total strategy, a massive assault is being mounted against the Republic involving 'diplomacy, industry, trade, technology, the written and spoken word, the public media, demonstrations, strikes, boycotts, subversion and so on' (cited in Callinicos, 1981, p. 101). Such a wide-ranging form of attack requires a similarly comprehensive response. To combat this 'total war', South Africa needs a 'total national strategy' in which a wide range of the Republic's policies are coordinated and directed towards the achievement of a common set of strategic objectives. The 1977 Defence White Paper, taking as its premise that South Africa is involved in a war, gives a clear summary of the basic thinking underlying the total strategy. It is seen as a

> comprehensive plan to utilise all the means available to a state according to an integrated pattern in order to achieve the national aims within the framework of specific policies. A total strategy is, therefore, not confined to a particular sphere, but is applicable to all levels and to all functions of the state structure. (Cited in Leonard, 1983, p. 200.)

The package of internal reforms and external initiatives that together are said to comprise the coordinated response of the South African state to this perceived total onslaught are by now well known. (For a brief summary of the components of the total strategy see: Jenkins, 1980; Leonard, 1983, pp. 198–221; Davies and O'Meara, 1984.) Internally a series of measures have been announced designed to improve the situation of the minority or urban blacks. Limited trade union rights have been granted to those black workers who join registered and approved unions. Job reservation has been terminated and commitments have been given to the idea of increased education and training for blacks. The system of influx control has been streamlined making employers more responsible for its operation in order to reduce the level of illegal black immigration to the cities. The privileges enjoyed by 'section-tenners', the minority of urban blacks statutorily exempted from the general prohibition on Africans residing in white areas, have been enhanced.[12] And the small but rapidly expanding African petty-bourgeoisie has been deliberately fostered by lifting some of the restrictions on black businesses.

More generally the government has announced its intention to 'liberalise' the South African economy and to reduce the level of state interference and regulation in a wide area of economic activities. Limited forms of non-white political representation have been introduced via the local community councils for urban blacks and the separate legislative parliamentary chambers for the Coloured and Indian communities. Nationalist thinking on this latter constitutional reform was summed up in a letter sent by Dr J. Grobler, chief information officer for the National Party, to Dr A. Treurnicht on the eve of the formation of the breakaway Conservative Party.

> we should associate the Coloureds as a block of 2.5 million people with whites at any price, so that we can broaden our powerbase and not deliver them to the 'black power' situation. (Cited in Welsh, 1984, p. 149.)

Finally, some of the excesses of petty apartheid have been eliminated in an effort to remove some of the sources of internal friction and to improve South Africa's image abroad.

These internal policy modifications have been complemented by a set of new regional initiatives across Southern Africa, all of which have strong military overtones but which are not determined by narrow military objectives alone. (See Price 1984 for a discussion of the different dimensions of South Africa's regional strategy.) The sponsorship of dissident groups and the campaign of destabilisation cannot be understood simply as an attempt to overthrow the MPLA government in Angola or the FRELIMO government in Mozambique, at least in the foreseeable future. Rather the purpose of destabilisation is twofold. First, it is designed to persuade the black African states themselves to assist in the neutralisation of the guerrilla threat posed by the ANC and by SWAPO. If the front line states can be forced to deny training facilities to guerrillas, and to restrict the size of the non-combative infrastructure that provides the support for military operations, then the security of the Republic will have been greatly enhanced. In this respect the much publicised 'peace accords' signed at Nkomati in March 1984 between Prime Minister Botha and President Machel of Mozambique appear to be a triumphant vindication of this strategy.[13]

Secondly, destabilisation is designed to weaken the economies of the independent black states and to reinforce South Africa's pivotal economic role in the region. In the long term South Africa's declared ambition is to preside over the establishment of a Constellation of Southern African States, including the bantustans, Angola, Botswana, Lesotho, Malawi, Mozambique, an independent Namibia, Swaziland, Zaire, Zambia and Zimbabwe. This grouping is explicitly seen as involving new political relationships as well as extensive forms of economic cooperation. More immediately if South Africa is to be able to continue to supplement its military pressure with economic leverage, it must work to undermine the Southern Africa Development Coordination Conference launched by the front line states in 1980. One of the primary objectives of this organisation is the foundation of an integrated transport network independent of that of

South Africa. If successful this would result in a very considerable loosening of the asymmetrical ties of dependency between the black states and South Africa. Therefore both UNITA and MNR have consistently sabotaged east–west road and rail links in Angola and Mozambique, which has had the effect of denying Zambia, Zaire and Zimbabwe access to the sea other than via routes that pass through South Africa. (See Price, 1984, for other examples of economic leverage.)

In summary, therefore, the total strategy appears to take the form of a two-pronged counter-attack designed to ensure the survival of white rule in South Africa. On the one hand it seeks to eliminate the potential threat of the ANC and to neutralise or subordinate those who would give it material support through a combination of military and economic interventions in the region. On the other hand it aims to improve the economic, social and political situation of the 'browns' and a minority of blacks in South Africa, in order to render these groups less susceptible to mobilisation in support of the aims of the ANC and so to create a buffer between the privileged whites and the mass of dispossessed blacks.

HOW 'TOTAL' IS THE TOTAL STRATEGY?

It is clearly in the interests of the ruling Nationalist regime to present its policies as if they formed a coherent total package, an integration of political and military initiatives designed to thwart the total onslaught against white civilisation. However, although the South African state may choose to present *itself* as a rational subject possessing the strategic skills and political acumen necessary to ensure its own survival, social scientists must at all costs avoid such simplistic assumptions. In particular a thoroughgoing analysis of the contemporary South African state must at least initially treat politically loaded terms like 'total strategy' with some scepticism and examine them as objects of analysis rather than appropriating them from the outset as useful explanatory concepts.

We have argued elsewhere that much of the recent writing on the South African state rests upon simplistic instrumentalist assumptions in which the state is conceived in unified and over-rationalistic terms (Mitchell and Russell, 1983). It would appear that similar assumptions underlie most considerations of the total strategy, with the result that there has been a failure on the part of most commentators to 'unpack' the notion of 'total strategy' or to problematise the degree of internal unity among its elements. Thus for example Price's very thorough discussion of South Africa's diverse regional interventions is premised upon the belief that these represent a carefully planned 'comprehensive strategy' exhibiting a 'coherent inner logic' (Price, 1984, p. 27).

There are a number of issues that need to be raised in order to probe in more detail the nature of the total strategy. In the first place, although South Africa is undoubtedly facing severe difficulties, it is doubtful whether the threat to the survival of the Republic is as serious as the idea of total onslaught suggests.[14] The SADF has more combat troops, more and better equipment and vastly superior resources to draw upon than the combined forces of all the front line states. The ANC, although able on occasion to pull off a dramatic success like the bombing in June 1980 of the Sasol oil-from-coal plants, cannot be considered to pose a serious military challenge to the South African regime. Indeed there is, as Rich has pointed out, a peculiar paradox at the very core of the ideology of total onslaught, since the idea of white supremacy is often premised on the belief that black people are 'inherently incapable of mounting a successful military attack' and are 'continually prone to bungling and internal political division' (1984, p. 73).[15]

If the ANC is not a serious threat to South Africa's survival and if blacks are believed to be inherently incompetent in military affairs, then what is the purpose of the total strategy? In part we would agree with Adam that the permanent state of emergency is an asset to the South African state since it can be utilised to secure minority white rule.

> While a government in a divided society may rhetorically deplore the potential instability, it also benefits from the institutionalisation of crisis: it keeps its constituency mobilized and provides the rationale for assuming wide discretionary power for maintaining law and order. If the 'total onslaught' were not real in some aspects, it would have had to be invented in South Africa. (Adam, 1984, p. 47.)

In addition, periods of crisis – real or imagined – are periods of change and by amplifying the notion of total onslaught, the South African ruling élite has more easily been able to break old alliances and cement new ones in the search for a more secure future. The shift from the traditional ideology of Afrikaner exclusivism towards a concern for white survival has been a difficult one for the ruling National Party to make. However, the cataclysmic portrayal of the threat to South Africa encapsulated in the idea of total onslaught has generated a kind of war psychosis which has in turn served to encourage this painful transition. As one government official has admitted:

> There is a threat as perceived by government, but the concept of this threat is used for other reasons than the real threat: to bring people together whom the government thinks should be together. (Cited in Charney, 1983, p. 149.)

Secondly in terms of the total strategy itself, there is the central issue of the degree of inner coherence of the initiatives themselves. To what extent do they comprise a total package of interdependent reforms each constituting one element of a carefully planned and systematic strategy? (See Mitchell and Russell, 1983, pp. 17–19 for a discussion of the internal contradictions of the total strategy.) For example the high degree of centralised autocratic direction from above implied in most aspects of the total strategy fits uneasily with the ideas of economic liberalism and the free market that have recently been espoused by the National Party leadership. Indeed, it is doubtful whether any society in an advanced state of war-preparedness could avoid the necessity for a top-down system of controls over private enterprise. Given the increasing militarisation of South African society it is highly unlikely that the Nationalist government will be able to set private industry free. As one commentator has noted:

> in the current South African case, the ideological theme of 'free enterprise' has become a means for legitimating areas of state intervention in the economy on the one hand, and a high degree of participation by big business in the affairs of the state, on the other. (Posel, 1982, p. 13.)

It also needs to be emphasised that the South African government is not in complete control of all the factors that will determine the overall success or failure of the total strategy. The economy remains highly dependent upon the export of gold which contributes over half of its foreign exchange earnings. This inevitably means, as the South African Reserve Bank has noted, that 'short run prospects for the South African economy necessarily remain tied to a significant extent to the vagaries of the gold price in the international market' (from an advertisement placed by the South African Reserve Bank in *The Economist*, 21 June 1980). In addition while it is undoubtedly the case that South Africa's strategic position improved as a result of the electoral successes of the New Right in Britain and the USA, there is no guarantee that this more favourable international climate will last. The recent upsurge of anti-apartheid sentiment in the USA and the concerted attempts to call a halt to further American investment in South Africa are forcing changes in President Reagan's policy of 'constructive engagement' with Pretoria. In general therefore we can appreciate that one of the central problems inherent in the idea of the total strategy is that it invests Pretoria with too much power and too much control. The South African state is not some kind of omniscient rational subject, planning its strategic moves in a gigantic game of chess in which it controls all the pieces.

The third problem concerning the total strategy is the extent to which the verbal commitments to change and reform have in fact been carried over into practice. Quotes from senior government ministers, or from the pages of the many reports and commissions that are such an important feature of South African political life, do not in themselves indicate that material changes have taken place. There is a world of difference between the conception of a new set of policies and their implementation.

Two rather different examples can be used to illustrate this problem, the first concerning the streamlining of influx controls, the second involving the restructuring of black education. It is commonly agreed that the proposals of the Riekert Commission on the reform of influx controls are a central element of the total strategy. The government has accepted the proposals in principle, and has committed itself to modifying existing legislation, especially the Urban Areas Act, to bring the law into line with the Riekert proposals. Yet attempts to legislate in this area have met with widespread hostility both from the right, who oppose any reform, and from the liberal opposition who want more substantial changes.[16] As a result on two occasions in 1980 and again in 1982, government Bills were withdrawn from the Parliament for further consideration. Additional uncertainty has been introduced to the situation by a decision of South Africa's highest court of appeal in May 1983, which appears to grant exemption under section 10 of the Urban Areas Act to tens of thousands of migrant workers.[17] As a result, government plans to streamline influx controls appear to have been blown off course.

The case of reforms in black education is a rather different manifestation of the same essential problem of the gap between stated intention and concrete practice. Both the Wiehan report on trade union reform and the Riekert report on influx control hinted that changes in the education and technical training of young blacks were needed. In 1980 the government appointed the De Lange Commission of Inquiry into Education which reported a year later. (For a discussion of the De Lange report, see Chisholm and Christie, 1983.) Its proposals dovetailed precisely with those of the earlier reports and were designed to modernise thinking on black education within the overall confines of apartheid. The 1981 government White Paper rejected even the modest reforms of the De Lange Commission, especially its central principle of 'equal quality' in educational provision to be administered by a single education department. Together with the previous example on the problems of modernising influx controls, this shows the continuing strength of white opposition to the package of reforms that comprise the total strategy. The departure of Dr Treurnicht and his supporters has by no means eliminated the opposition to change from within the ranks of the National Party and its associated institutions. (For a discussion of the network of institutions that contribute to the workings of Afrikaner politics, see Giliomee, 1979.) In particular many sections of the Verwoerd-appointed Afrikaner civil service appear to be reluctant to follow President Botha and General Malan in their search for new strategies for survival.

But it is not only white opposition that has opened up a serious gap between the theory and practice of the total strategy in contemporary South Africa. A variety of forms of black resistance have been crucial in undermining all attempts to engineer new forms of control from above. The South African government has experienced great difficulty in attempting to contain and control black trade unions, with the result that there has been a maintenance of levels of industrial militancy despite the effects of the recession. (For a discussion of the levels of industrial militancy in different industries in 1982, see Lambert and Lambert, 1983.) Further attempts to restrict and limit black trade union activity would almost certainly result in an even greater politicisation of industrial conflict – something that the South African government must be anxious to avoid.

In addition the attempts by the South African regime to create limited forms of political representation for non-whites have also proved to be a conspicuous failure. The elections for the black community councils in urban areas have produced derisory turn-outs and councillors and their supporters have become the objects of hostility, abuse and violence. (Detailed information on the workings of the community councils is given in Hughes and Grest, 1983.) And the elections for the Indian and Coloured chambers in the new tricameral parliament in 1984 attracted a much lower turn-out than had been expected. Indeed, by providing a focus for hostility and resentment, these reforms have turned out to be counter-productive for the Nationalist Government in its search for greater political stability.

In conclusion therefore we can see the implementation of the set of reforms integral to the total strategy has been highly problematic for the South African government. Even if we take the stated commitment to change to be genuine, the capacity of the regime to carry through even moderate changes in the face of widespread hostility from sections of the white community and from the majority of brown and black South Africans is severely limited. The result has been a growing gap between the rhetoric and the reality of the total strategy.

CONCLUSION

Any hopes that the economic and political reforms of the total strategy could serve as a blueprint for white survival ought by now to have been extinguished. Whilst political commentators have usually highlighted the reformist dimensions of Mr Botha's 'adapt-or-die' message, Government policy has in reality exhibited a different emphasis. In practice, the Nationalist strategy for survival has revolved around an ongoing militarisation process in which the logic of a war against 'the enemies of the Republic' has been the central driving force. We have suggested in this chapter that an adequate account of this process needs to focus on those features of the South African situation which have been unduly neglected in most recent state theory.

The Nationalist regime has had to use an uneven combination of repression and reform to maintain its grip on South African society and has come increasingly to rely upon a variety of forms of coercion and constraint to secure its rule. Their unsuccessful search for legitimacy – internally and internationally – has meant that extensive state intervention, repression and military force, both inside and outside South Africa's borders, continues to provide the principal safeguard for the survival of white rule. The National Party's determination to maintain white control of the state apparatus at all costs gives relatively little scope for generating widespread popular consent. In addition there is little in South Africa's recent economic performance to suggest that it can seriously expect to achieve greater 'legitimacy by results'. Consequently policies designed to generate broader support for the regime – in particular from 'brown' South Africans and from 'urban insiders' – have been consistently outweighed by coercive policies and practices calculated to induce acquiescence from the majority of the black population. The tightening of the mechanisms of control and the suppression of internal dissent have become the preserve of an extensive network of coercive apparatuses which, despite encountering a variety of forms of opposition and resistance, appear so far to be capable of imposing political rule. There is also every indication that the South African state has the capacity to unleash a much greater degree of repression than has so far been evident.[18] The power and resources that it has at its disposal to enforce compliance and to suppress insurrection convinces us that to exaggerate the vulnerability of the South African state is a mistake.

Whilst the South African military exist as the principal source and the most potent symbol of this extraordinary state power, our purpose in this chapter has not been to concentrate solely on the power of the military as such. Instead we have tried to highlight the thoroughgoing militarisation of the entire state system and the wider society. The mobilisation of white South Africans for war, the militarisation of policy processes and the sustained military aggression in the region together represent Pretoria's strategic response to the specific constellation of international and national pressures that have confronted the South African state since the mid-1970s. The emergence of a highly autonomous executive at the summit of the South African state is in the main a consequence of the logic of war and of the associated requirement for an increased level of direction and control over the state. In this way the militarised South African state has sought to secure white domination within the Republic and to consolidate its military and economic domination throughout Southern Africa. We believe that the effect of this is more likely to result in a vicious spiral of increasing militarisation, black resistance and state repression, than it is to achieve the economic modernisation and political stability envisaged by the architects of the total strategy.

NOTES

1. This chapter was written prior to the intensification of crisis and conflict which has accompanied the South African government's July 1985 declaration of a state of emergency. Nevertheless, we believe that subsequent developments can in many ways be taken as a confirmation of

our general analysis and we have therefore avoided any significant redrafting of the chapter in the light of these more recent events.

2. Our ideas in this introduction have been informed by the recent work of David Held (1983; 1984).
3. Leonard (1983, pp. 102/3) notes that in 1974 the permanent staff of the army was 85 per cent Afrikaner. In the air force and the navy the equivalent figures were 75 per cent and 50 per cent respectively. The army is by far the largest branch of the South African Defence Force, accounting for more than 80 per cent of its troop strength.
4. BOSS is an acronym for the Bureau of State Security set up by the Vorster government. It was renamed the Department of National Security (DONS) in 1978. The close relationship between Prime Minister Vorster and General Van den Bergh is emphasised by Leonard (1983, pp. 7/8).
5. Thompson and Prior (1982, p. 135) state that in 1980 the SSC met fortnightly under the chairmanship of Prime Minister Botha.
6. The office of President was created under the recent package of reforms which were implemented in 1984. The post of executive President combines the former powers of the State President and the Prime Minister. In addition the incumbent will head the new tricameral parliament, as well as having supreme authority over the SADF. Predictably, Mr Botha has taken up the post.
7. There is an important distinction between 'state' or 'authoritarian' corporatism developed from above and the 'societal' or 'liberal' corporatism more characteristic of the Western democratic capitalist states. Cawson (1982) and Martin (1983) both discuss this distinction in some detail.
8. Armscor is an acronym for the Armaments Corporation of South Africa. It grew out of the Munitions Production Board first established in 1964 by the Nationalist government after the United Nations embargo on the export of arms to South Africa. Although a state corporation, it works closely with private arms manufacturers. It is currently the third largest corporation in South Africa (Leonard, 1983, pp. 137–9).
9. Figures for defence spending are derived from information contained in: *Apartheid – the Facts* (1983, p. 68); Evans (1983, p. 43); and the *Guardian*, 19 March 1985. It should be noted that these figures significantly underestimate the full cost of the military programme because of the secret purchases of arms and equipment from abroad.
10. Allowances for inflation have been made on the basis of information derived from the international financial statistics of the IMF, quoted in *Official Yearbook of the Republic of South Africa* (1984, p. 344).
11. The Commandos are said by Leonard (1983, pp. 115–16) to be local Defence Force units modelled on the militias used historically by the Afrikaners, especially during the Boer War. They tend to have a fairly large proportion of volunteers although more men, especially older men who have missed National Service, are being conscripted into their ranks. The Citizen Force, the national back-up corps for part-time service, has more conscripted men who have already completed their two years of National Service. Both bodies are now of roughly equal strength, each making up 35 per cent of the total Defence Force.

12. Under Section 10 of the Urban Areas Act, two kinds of exemption are possible to the general rule denying the right of permanent residence to Africans outside their designated 'homeland' areas. Statutory exemption is possible for individuals who qualify on the basis of birth or a long period of continuous residence in one area. Administrative exemption may be granted to individuals recruited to specific areas on temporary labour contractors. Only the former are customarily known as 'section-tenners'.
13. Less publicity has been given to the equally important treaty on non-aggression and to the agreement on disengagement negotiated between South Africa and Swaziland and Angola respectively.
14. We would disagree with those commentators who have interpreted the recent escalation of violence in the townships as indicative of the imminent collapse of white rule.
15. Chief of Defence Force General C. Viljoen seemed to be expressing this belief when he stated in July 1981 that the ANC 'has not nearly shown itself to be a worthwhile military organisation' (cited in Rich 1984, p. 75).
16. One of the reasons why the proposed government legislation received such a high level of criticism from the liberal opposition was that in certain respects, the proposals seemed to intensify rather than liberalise the controls on urban blacks. For a discussion of this and other issues concerning the fate of the Riekert Commission's proposals, see Hindson and Lacey (1983).
17. The case involved Mr M. Rikhoto who had claimed that, since he had worked as a migrant labourer for the same Johannesburg employer for ten years, he should be entitled to permanent exemption from the general prohibition on blacks residing in urban areas. The Appellate Division of the Supreme Court upheld his claim. Previously it had been assumed that since labour contracts could only be issued for a maximum of twelve months, migrant workers would never be able to qualify for statutory Section 10 exemption. See also note 12 above.
18. The recent declaration of a state of emergency and the rise in the numbers of blacks killed by the security forces is a clear indication of this.

REFERENCES

Adam, H. (1978) 'Survival politics: Afrikanerdom in search of a new ideology.' *Journal of Modern African Studies*, vol. 16, no. 4, pp. 657–69.

Adam, H. (1984) 'South Africa's Search for Legitimacy.' *Telos*, no. 59, pp. 45–68.

Apartheid – the Facts (1983) London: International Defence and Aid Fund.

Callinicos, A. (1981) *Southern Africa After Zimbabwe*, London: Pluto Press.

Cawson, A. (1982) *Corporatism and Welfare*, London: Heinemann.

Charney, C. (1983) 'Restructuring White Politics: the Transformations of the National Party', *South African Review One*, pp. 142–54.

Charney, C. (1984) 'Class Conflict and the National Party Split,' *Journal of Southern African Studies*, vol. 10, no. 2, pp. 269–82.

Chisholm, L. and Christie, P. (1983) 'Restructuring in Education', *South African Review One*, pp. 254–63.
Cullinan, S. (1983) 'Military Policy and the Namibian Dispute', *South African Review One*, pp. 33–41.
Davies, R. and O'Meara, D. (1984) 'The State of Analysis of the Southern African Region: Issues Raised by South African Strategy', *Review of African Political Economy*, no. 29, pp. 64–76.
Evans, M. (1983) 'Restructuring: the Role of the Military', *South African Review One*, pp. 42–9.
Frankel, P. (1984) *Pretoria's Praetorians: Civil–Military Relations in South Africa*, Cambridge: University Press.
Giliomee, H. (1979) 'Afrikaner Politics: how the System Works', in Adam, H. and Giliomee, H., *Ethnic Power Mobilised: Can South Africa Change?*, New Haven and London: Yale University Press, pp. 221–32.
Held, D. (1983) 'Central Perspectives on the Modern State', in D. Held *et al.* (eds), *States and Societies*, Oxford: Martin Robertson, pp. 1–55.
Held, D. (1984) 'Power and Legitimacy in Contemporary Britain', in G. McLennan, D. Held and S. Hall (eds), *State and Society in Contemporary Britain*, Cambridge: Polity Press, pp. 299–369.
Hindson, D. and Lacey, M. (1983) 'Influx Control and Labour Allocation: Policy and Practice since the Riekert Commission', *South Africa Review One*, pp. 97–113.
Hughes, H. and Grest, J. (1983) 'The Local State', *South African Review One*, pp. 122–41.
Jenkins, S. (1980) 'The Tribal Glue,' *The Economist*, 21 June.
Lambert, R. and L. (1983) 'State Reform and Working Class Resistance, 1982', *South African Review One*, pp. 218–250.
Laurence, P. (1984) 'Why Military Minds Intervene in Political Role.' (sic), the *Guardian*, 24 October.
Leonard, R. (1983) *South Africa at War: White Power and the Crisis in Southern Africa*, Connecticut: Lawrence Hill and Co.
Martin, R. (1983) 'Pluralism and the New Corporatism,' *Political Studies*, vol. 31, no. 1, pp. 86–102.
Mitchell, M. and Russell, D. (1983) 'Restructuring Apartheid', unpublished paper presented to the Annual Conference of the British Sociological Association at University College, Cardiff.
Official Yearbook of the Republic of South Africa (1984) Pretoria: van Rensberg Publications.
Posel, D. (1982) 'State Ideology and Legitimation: the Contemporary South African Case', unpublished paper cited in Charney (1983).
Price, R. (1984) 'Pretoria's Southern African Strategy', *African Affairs*, vol. 83, no. 332, pp. 11–32.
Rich, P. (1984) 'Insurgency, Terrorism and the Apartheid System in South Africa', *Political Studies*, vol. 32, no. 1, pp. 68–85.
South African Review One: Same Foundations, New Facades? (1983) Johannesburg: Raven Press.
Thompson, L. and Prior, A. (1982) *South African Politics*, New Haven and London: Yale University Press.

Vale, P. (1983) 'Pretoria and Southern Africa: from Manipulation to Intervention', *South African Review One*, pp. 7–22.
Welsh, D. (1984) 'Constitutional Changes in South Africa', *African Affairs*, vol. 83, no. 331, pp. 147–62.

6 Israel: Conflict, War and Social Change

Avishai Ehrlich

The case of Israel may serve as an example of the contention that conflict and war bring about creation, modification and change, transformation or destruction of social formations. It seems probable that the longer lasting, the more comprehensive and intensive the conflict, the more salient will be its effects upon the social structure. Israel is thus an example, one of a few in modern history, of a permanent war society.

In this chapter, I shall argue and try to demonstrate that the Israeli-Arab conflict is a social process which has a great formative effect on the Israeli social formation. In the first part of the chapter I shall trace the evolutionary aspect of the conflict and its transformations. Clarification of what is meant by the conflict determines the conceptions about its effects. In the second part I shall sketch briefly the way that Israeli sociology has dealt with the conflict and point out some deficiencies in the various Israeli approaches. I shall argue that the conflict, despite its centrality is not allowed as a separate, independent and comprehensive field of research and as a result its effects are belittled or ignored. In the third part I give an example which shows the pivotal importance of the conflict to the shaping of the Israeli social formation in the past and at present.

THE CONFLICT

Azar, Jureidini and McLaurin (1978) typified the Israeli-Arab conflict as a 'protracted social conflict' along with conflicts such as: the Sino-Soviet, Northern Ireland, Somalia–Ethiopia, North Korea–South Korea, China–Taiwan, Cyprus, Lebanon, etc. They characterise protracted conflicts by their long *duration*, *fluctuation* of intensity, their *comprehensiveness* – extending to all domains of communal and international relations – and by the *absence of a distinct termination point*. They have argued that protracted conflicts are not specific events or even clusters of events at a point in time but are processes. As processes, it is argued here, they each have their structure and evolution which differ from one protracted conflict to another.

Unlike some of the conflicts mentioned above, the Israeli-Arab conflict has one particular feature which makes it even more important in shaping Israeli society. This is the fact that the conflict can be traced to the very beginnings of the modern Jewish-Israeli settlement in Palestine. As early as 1920 the conflict became a national conflict rather than an interpersonal or local one. The significance of the early eruption of the conflict is its emergence before the social structure had formed or taken a specific shape. Thus it is a historically continuous central factor in the shaping of the social formation from its meagre beginnings. Before demonstrating how the conflict shaped and changed Israeli society, it is necessary to define and clarify some key notions about the conflict.

(1) The Israeli-Arab conflict has as its core the efforts of the Zionist settlers to create an exclusivist Jewish society in Palestine and the resistance, first of the native Arab Palestinians, and later of states, Arab and other, to this colonisation project. In this respect the conflict is perceived by both sides in zero-sum terms and in opposing symmetrical concepts: the social, national and state building processes of Israel are seen by the Arabs as processes of destruction, dispersion and destructuration of Palestinian Arab society.

(2) Though the core of the conflict has not changed it has evolved historically. The history of the conflict can be periodised into three major phases, each having its own characteristics:

(a) 1920–1947: an intra-state conflict between two national communities;
(b) 1948–1967: an inter-state conflict between Israel and the surrounding Arab states both backed by international allies;
(c) 1967–1985: inter-state conflict internationalised, becoming one of the central arenas in the superpowers' competition for global hegemony.

The extension of the conflict and the change of phases did not mean the disappearance of features characteristic of previous phases. New variables were superimposed on existing ones, changing the locus of the conflict and the significance of previous variables in its overall structural matrix. The features of previous phases thus continue but are transposed within a different, wider, context.

In the first phase the nature of the conflict between the Jewish-Zionist community and the Arab community in Palestine is overdetermined by the fact that the state and its main apparatuses were in the hands of a third power – the British. It is this external power which sets the limits on the possible evolution of each community's aspirations and determines the means by which they can be achieved. The particular development of the Jewish Yishuv in Mandatory Palestine has to be understood in the light of the fact that colonisation could not be achieved – as in many other colonial contexts where there was no external, superior, power in government – by force and legal coercion. Instead it had to rely on the development of capitalist market mechanism for the acquisition of land, and on immigration laws for entrance. It is only in this context that the specificity of the Zionist structure can be comprehended.

The existence of the foreign, British, state was perceived as a fetter for national development by the Arabs, as it blocked their majority rights in law-making and neutralised their ability to use force. The Palestinian national movement thus strove for independence and statehood as a precondition to the resolution of the conflict (the 1936–9 Arab rebellion) – but failed. The Zionists felt the British state as a fetter on their further development after 1939 when the laws on land acquisition and immigration closed off further possibilities of extending the Jewish Yishuv, thus freezing it in a minority status. After 1945 it was the Zionists who demanded independence.

Under the conditions prevailing in the first phase the modes of expression of the conflict were limited to pressure on the government for favourable policies, boycotts of economic exchanges, the separate development of sectors and sporadic limited localised hostilities. The conflict could not become an all-out war by the fact of the enforcement power of a superior coercive apparatus – the British Government. This fact does not mean that the conflict was not intensive or comprehensive: indeed it overshadowed every aspect of life.

The withdrawal of the external power made possible the first full-blown war which raged over the issue of whether a Jewish state should be founded, and its territorial extent. The outcome of this war was the foundation of the state of Israel. The 1948 war is a most profound example of the effects of war on society. The Palestinian defeat resulted in the break-up of their social structure and their physical dispersal.

With the foundation of the Israeli state in 1948 and the military intervention against it by seven Arab states the conflict entered its second, inter-state, phase. Palestinian resistance continued – albeit under new conditions of struggle. Its main military mode was now guerrilla activities carried out inside Israel and from across the borders – by irregulars. Thus even in the inter-state phase internal security remained an important aspect of the conflict. Palestinians in Israel were subjected to unequal status by the Emergency Regulations Act 1945 which restricted their movement, human rights and employment. Above all the process of colonisation of their lands intensified. The main mode of resistance of the Palestinians in Israel was political struggle for democratic rights and limited recourse to the law (Lustick, 1980). From the Palestinian point of view, however, the main effect of the involvement of Arab States was the shift in the locus of the conflict. The core mode of conflict became inter-state activities; the Palestinian case had been taken over now by Arab states. The Palestinians and their struggle became subordinate, controlled and used according to each state's interests and to inter-Arab relations.

The inter-state phase is characterised first of all by its long duration. As Israel could not force the Arab states to conclude a peace agreement and as the Arabs were not inclined to do so, a state of war, though not necessarily actual wide-scale fighting, became the permanent state of affairs. This situation covers a wide spectrum of activities ranging from full, all out, wars in 1948, 1956, 1967, 1973, 1976 and 1982 to numerous, more limited, campaigns, raids and skirmishes some of which, such as in the mid-1950s and following the 1967 war, were almost daily fights on quite extensive scales (the war of attrition). The first consequence of the permanent war situation was the inevitable military build-up. In contrast to the pre-statehood phase where external security was in the hands of the British, Israel had to devote much of its financial and manpower resources to security. The ratio of military expenditure out of total resources rose continuously becoming a heavier and heavier burden. Although the initial Arab intervention had to do with the actual foundation of the state of Israel and the plight of the Palestinians, the state of war gave birth to additional issues of hostility. Israel's conquest and holding of Arab states' territories in the wars that followed thus became causes for future wars (e.g. 1973).

The radical nature of Arab opposition to Israel, that is that the conflict was not about the territorial expanse of the state but against its very right to exist gave the situation a deep ideological dimension of total war (Harkabi, 1968). The objective situation of a state surrounded by hostile states was made into an ideology and a siege mentality, 'a nation with its back to the sea'. The Arab aim was seen as 'Politicide' and was superimposed on the collective memory of Nazi genocide against the Jews. This mentality was, and still is, the basis of Israel's political consensus.

The escalation of the conflict into an inter-state phase adds also the dimension of international relations as another arena in which the conflict is being acted out. The aim here is to harm Israel's international standing, to castigate and delegitimise it, isolate it and thus weaken its ability to gain support. The purpose is to prevent the acceptance of Israel as a normal fact: exacting a price on Israel's good standing among nations in international bodies by economic boycotts, and by preventing tourism, scientific, cultural, educational and sport exchanges. Thus sports or even scientific conferences became modes of expression of the conflict. This means that from Israel's point of view all these contacts are valorised and charged with national security meaning beyond their actual content.

Another aspect of the inter-state phase is the involvement in the conflict of additional powers. Although states do meddle in intra-state conflicts this is regarded as interference. Alliances among sovereign states, on the other hand, are legitimate in international relations. The involvement of other powers increases the complexity of the initial conflict as third parties' interests are superimposed on the initial contentions. Third parties can provide Israel with weapons, war materials, technologies and testing grounds thus extending its capabilities. Third parties can provide strategic economic materials as alternatives to economic boycotts, can act as economic agents with countries where there are no economic relations due to the diplomatic and economic aspects of the conflict. Third parties can provide direct aid – financial, diplomatic, military – thus influencing the ability and willingness to open hostilities, restrain them, or even move towards normalisation of relations. Last but not least, alliances also mean that direct adversaries provide bases and support for third party's operations against the enemy, that they act directly in tandem with a third party against their enemy or can act as proxy for a third party against the enemy or its allies – covertly or openly. All these effects of the inter-state phase lead almost inevitably to its internationalisation, especially due to its long duration and the growing involvement of the superpowers.

The internationalisation of the conflict reaches its apex with the growing intervention of the two superpowers who are drawn into it by the effects that it has on their global interests, by the involvement of their cliental states and as part of their scramble for strategic influence. The Middle East borders on Soviet territory and has essential significance for Western economies.

The entry of the superpowers into the conflict alters completely the grid within which it was previously framed. Hostility between states, regardless of its contents, is a means through which superpowers enter and subsume the contending states – turning them into dependent clients. Henceforth the manifestations of the conflict are controlled by the patrons and the events of the conflict are scenes acted out on the superpowers' global stage. A 'cold war' situation between the superpowers can be fought by means of very 'hot' wars in the periphery! This third phase, superpower clientelism is not necessarily a conscious deliberate decision. It can be the outcome of a step-by-step slippage – the consequence of previous moves, or made necessary by countermoves of the adversary. Be that as it may, the root cause is the inability, for whatever reason, to achieve an independent resolution of the conflict.

The degree of autonomy or subordination to superpowers of the adversary states in the Israeli-Arab conflict is the outcome of the course of the conflict. There may be an argument about the beginning of this phase: it can be argued that it precedes 1967, however, it is mainly after the June war that its effects are manifested inside Israel.

One of the main reasons for the appeal to a superpower is the inability, or the fear thereof, to continue in the mode and scale of the conflict imposed by the adversary. The involvement of the superpower thus provides the means for the continuation of the conflict while acting as a deterrence against its escalation. However, the escalation depends on the adversaries' ability to commit its superpower to the new mode and scale reached. The first important effect of the superpower phase of the conflict is the qualitative change in the size, sophistication and costs of the military build-up (Offer and Kober, 1984, esp. pp. 33–43, 117–125, 161–206).

The military might exhibited in the conflict does not now reflect, to the extent that it did before, the independent economic resources of the states involved but is a transfer, paid or unpaid, from the superpowers' capabilities. The economic mode of giving military aid has important effects on the economic alternatives faced by the recipient: on its present and future liabilities and thus on the ratio of resources which will be left for national consumption and investment. The effects of the qualitative army build-up are reflected also in a major diversion of manpower resources from the productive to the non-productive sectors of the economy, an additional burden on the economy. Furthermore, to the extent that large foreign aid is given to internal production of military hardware, this brings about major changes in the entire structure of the economy, making much of the social structure dependent on the military and military production; hence, to the development of a military–industrial complex which has in turn major political repercussions. To the extent that military aid is augmented by major additional civilian aid, as government to government loans or unilateral transfers, this has repercussions on deficit spending and the national debt and on the autonomy of the government which does not rely any more for much of its income on taxation, internal borrowing or donations. This spending also has repercussions on the general standard of living, the distribution of wealth, sectoral composition of the economy and on the political system.

Another most important change resulting from the alliance with the USA was the ability of Israel to retain and colonise additional territories conquered in war. The 1967 war was a turning point in this respect, as Israel captured and was allowed to hold territories which were not part of Mandatory Palestine. This could have been achieved only through US backing. It meant that the situation escalated from a conflict within the territorial bounds of Mandatory Palestine to a regional conflict which threatens the territorial status quo and integrity of the surrounding Arab states. This was further demonstrated by the 1976 and 1982 wars in Lebanon. It was this wider scope of the war which drove some Arab states towards Soviet clientelism.

The backing and support of the US has also transformed the other, non-military, modalities of the conflict: the diplomatic campaign against Israel in international organisations has been foiled through the US veto and mobilisation of the Western alliance. Economic boycott became ineffective as the US resisted it and supported its infringement by others.

The superpower phase also renewed the salience of the Palestinian factor which had been subsumed by the Arab states. The occupation by Israel of the West Bank and Gaza brought forth Palestinian popular resistance in which the PLO, founded in 1964, assumed leadership. Arab attempts to dislodge Israel from territories conquered in 1967 resulted in the attrition war and guerrilla activities in which the Soviets became deeply involved. The failure of these attempts to achieve Israel's withdrawal split the confrontation states. Egypt concluded that only via re-alliance with Israel's superpower might it dislodge Israel from the conquered territories. Thus it cooled off its Soviet alliance, and after the 1973 war moved towards a negotiated settlement under the auspices of the US which was concluded in 1979. Syria, on the other hand, persisted in the military mode and moved deeper into Soviet clientelism.

As long as the superpowers compete and as long as the main confrontation states are divided, a comprehensive agreement can be blocked. Soviet support for the PLO has also to be understood in the context of the superpower competition. As the intensity of the conflict is greatest between Palestinians and Israel and negotiated agreement between them most difficult, Palestinian resistance is a bulwark, along with Israeli obduracy, against a US negotiated agreement. Soviet backing of the PLO was thus part of blocking US hegemony. On the other hand, the PLO's ascendancy and its international stature cannot be explained without Soviet backing. The PLO was the linchpin of the 'rejection front' and was cultivated by the Soviets against appeasement tendencies among the Arab states (Ochana and Yodfat, 1985, esp. pp. 171–217). The wars against the PLO in Lebanon in 1976 and in 1982 were the result of the blocking function it assumed and its growing autonomy under Soviet auspices. The result of the war was the curtailment of the autonomy of the Palestinian factor and its subordination to the Arab states. It is now the internal unity of the PLO, its only achievement, which is at stake as its different wings are pulled apart by their Arab hosts.

ISRAELI SOCIOLOGY AND THE ISRAELI-ARAB CONFLICT

In the previous section the Israeli-Arab conflict has been shown to be many faceted and composed of several tiers. In assessing the influences of the conflict on the structure of the Israeli social formation and on its dynamics, it is imperative that the different modes of expression of the conflict, the economic, the ideological and cultural, and the diplomatic-international, should all be taken into consideration. Although one modality may be dominant it does not encapsulate the full effect of the conflict on the overall structure of society. Furthermore, although at different phases different actors assume major roles: the superpowers, the Arab states or the Palestinians, it is wrong to ignore at each phase the role of the minor actors. For example, the Palestinian theme expresses itself internally, in newly occupied territories, and on the international scene even at the inter-state and superpower phases.

Despite its centrality in everyday life, the Israeli-Arab conflict is still a neglected marginal area of research in mainstream Israeli sociology. A survey of existing literature shows a paucity of research on the connections between aspects of the conflict and major spheres of Israeli social structure: economics and stratification, politics, culture and values, socialisation and the family. Even fewer are researches which deal with consequences of the conflict on Israeli structure from a macro-societal point of view using a historical-comparative method or trying to establish connections between the dynamics of the conflict and processes of social change in Israel. There does not exist yet in Israeli sociology, and not due to its underdevelopment, a trend or school which takes the conflict and its multiple aspects as a starting point for the explanation of the specificity of Israeli society. It seems as if most Israeli sociologists either recoil from researching the conflict or have difficulties in treating it as a legitimate, comprehensive, separate and independent field. The relative scarcity of research on Arabs by Israeli sociologists has already been pointed out some years ago by Smooha and Cibulski (1978). Karl Deutsch has referred again to the lack of research on Arabs and by Arabs as the blind spot of the profession in an introduction to a most recent anthology of Israeli political sociology (Krausz, 1985). Thus it is not that the problem is unknown or new; and yet the lacuna is not being filled.

In my view the problem is wider than seen by Smooha and Deutsch and does not only pertain to research on, or by, Arabs but to Israeli sociologists' dominant view of their own social formation. As it is beyond the scope of this chapter to survey in detail Israeli research, I shall limit myself to a brief typology which demonstrates my contention that Israeli sociology is blinkered by an hegemonic conception of the conflict which is shared by most Israeli sociologists and which is part and parcel of the Israeli political consensus in which they are embedded.

The way in which the conflict and its full implications for the Israeli social formation are circumscribed has to do with the way its main components are understood and defined: *Israeli society*, *Palestinian Arabs in Israel, 'the conflict'*; whether each component is related to the two others or is treated separately; the width and scope of each element and of the type of connections made between elements; whether the Israeli case is related in a historical and comparative way – and to whom and what.

In the following matrix I suggest a classificatory scheme which sums up existing areas of Israeli research together with 'lacunae', areas which are avoided or are not linked together. It is my contention that the comprehensive study of the impact of the conflict on the Israeli social formation necessitates an integrated field which deals with all three components within one analytical framework. Each category of research is numbered and expounded below:

Existing and necessary areas of research within Israeli sociology

Category of research	Arabs	Israeli-Jewish social structure	Conflict
(1)	–	+	–
(2)	+	–	–
(3)	+	–	+
(4)	–	+	+
(5)	+	+	+

(1) In this approach 'Israeli Society' is understood as tantamount to Jewish-Israeli society. Arabs in Israel are marginally mentioned and are not related to the analytical framework, nor is the conflict. This type of research has its origins and tradition in the pre-state period. The thrust of Zionist policy then was the separate development of the Jewish sector and the segregation of the social-political and economic life of the two communities as a precondition for a future separate Jewish state. The mental conception of separatism was also carried into research, analytic separatism preceded political independence. In this context research itself was divided. The Arab community, developments therein and the conflict were studied mainly by a

separate specialised group of experts, the 'Arabists'. This approach became, after the foundation of Israel, the mainstream of Israeli social science. In the discourse of mainstream Israeli sociology, the field of research is the Jews and what happens to them. The evolution of the 'Yishuv' (the Jewish sector in Palestine) is related to the situation of the Jews elsewhere and to internal developments in the Jewish community (Eisenstadt, 1967; Shapiro, 1977; Horowitz and Lissak, 1978). The conflict, as the most basic aspect of the developments in Palestine, is not integrated analytically into the theoretical framework of the sociological discourse: it is not taken as an inherent aspect of the Zionist project. It is not taken as a major condition which Jewish settlement instigated and to which it had to adapt and respond as it evolved. The conflict is not perceived as a continuous formative process which shaped the institutional structure and the mentality of the Israeli social formation (as well as that of the Palestinian Arab society). At best, if at all, the Arabs and the conflict are regarded as an external addendum, an appendix to an internally self-explanatory structure: an appendix which erupts from time to time in a temporary inflammation. The Arabs and the conflict are thus viewed as external to the structure and process of Israeli society.

(2) This type of research category studies the Arabs in Israel but is complementary to the first type. It ignores the exclusivity of the Zionist-Jewish state structure and the inassimilability of the Arabs within this structure. It ignores the evolution of the structure of the Arab society in Israel as the outcome of the conflict and conquest and as a dominated and discriminated minority. The discursive field of this type of research category views Arabs as 'a modernising and adjustable minority in Israeli society' (Smooha, in Smooha and Cibulski, 1978). It thus avoids deliberately the problematics of the specificity of Israeli-Jewish society and treats it in terminology akin to 'western pluralist democracies' as if Jewish collectivity and membership in it were of the same type as, shall we say, US citizenship. The treatment of Arabs in Israel in the terminology of 'modernisation' also shuns the main particular issues. This is not the place for a critique of the concept of 'modernisation' in general but its extension to the conditions of the Arabs in Israel shifts the perceptual focus from their conquest, dependency and discrimination to the 'benevolent' Third World Discourse of Rostow or the North-South Brandt report. The terminology used here is thus obfuscatory and distorting. The terminology creates an analytical analogy between separate phenomena and thus shifts the discursive grid away from the context of

the colonial-settlers type societies to the general context of underdevelopment.

(3) This approach also deals with the Arabs in Israel but relates their situation in an explanatory manner to the existence of a state of war between Israel and Arab states. Unlike the previous approaches, it takes cognisance of some of the specific discriminations of the Arab population in the Jewish state, however, it does not make the connection between the status of the Arabs and the structure of the state. The discriminations are attributed to the *situation* (war) rather than to the *structure* (Jewish exclusivism). The Arab citizens of Israel are seen as ethnically a part of a hostile nation in a state of war with Israel (like the Germans in Britain during the Second World War or the Japanese in the USA). The discriminations are perceived and explained as a security necessity born by the war. This approach, by the nature of its explanation, is confined to the post-independence period when the inter-state war ensued. Thus the inability to integrate into one analytical framework all three basic elements of the formation: Arabs, Israeli-Jewish structure, conflict leads to: (a) a limited perception of the inequalities, (b) a discontinuous explanation of the history of the social formation, (c) a narrow understanding of the conflict. The conflict is not viewed as inherent in the colonial-settlers project but as an external occurrence. The cause and effect of the war is reversed: rather than the inter-state war being seen as an extension of the internal resistance to colonisation, Arab modes of resistance in Israel and newly occupied territories are seen as outcomes of the Arab states' hostility, i.e. externally instigated (Schwartz, 1959; Stendel, 1973).

(4) In this type I include a large body of research which deals with the relations between the military and society. Among the themes dealt with by this category of research are: the role and impact of the army in the absorption of immigrants, ethnic divisions (oriental versus occidental), the socialisation of women. Other topics include the relations between the military and the political system, the nature of boundaries between the army and politics, the politicisation of the army and the militarisation of politics. The growing role of army in government (military government) since 1967 is also a topic of research, and the growth of a military–industrial complex and the burden of military expenditure. Another, broader, theme is the military system and the characterisation of the regime in Israel – the 'garrison state' versus 'the nation in arms' debate.

In a certain way this approach is a subspecies of the first category as neither Arabs nor the conflict appear as direct subjects of discourse. The research deals with Israeli-Jewish social structure, more precisely, with inter-relationships between institutional spheres – military and polity, military and economics etc. In another respect, however, it is within this category that many interesting studies have been written about the effects of the conflict on the Israeli social formation, albeit in a circumscribed way. The conflict does not appear directly as a discursive subject and it is not from its vicissitudes that changes in the military and society are examined. The military is a mediation of the conflict *in* the social structure and it is only through the aperture of the military that the conflict is viewed. As was argued above, the military confrontation is but one dimension of the conflict and thus the military aspect, though most important, is far from exhaustive, and gives a narrow picture of the effects of the conflict.

The 'problem stellung' of this category of research is the effects of the *wars* on Israeli society and wars are defined usually as the all-out 'big' wars (Kimmerling, 1979, 1983a). Even when the conflict does mention 'armed struggle' in general (Lissak, 1984) it concentrates on the bigger wars and does not take into account the indirect effects of a continuous guerilla war and the modes of conflict which are not armed struggle. The best example is Kimmerling's thesis of Israel as an 'interrupted system' where it is explicitly maintained that Israeli society moves between two phases: the routine, which is portrayed as a 'Western pluralist democracy' in times of no big wars or total mobilisation; and the so-called 'interrupted' phase which is when the society is at war and the war takes precedence over all other social processes. War is thus depicted as a short attack of, say, influenza (the model is the six-day war of 1967, not Lebanon 1982) which interrupts the 'healthy', 'normal', 'routine' and to which the body politic returns after it has dealt swiftly with the emergency. This attitude is ideological in the sense that it minimises the definition of the conflict and it excludes from comparative examination the specific nature of the so-called 'routine' and the way in which every aspect of this 'routine' is permeated with the national conflict situation and siege mentality. The typification of Israeli society is ideologically postulated rather than comparatively studied and the contours of the 'democratic pluralist' model are carefully drawn around the Arabs under Israeli jurisdiction so that their situation does not stain the mythical picture.

This is not to say that some of this research is not critical and concerned about recent developments. It points out the growing politicisation of the army and the loss of civilian control, and the extension of the army's intervention in the social fabric. Also noted are the chauvinist and anti-democratic effects of occupation and war, the subordination of the economy to the military and the growing dependency of Israel on the USA. Yet this type of research demonstrates best that in a total protracted conflict most scholars in the situation are themselves, and probably cannot but be, committed politically to the national consensus of Jewish-exclusivism. It is here that Karl Deutsch's remark on the lack of Arab scholars is most pertinent: 'Israeli sociological research still is at a stage where it resembles the work of an honest and hardworking veterinarian whose patients do not talk.' (Krausz 1985, p. 4). What is lacking, I would add, is not just Arabs in Israel writing about Arabs in Israel but about Israeli society in general – of which they are a part, from the point of view of the animal being operated on.

(5) The fifth approach integrates a characterisation of the Israeli social formation, the Arabs in it and the process of the conflict under one analytical framework, namely: the settler-colonial model. It is significant that although the model is well known in Israel, it is hardly practised by sociologists working in Israel as it does not accept the basic ideological premisses of Zionism uncritically underlying mainstream Israeli sociology.

Thompson's (1963) argument against sociology's treatment of the notion of 'class' as a-historical and as a 'thing' rather than an inter-relationship is very appropriate also to protracted national conflicts. The 'Yishuv' (Jewish society) and Palestinian society are not independent 'categories' or 'structures' to be studied separately and then brought together, but should be seen as forming and reshaping each other through the historical process of the conflict. 'Structure', 'process' and 'conflict' are concommitant.

A similar approach is also necessary, and has not been taken, in Israeli sociology to the study of internal strains and conflicts. It was shown earlier how the relations between the military and the economy or the polity were studied without reference to the actual constraints imposed by the process of the conflict. In the same vein, the research on group conflicts inside Israel separates each conflict rather than focus on their inter-relationship and above all does not relate them to the over-determining Israeli-Arab conflict. Smooha's (1978) and Swirski's (1981) critical studies are the best examples. Smooha describes Jewish–Arab relations (but only in pre-1967 borders) Oriental–Occidental relations and religious–non-religious relations but does not interconnect them, neither does he correlate them to the overriding process of the Israeli-Arab conflict. Swirski uses Frank, Wallerstein and Hechter to develop a dependency model of the division of labour among Oriental and Occidental Jews but does not even mention the Arabs in Israel: how their position affects Oriental–Occidental relations or how the overall Israeli-Arab conflict affected the position of Oriental Jews in the Jewish state.

In the third part of this chapter, I shall give an example of the effects of the conflict on a specific structure of the Israeli formation and how the evolution of the conflict brought about changes in this structure.

CONFLICT, STRUCTURE AND PROCESS – THE CASE OF LAND AND SETTLEMENT

A crucial sense in which Palestine has become Jewish, in the wake of the 1948 war, is in the possession of the land and its settlement. The only way in which Jewish colonisation could evolve before 1948 was by purchases of land. These became possible due to the growing commodification of land since the late Ottoman period and due to the large importation of Jewish capital, private and national. Until 1948 buying through the market was the only means of acquiring land as the Jewish settlers had no coercive power over the indigenous Arab population and they did not control the state. The limitations of this method can be seen by the fact that by 1948 all land purchases by Jews amounted to only 7 per cent of the total area of West Palestine.

The UN resolution on the partition of Palestine called for the creation of two states in West Palestine and allotted 55 per cent of the area to the Jews. As a result of the 1948 war the area which was supposed to be Arab Palestine was seized by Israel, Jordan and Egypt with Israel holding about 80 per cent of West Palestine. Within the area that was to become Israel there were, prior to the 1948 war, 447 Arab agricultural villages and towns (these included also towns with mixed Arab and Jewish populations). After 1949, only about 95 Arab settlements remained (Keyman, 1984). Many villages were evacuated and their residents forbidden to return. The villages themselves were either demolished or taken over and resettled by Jews.

Land which was not under private or common ownership, in fact most of the uncultivated land, was Government land and with the creation of Israel automatically became Israeli Government land. Land and property owned by Arabs who were outside the borders of Israel or who resided in Israel but not allowed to return to their property was sequestered and held by a specially created authority. In the early 1950s this was augmented together with the Government Land and the 'Jewish National Fund' Land to create in 1960 the 'Land Authority of Israel'. The regulations of the Jewish National Fund which forbade the sale, lease or even cultivation by non-Jewish labourers was now adopted by the new authority and extended to all lands under its jurisdiction. This foreclosed the possibility of Arabs buying or possessing any new land in Israel in addition to land which was retained by them after 1949. Most land ownership was thus transferred to Jewish authority and Arab land ownership was frozen. (The amount of private agricultural land which can be sold is very small.) Continuous confiscation of Arab land since 1949 has reduced even further the amount of land owned by Arabs and has become a major focus of conflict between the Israeli Government and the Arab citizens of Israel. The development of Arab land ownership and landed property has been completely blocked in Israel and is being continuously eroded. Loss of land was one of the major factors of the proletarianisation of the Arabs.

Water for irrigation in this semi-arid area is a condition without which there could not be modern agriculture. Water is more abundant in the north. The settlement of southern parts required centralisation of water development and usage in a national water authority. Water, like land, is nationalised and private ownership does not extend to water sources on private lands. The use of water for agriculture is planned and rationed, water 'quotas' are used as the most effective limiting means of control of agricultural produce. The nationalisation of water and the subordination of its usage to national, political, settlement and development also limits (beside land shortage), the development of agriculture in the Arab sector. Since 1967 the same conditions apply also in the West Bank and Gaza. This control over both land and water resources has been manipulated for political reasons.

The land situation in the 1967 occupied (and not officially annexed) territories is somewhat similar – though with some differences. Government land is held by the military government which prevents its use by Arab local authorities and allocates lands for Jewish settlement. The military government also restricts possession without ownership, confiscates private Arab lands and closes off private land from its owner's use in order to create pressure to sell to Jewish settlers.

Settlement in the pre-state period was a means of making ownership concrete, of possessing the land through cultivation and presence

(Kimmerling, 1983b). Settlement thus had, besides its economic and immigration-absorptive aspects, also a political strategic dimension of conquest. Formal ownership was not felt to be sufficient under conditions of no sovereignty and had to be reinforced by direct possession. The outer limits of the Jewish zone were demarcated by its frontier settlements. There were 51 Jewish agricultural settlements in 1920 and 302 at the end of British rule in 1948.

The specific forms of Zionist settlement which evolved in Palestine were also a result of the development of the conflict. Towns were frowned upon, they preceded Zionist colonisation and were not seen as fulfilling a colonisatory role. *Moshavot* were the early form of Zionist settlement mostly on privately bought land and were privately run utilising hired labour. The establishment of new *Moshavot* was later stopped owing to economic and social crises which abounded in them. By 1948 there were 85 *Moshavot*.

The two novel forms of settlement invented in Palestine were the *Kibbutz* and the *Moshav*. The *Kibbutz*, a production and consumption co-operative based on communal principles was a particularly suitable form of settlement under conditions of economic hardship and lack of security. Its idealism and close group intimacy made it into a missionary order combining military and productive capacities. The *Kibbutzim* were the spearhead of Zionist colonisation. By 1947 there were 148 *Kibbutzim* with 7.5 per cent of the Jewish population, the peak period of *Kibbutz* ratio in the population.

The *Moshav* is founded on nationalised land, on familial rather than communal units, which utilise mainly self, not hired labour. They incorporate mutual aid and cooperation in equipment and services but are familial in consumption. While the borders of Jewish settlement were demarcated by *Kibbutzim*, the depth and filling of territories was done mainly by *Moshavim*. From 1921 to 1948 94 Moshavim were founded. (Figures in the following discussion are derived from Efrat, 1981; Gvati, 1981; Bein and Perlman, 1982; Gorni, 1983.)

The establishment of a Zionist state has meant that colonisation could be implemented not just via the market mechanism but through legislation and by the legal enforcement of the law using coercive measures. This opened new vistas and was exploited to the full by the reduction of the Arab population and by the seizure of their land and property. However, the new sovereign state with new expanded territory beyond the UN partition Resolution was not accorded recognition by many states and even those who recognised it did not, in many cases, recognise its *de facto* borders as legitimate. (This non-recognition still continues to the present, i.e. the status of Jerusalem as Israel's capital.) The neighbouring Arab states signed armistice agreements with Israel, not peace and did not recognise its borders. Neither did the Palestinian refugees who sought to return or to take revenge and, encouraged by their host states, kept infiltrating those borders daily. These conditions, international non-recognition and security deterioration, coincided with yet another factor – the massive wave of immigration which brought to Israel 700 000 Jews in three years (1948–51) and more than doubled its Jewish population. These immigrants had to be absorbed, that is, housed and employed.

The existence of more than 300 evacuated Arab villages and towns was a partial solution to some of these problems. The settlement of many of these villages would have created Israeli-Jewish presence along the new borders, thus creating a new reality which, with the passage of time, it was hoped, would be recognised. It would also have filled up the vacuum between the new borders and old settlements thus creating in fact the new frontier of the Jewish state. The settlements would also be a defence line against infiltration and future hostilities and, last but not least would solve the immigration absorption problem which threatened the economic and social viability of the state. Settlement of existing villages and previously cultivated areas was also the cheapest and quickest means of absorption as it utilised already existing means of production and capital. The years 1948–1952 saw the establishment of about 300 new Jewish settlements, more than the total number of settlements established from the inception of Zionist colonisation in 1882 until the foundation of the state in 1947.

This period of mass settlement saw also the creation of a new form of settlement: the '*NAHAL*' which were formed in 1949. These are military units made up of conscripts doing their compulsory service who combine military service with settlement. *NAHAL* was used mainly to hold and establish presence in zones of hard natural or security conditions and prepare the conditions for their subsequent civilian settlement, in many cases, by the same people after their demobilisation. Since its inception *NAHAL* has established or augmented more than 100 settlements. Since 1967 *NAHAL* settlements have been created mainly in the occupied territories. *NAHAL* is an example of the link between the Israeli-Arab conflict and settlement and how settlement is a political–military act.

Another two major forms of settlement invented during this period were the *Moshav Olim* (immigrants' *Moshav*) and *Development Towns*. The *Kibbutz* movement which was based on ideological commitment to communal settlement had its main reserves in Zionist youth movements in Europe which were depleted by the Nazis. The rapid settlement of the first years after the foundation of the state exhausted the manpower reserves of the *Kibbutz* movement. To the new immigrants mainly from Arab countries, the ideas of the *Kibbutz* were alien. The *Moshav Olim* and *Development Town* were thus the two most common forms of settlement with more than 200 settlements out of 300 belonging to these forms.

After the 1967 war Jewish settlement in the West Bank evolved in several stages. In the first phase, under the Unity and Labour governments until 1977, the main settlement programme was the 'Alon Plan'. It advocated settlement along the Jordan Valley and on the eastern desert, slopes of the Judean Hills. Its intention was to cut off the West Bank from Jordan by a wedge of Jewish settlements while, also, avoiding settlement in the heavily Arab populated shoulders of the mountain range. The settlements under the 'Alon Plan' took the forms mainly of *Moshav*, *Kibbutz* and *Nahal Heachzut* – that is, agricultural type settlements. To date there are in this zone about 35 settlements with only about 3500 inhabitants (Efrat, 1984).

Strong objection to the limitation of Jewish settlement in the newly occupied territories was raised by the Greater Israel Movement, by Begin's Likud party and later by Gush Emunim. The Gush – the most militant, mainly religious, extra-parliamentary movement – challenged the government by founding a few 'unauthorised' settlements in 1974. After the Labour government's failure to evacuate them, more settlements – twelve in all – were founded and eventually they won recognition and financial aid.

In 1977 Begin's 'Likud' won the elections and formed a coalition government committed to settlement without restraints at maximal speed. New programmes of massive settlement were drawn disregarding financial, political or manpower realities. These programmes were based on principles of maximum seizure of land and presence of Jewish settlers everywhere in the West Bank – even inside heavily populated Arab areas. In 1979 it was decreed that land without deeds (and much of the land was traditionally cultivated without deeds) belonged to the government thus, by fiat, 64 per cent of lands in the West Bank were confiscated (Efrat, 1984, p. 91) and opened for Jewish settlement in addition to what had previously been the official Jordanian Government land on which earlier settlements were founded. At the same time the government also allowed private land companies to purchase Arab lands. Thus in contrast to the pre-state market mechanisms of land acquisition, coercive-legal methods were now heavily employed. Even purchases, as it now transpires, were done by forgery and by coercion of the legal owners. It is estimated that by 1984 there were about 115 settlements in the West Bank with about 28 000 inhabitants (Efrat, 1984, pp. 91–5).

New forms of settlement have also emerged: *Kfar Khilati* – a small settlement, somewhat like a *Moshav* but not based on agriculture; *Yishuv Khilati* – a larger form, less selective of its members – most of its inhabitants commute to work in the urban conurbations of Tel Aviv and Jerusalem; and *Toshava* – an urban suburb in its earlier forms, also based on commuting (Newman, 1985). Unlike the pre-state settlements which emphasised self-reliance, the new settlements are heavily dependent on the army for security and on the economic hinterland of Israel. The motivation of the settlers is either religious messianic as among the 'Gush Emunim' members or opportunistic as among the urban settlers who flocked to the West Bank as a means of improving their standard of living. Be it as it may in numerical terms the settlement drive has been a failure – only about 25 per cent of the inhabitants of the West Bank are to date Jewish (excluding Jerusalem).

CONCLUSION

Shortage of space precludes further examples. I hope to develop these themes, with others, in forthcoming papers. Ideally, one would want to show how all major aspects of Israeli society have been structured by the conflict: the dependency on unilateral transfers in the economy, the political system and its divisions, the special nature of the state, relations among Jewish ethnic groups – occidental versus oriental – the evolution of fundamentalist messianic trends in Jewish religion, etc.

The development of the research into the effects of the conflict calls forth a critique of existing approaches dominant in the social sciences in Israel, and of the dividing lines between fields of study and the basic premises, which have been influenced by political commitment to the existing order. The price exacted by the conflict on Israeli society can only be comprehended by making the conflict itself an independent and integrated field of research.

REFERENCES

Azar, E. E., Jureidini, P. and McLaurin, R. (1978) 'Protracted Social Conflict: Theory and Practice in the Middle East', *Journal of Palestine Studies*, no. 29, pp. 41–60.

Bein, A. and Perlman, R. (1982) *Immigration and Settlement in the State of Israel*, Jerusalem (Hebrew).

Efrat, E. (1981) *Settlement Geography of Israel*, Tel Aviv: Ahiasaf (Hebrew).

Efrat, E. (1984) *Geography and Politics in Israel*, Tel Aviv: Ahiasaf (Hebrew).

Eisenstadt, S. N. (1967) *Israeli Society*, Jerusalem: Magnes (Hebrew).

Gorni, Y. (1983) *From Rosh-Pina and Degania to Demona*, Tel Aviv: Ministry of Defence (Hebrew).

Gvati, C. (1981) *A Century of Settlement*, Tel Aviv: Hakibutz Hameuhad (Hebrew).

Harkabi, Y. (1968) *The Arab Position in the Conflict with Israel*, Tel Aviv: Dvir (Hebrew).

Horowitz, D. and Lissak, M. (1978) *The Origins of Israeli Politics*, Chicago: University of Chicago Press.

Keyman, C. (1984) 'After the Disaster: The Arabs in the Israeli State 1948–1950', in *Mahbarot Lemechkar U'lbikoret*, no. 10, Haifa: December (Hebrew).

Kimmerling, B. (1979) *Social Interruption and Besieged Societies: The Case of Israel*, Buffalo, New York: Special Studies Series, Council on International Studies.

Kimmerling, B. (1983a) 'Making Conflict a Routine: Cumulative Effects of the Arab-Jewish Conflict Upon Israeli Society', *The Journal of Strategic Studies*, vol. 6, no. 3.

Kimmerling, B. (1983b) *Zionism and Territory*, Berkeley: The Institute of International Studies of the University of California.

Krausz, E. (ed.) (1985) *Politics and Society in Israel*, New Brunswick: Transaction Books.

Lissak, M. (1984) 'The Social Cost of the Wars of Israel' in Offer and Kober (eds), *The Price of Power*.

Lustick, I. (1980) *Arabs in the Jewish State: Israel's Control of a National Minority*, Austin: University of Texas Press.

Newman, D. (ed.) (1985) *The Impact of Gush Emunim*, London: Croom Helm.

Ochana, Y. and Yodfat, A. (1985) *PLO – A Portrait of an Organisation*, Tel Aviv: Ma'ariv (Hebrew).

Offer, Z. and Kober, A. (eds) (1984) *The Price of Power*, Ministry of Defence, Tel Aviv (Hebrew).

Schwartz, W. (1959) *The Arabs in Israel*, London: Faber & Faber.

Segev, T. (1984) *1949: The First Israelis*, Jerusalem: Domino (Hebrew).

Shapiro, Y. (1977) *Democracy in Israel*, Ramat Gan: Massada (Hebrew).

Smooha, S. (1978) *Israel – Pluralism and Conflict*, London: Routledge and Kegan Paul.

Smooha, S. and Cibulski, O. (1978) *Social Research on Arabs in Israel, 1948–1977*, Ramat Gan: Turtledove.

Stendel, U. (1973) *The Minorities in Israel*, Jerusalem (Hebrew).

Strausz-Hupe, R., Kintner, W. R., Dougherty, J. E. and Cottrell, A. J. (1959) *Protracted Conflict*, New York: Harper & Brothers.
Swirski, S. (1981) *Orientals and Ashkenazim in Israel*, Haifa.
Thompson, E. P. (1963) *The Making of the English Working Class*, Harmondsworth: Penguin.

7 The Rise and Fall of the Military–Democratic State: Britain 1940–85[1]

Martin Shaw

The year 1985 saw the commemoration of the 40th anniversary of the ending of the Second World War: in May, the accent was on victory in Europe, but by August, the festive atmosphere had soured as it was Hiroshima's turn. In Britain, the event was officially celebrated as marking four decades of 'peace' and 'democracy', under a Prime Minister who claimed Churchill's mantle for herself. Critics were quick to point out how militarily fraught has been the 'peace' of the post-war period, and how little connection today's nuclear weaponry has with the sort of war which ended 40 years ago. There was less comment, perhaps, on the claims for 'democracy', although it can be argued that in Britain especially the Second World War inaugurated a particular form of the 'democratic' state, based on social welfare rights, which the present government is consciously attempting to undermine. In this sense, Mrs Thatcher is the leader least suited to claim the legacy of the Second World War struggle for democracy.

This chapter was originally offered, therefore, partly to sharpen up thinking about how we appropriate the memory of 1939–45. But it was always about more than that, and certainly does not propose an uncritical version of the 1940s welfare state. The aim is, rather, to develop a conceptualisation of the democratic forms inaugurated by the Second World War which emphasises their inherently contradictory character; to locate this contradiction in the relationship between militarism and society in that period; and to re-analyse the crisis of the post-war settlement in a way which takes account of the systematically neglected factor of the relationship of militarism and society.

There has been no shortage of recent commentary on either the welfare state in general or its present crisis. Indeed Stuart Hall has recently defined the 'Keynesian welfare state' in a way which is highly acceptable: as a contradictory structure, 'a "historic compromise", which both achieved something in a reformist direction for the working class *and* became an instrument in disciplining it' (Hall, 1985). But neither he nor most other contributors to the literature have successfully located this state-form in its military–historical context. This is the intention of this chapter, as an intervention in the debate about the state in British society and indirectly in the wider debate about states in Western capitalist societies in general.

The discussion here draws implicitly on an impressive accumulation of argument which denies the Marxist orthodoxy, briefly dominant in the 1970s revival of state theory. This had made – usually without arguing – the methodological assumption that 'internal' social contradictions predominate in the state over 'external' contradictions deriving from inter-state relations. Referring back to Hintze (1975), writers such as Nairn (1977) and Skocpol (1979) pointed out that states are 'Janus-faced', looking both 'in' to their national societies and 'out' to the world of states, and determined by the interaction of the two; the argument has recently been extended by Mann (1984) and Shaw (1984a, 1985). Although often trenchantly put, the arguments have not universally been incorporated into either Marxist or 'post-Marxist' thinking about the state, as witness a recent trend report (Pierson, 1984) which almost completely overlooks them.

Rather than renew the attack on the general level of the theory of the state, this chapter tries to apply the fundamental insight of the new state theory – that external state conflicts are as crucial as internal class conflicts to the form of the state, and that the job of analysis is to examine the relationship of the two. The field of application is the state in Britain in two periods: firstly the Second World War, which in social terms lasts effectively from the end of the phoney war and the formation of the Churchill coalition in 1940, until the conclusion of the Labour Government's main reform programme with the NHS in 1948; and secondly the period of the Cold War and East–West conflict, which begins to have clear political form, and social effects, from about 1947 even if its military–diplomatic roots go back to the actual war period. The first period, of the war and its immediate aftermath, is one in which all historical writing must obviously recognise the relationship of military to social and political forms; it is relatively well served by historians such as Calder (1969), Addison (1977) and the sociologically-aware work of Marwick (1968, 1977). There is thus a good historiographical foundation for sociological generalisation about this period.

The problem arises with the 'post-war' period (that the contemporary is still defined in relation to wartime experience says much about the latter's centrality). Here the military context becomes, necessarily, less total and less visible, and tends to be almost wholly replaced – even in the work of a social and political historian like Middlemas (1979) who recognises the centrality of war in earlier periods – by the socio-economic issues which, obviously, are at the front of the stage. A sample of otherwise very good recent sociological textbooks concerned with the problems of political power and the decline of consensus (Leys, 1983; Coates, 1984; McLennan *et al.*, 1984) confirms that these are being defined largely without reference to the context of military power. Here social theory is clearly lagging behind social consciousness, for since 1979 international and military issues have been central to problems of the state in Britain and other Western societies. The argument of this chapter is that, although they were not front-stage in much of the earlier post-war period, the military context was essential to the framework of social institutions and is neglected at our peril.

In particular, what this chapter attempts to do is to apply a central sociological idea about the Second World War – arguably the key proposition of the sociology of war – to the changed context of the 'post-war' period with its different relationship of militarism and society. The idea of a 'Military Participation Ratio' – 'the proportion of militarily utilised individuals in the total population' – was of course first put forward as a general concept in the sociology of war by Andreski (1968). Modified to the wider 'wartime participation' by Marwick (1977), it became a central concept in understanding how 'total war' – itself defined as warfare in which the economic, social and ideological mobilisation of the population is central to the military struggle – resulted in major social change. Although Marwick's comparative study (1977) shows a full awareness of the varied forms of civilian participation and their social effects, in different national contexts in the two world wars, his earlier popular study of Britain (1968) crystallised a particular meaning of wartime participation. In line with other studies of Britain in the Second World War, this society is seen as one in which the active participation of citizens in wartime struggle *results in* a major process of social reform. Mann (1985) now translates this into a general law of 'the period of citizen wars' (1914–45): such wars, while characterised by great attrition, destruction and draining of public resources, and hence (possibly?) 'irrational as a means to the stated ends' are nevertheless 'rational as a contribution to citizen well-being'.

It seems necessary to comment that this is a drastic over-generalisation, both in the narrow sense that the British case (which was highly unusual in important ways) cannot be seen as typical, and in the wider sense that to the extent that 'citizens' in most states 'benefited' from the outcome of the Second World War this was the result not of the inner logic of 'citizen war', but of the victory of one model of mobilisation for total war, 'democracy', over another, 'fascism', as well as of the economic circumstances of the post-war world. Where a different model of wartime mobilisation was successful, as in Eastern Europe in 1944–5, the result was much more ambiguous, at best offering welfare rights without democratic freedoms; had the Axis powers been successful, an even worse balance would clearly have been the general result of the entire period of total war. Where economic conditions were different, as after the First World War, the popular blessings were also far more mixed.

Mann's concept of 'citizen wars' is the middle one in a threefold historical categorisation: Clausewitzian (1648–1914: limited in scale and in its effects on society; rational as means); Citizen (already described); and Nuclear (post-1945 or 1955: absolutely irrational, but 'deterrence' permits subsidiary forms of militarism). If such a threefold division makes sense, it is probably necessary to revise it as follows: (a) to present the different types of war as overlapping rather than distinctly consecutive phases; (b) to recognise that modern total war, with mass citizen mobilisation, goes back to the Revolutionary and Napoleonic Wars – which inspired Clausewitz, whose name should not therefore be given to the first type; and (c) to see that the label 'citizen wars' prejudges an important issue in what is more generally called total war: that there are highly variable models of civilian participation.

The very term 'participation' is of course open to weak (neutral) and strong (positively evaluated) interpretations. The population always 'participates' in total war in the sense that it is mobilised, used, forced to work, fight and die by the state; it does not always 'participate' in the sense of being able to influence the aims and conduct of the war, or of enhancing its post-war influence on social and economic organisation or its post-war social rights. Total war is *at best* a two-way process, in which the state coerces the population but the population also improves its position in and influence on the state; at worst, as in the cases of Nazi Germany, Imperial Japan and Stalinist Russia, only the coercive side remains. It seems wrong to see these cases, as Mann does, as exceptions to this phase of militarism. Rather, they represent major models of militarism in the age of total war, mass armies and mass mobilisation; they could very easily have been the successful ones.

Civilian war participation must, moreover, be evaluated not only by reference to the aims, methods and ideologies of states, but also in relation to the actual wartime experience of the people. This will depend on factors outside the control of the individual state: its success or failure in the war, the weaponry used against it, the economic conditions which result, etc. Viewed in this context, the British experience in the Second World War was unique among the major combatant states in a number of crucial respects. Unlike the Axis powers or the Soviet Union, it possessed a parliamentary democracy before the war. Unlike all European states and Japan (and like only the US and the Dominions), it was both uninvaded *and* ultimately victorious in the sense of participating fully in military success. Unlike most European countries and Japan, it suffered relatively small civilian losses (some 60 000 compared with the millions of the USSR and Poland at the other extreme), and no single catastrophes on the scale of those experienced at Hamburg and Dresden, Hiroshima and Nagasaki, not to mention the mass exterminations of Jews, Poles etc. as a result of Nazi policy. Unlike the US and the Dominions, however, Britain *was* directly militarily threatened, it did experience civilian casualties – which by any other measure than those of Europe and Japan in the same war were a deep blow to the normal social order – and it experienced economic shortages.

As an example, the city of Hull, in which the BSA's 1985 Conference was held, with a population then (as now) of around 300 000 – comparable with that other port, Hiroshima – was (apart from London) the most regularly bombed of all British cities. Its death toll was 1200 over six years, which may be contrasted with the disasters of Hiroshima or Dresden as a gauge of the British experience.

It was then the unique position of Britain – in the range of wartime experience, as well as geographically, standing in between the security and even prosperity of the US and Canada and the deprivation and mass slaughter of large parts of Europe and Asia – which determined the particular socio-political results of war in the British case. In view of the fact that nearly all major industrial countries, apart from the USSR and those states which came into its sphere of influence, have remained or become parliamentary democracies since the Second World War, it is important to specify the individual nature of the link between wartime experience and the *content* of democracy which operated in the British case. Unlike the US and Canada, and also neutrals such as Sweden, post-war British democracy was forged as a direct result of a severe test of state and society, in which the state directly mobilised society and society was in turn able to secure (within a short period of the end of the war) major reforms in the state. Unlike the defeated and occupied countries, where mass mobilisation had led only to mass deaths and misery by 1945, and where only minorities had been involved in resistance, in Britain social reform and the state form were not something imposed or fostered by occupying powers, but the direct results of mass participation in victory.

Britain is not therefore a typical, but an *exceptionally* strong, case of what Mann (1985) calls 'the dialectic of development of civic and military participation'. The resulting state form was therefore relatively unique: an adaptation of existing parliamentary institutions to the demands for social reform generated in the population as a result of the war effort. The post-war British government, under Attlee who had been deputy prime minister in charge of the 'home front' for five years of the war, symbolised not just the social-democratic bias of the post-war 'settlement' of British society, but the continuity with the framework of social policy and participation generated in the war.

It has been suggested that, far from democratic military mobilisation being the inevitable consequence of the era of mass armies and total war, this represented one particular model of military and wartime mobilisation. It is instructive to place it alongside not just the particular totalitarian models which are available, but also certain theorisations of the problems of total war which stress the likelihood or even inevitability of overwhelmingly repressive forms of mobilisation. Marxist critics in the First World War, for example, widely expected that war would destroy parliamentary or liberal democracy and expose a nakedly repressive state power. For Lenin (n.d.), war could only lead to the creation of 'monstrously repressive', 'military-bureaucratic' states; for Bukharin (1976) the problem was that of the 'imperialist pirate state'. As I have pointed out elsewhere (1981), it is a supreme irony that one of the clearest cases of a state in which war did eliminate democratic forms is that of Soviet Russia itself in the civil war.

Against these expectations, and the very different experiences of total war in other state systems, I propose that we should describe a state such as Britain, in which democratic forms are actually extended as a direct result of wartime participation, as a 'military-democratic' state. The value of such a term is not merely to draw attention to the historical context in which important modifications of democratic institutions have occurred. It is also to indicate the double-edged nature of democratic advance: to show that democratic forms are conditioned, and may therefore be limited, by the demands of military mobilisation; and that the continuing military context may be very important to the further development of democratic institutions.

In the British case, it is extremely clear that the circumstances of wartime mobilisation gave a particular character to the democratic advances which were made. Democracy issued from above: the government, and 'experts' such as Keynes and Beveridge whose ideas and reports helped to shape the desired better society, were the sources of initiative, responding to perceived demands from the people, and to feedback from them, but with very limited scope for direct popular initiative. Participation – the ambiguity of the term has already been noted – did not mean direct democracy from the bottom. The state, which was centralised for war, remained centralised for peace: indeed, social reform was to a large extent a matter of converting the wartime machinery of planning to the problems of peace. Democracy consisted in the expectations of and support for this development which undoubtedly existed among the majority of the population – rather than in direct mass involvement. The post-war Labour government was noted for its centralist, bureaucratic style: its apparatuses of nationalisation and planning eventually became the target of grassroots democratisers on the left as well as economic libertarians on the right.

The centralism of welfare state social democracy, often ascribed to the statist ideology of Fabianism, in fact issued from the centralism of the war-state and war-economy. The contradiction of post-war democracy was the contradiction of Second World War democratic militarism: between the imperatives of control and mass manipulation by a centralised, secretive state, and the democratic, reform-based input of mass participation. The tension was largely controlled, during the actual war years and the immediate aftermath, although popular expectations did run ahead of state action. It has gradually become apparent, and finally developed into a fundamental cleavage, in the post-war period of 'peace'.

The central question which this chapter seeks to raise is this: how far can we extend the concept of wartime participation, as a key to social change, to participation in war-preparation? Following from this is the question of the relationship of military participation to other, more commonly considered, factors, in the transformation of the British state in recent decades. The chapter can only provide schematic answers which, hopefully, will provoke further work.

It does not appear to have occurred to previous theorists of military/wartime participation that there is any serious analogue in war-preparation-participation. Perhaps this is because, although war-preparation has been the central activity of states for millennia (Mann, 1980), it has not generally impinged very directly on society as a whole. Only total war creates a situation in which the economic, political and ideological mobilisation of society during the previous period of 'peace' is necessary for the subsequent phase of 'war'. Only the modern transformation of warfare has resulted as Pearton (1982, p. 11) puts it in a society where

> the polarity of 'peace' and 'war' has ceased to be axiomatic. Preparedness for war is no longer a matter of keeping barracks manned and powder dry. It is a continuous activity, reaching into all aspects of society and eroding, even nullifying, conventional distinctions about the 'civil' and 'military' spheres of life.

Modern industrial societies are not just, or even primarily, economic systems, adequately described by a theory of 'industrial' or 'capitalist' society; they are also societies bounded and dominated by states, one of the core functions of which is military. Such societies, as E. P. Thompson has put it, 'do not *have* military–industrial complexes: they *are* such complexes' (Thompson, 1982). The military function of the state enters society through the military–economic sector, its role in determining the balance in state spending (warfare/welfare), its absorption into the political framework, its centrality to the ideological formation of citizens.

To say that militarism has become a core, defining reality of societies in 'peace' as well as in 'war' does not, of course, mean that peace is the same as war. Nor does it mean that military participation is identical, or even similar, in either quantitative or qualitative terms. And to say that militarism has become a defining reality of all major societies does not mean that this is true to the same extent for all societies, or in the same society at different times. Changes within militarism may result in major changes in military participation. This, in essence, is my argument about Britain in the 'post-war' period.

Before we reach this point, a digression may be necessary on the concept of 'total war'. There is a sense in which, as Clausewitz indicated in his discussion of 'absolute war', war always tends to become total, i.e. absolutely destructive. This tendency is, however, inhibited by what Clausewitz calls 'friction', the inherent problems of terrain, supply, logistics etc., as well as by the often limited political goals of states which go to war. The concept of 'total war' generally employed in discussions of twentieth-century war, and used so far in this chapter, indicates a specific development, where warfare develops to the point at which the society is mobilised in an economic, political and ideological sense to support the military struggle. Total war in this sense does not initially entail extending the absolute destructiveness of war to the civilian populations; thus in the First World War, with aerial warfare in its infancy, civilians away from battle zones did not generally become directly involved in the military struggle. However, it is in military terms a logical extension, and with the development of aircraft a technically possible one, that once the entire society becomes incorporated into the logistical side of warfare, it should also be incorporated into the battlefield and become a target for bombardment. Twentieth-century 'total war' thus contains a crucial internal development, in which Clausewitz's tendency to absolute war is applied to entire societies. What is important for our purposes is the way in which this development affects the 'military participation' aspect of total war.

In the early phases of modern total war (including the First World War and most of the Second World War), the development of techniques of aerial bombardment of civilian populations only intensified the participatory character of war. Sporadic air attacks did not fundamentally disrupt industrial production, nor fatally undermine morale. If anything, as the British concluded from the effects of German air attacks on cities such as Hull and Birmingham, they strengthened civilian support for the war (Brooks, 1983). However, the lesson drawn from this was the need for much more destructive air power, leading both to a quantitative increase in conventional explosive power (Dresden, Hamburg) and to a qualitative leap in technology (Hiroshima, Nagasaki), both of which were so absolutely murderous that they were successful in breaking civilian morale. This is the point at which the participatory logic of total war undergoes a fundamental change. Civilian populations still participate in the supply side of war, and are ever more targets for it, but the military power directed at civilians far outstrips their capacity to respond. While civilian mobilisation is still important in war-preparation, strategic planning for actual war can no longer give such mobilisation an important place. With the development of intercontinental ballistic missile war, civilians are almost infinitely dispensable. The assumption is generally made that the exchange will be brief; civilian participation is transferred back into the phase of war-preparation. The absolute destructiveness of war inhibits its actual outbreak, so that the fighting of wars is replaced – for how long, no one can know – by the elaborate strategic game of 'deterrence'. At the heart of deterrence is the contradiction between the aim of war-avoidance and the necessary means of making war-fighting credible. (Plans for theatre nuclear war can be seen as the logical outcome of this central contradiction.)

The issue which concerns us here is that of the implications of nuclear warfare and deterrence strategy for military participation. In the early 'post-war' period, the shift which had been indicated by Dresden and Hiroshima was only imperfectly incorporated into military planning. Up until the mid-1950s, planning was based (in the UK) on the assumption that a future war would be fundamentally similar to that of 1939–45, atomic weapons being seen as an important specific modification within this framework. Although obviously there was a large-scale demobilisation from the levels of the Second World War, 'peacetime' military preparations continued fundamental features of wartime military participation on a lesser scale. The armed forces remained based on conscription (for the first time outside actual war), and a comprehensive system of civil defence remained in place. This was also a phase of intensive ideological mobilisation for the Cold War, under, moreover, governments headed by Britain's Second World War leaders, first Attlee and then Churchill himself. It could generally be said that military participation in the first decade after the war was a paler version of the actual wartime model.

In the mid- to late-1950s, under the stimulus of (a) technological developments – the H-bomb and missilery – which moved warfare clearly beyond any version of the 1939–45 experience; and (b) the growing recognition that this made all-out East–West war less likely, major policy changes occurred. The April 1957 Defence White Paper outlined a radical shift involving the end of conscription, a reliance on the 'independent nuclear deterrent', and related reductions in defence spending. Within two years there were moves to demobilise civil defence, followed in 1968 by its virtual disbandment. At the same time there was a gradual loosening of the ideological straitjacket of the Cold War, leading eventually in the 1960s to *détente*.

The changes in 1957 and afterwards signalled a growing separation of the state and the military establishment from the people. The state would dispense with the people in a future nuclear war; it had largely dispensed with the pretence of involving them in preparing for war too. The secret, capital-intensive part of the state's military power was to be developed; the people were not expected to discuss or decide, but merely to give their passive consent. The only popular participation in the defence debate was the one forced, against the state, by CND in 1958–63. When this fell away the state enjoyed 15 years of virtually complete popular indifference to its military preparations, ended only by the cruise debate in 1979.

Debates about Britain's military role, and especially about its nuclear core, were so marginal in – if not absent from – British politics in these 15 years that it is difficult at first sight to credit the idea that military participation can tell us anything significant about the overall trajectory of the British state in this period. And yet it can indeed be argued that the relative absence – or to be precise, the decline and near-invisibility – of what had been a crucial social cement, holding together the post-war social order and state, was as crucial as its presence. Hand in hand with wartime participation had gone economic and social participation; along with military duty had come economic and social rights. The connection of the two had been central to their general acceptance; in particular to the support of the political right in the Conservative Party for reforms which before the war would have seemed to it dangerously left-wing. Wartime participation was, in this sense, essential to the post-war consensus. Even if economic and social participation, as values, achieved a centrality of their own – the core of the consensus being located in full employment, planning and the welfare state – they were more easily jettisoned when their underpinning in military participation had gone. The decline of military participation was a necessary, if not a sufficient, condition for the break-up of the consensus. The disappearance of militarism from the public consciousness was not a disappearance of militarism from society, rather a separation of militarism from any connection with the sources of social democracy.

At the level of political parties, of course, an Atlanticist consensus on 'defence' survived until 1979, when the socio-economic consensus had been under open strain for a decade. The Labour government of that year, under Callaghan, David Owen (as Foreign Secretary) and Fred Mulley (Defence Secretary), had authorised NATO's 3 per cent p.a. real increase in defence spending, was negotiating with the US about Trident, and was participating in the NATO policy discussions which led to the installation of cruise missiles. Within 18 months or so the Labour Party (now in opposition, granted) had swung against not only cruise and Trident but nuclear weapons as such, under the impact of a new peace movement, breaking the consensus on defence. To understand this sort of turnaround – which reflected the trade union movement (see Pimlott, 1982) – it has to be understood that the Atlanticist consensus of the main parties had long since come to rest not on any active basis of ideological support, let alone real military participation, but on a passive, at best routinised, acquiescence of the population in the military preparations of the state.

What survive, in curious ways, are the ideological residues of military participation, so effectively but ultimately incongruously exploited by Mrs Thatcher in the Falklands War. Barnett (1983) has analysed what he calls 'Churchillism', the ideological framework of the 1940 coalition government, which shaped the basis of post-war British politics. He also suggests that its echoes in the Falklands War are hollow and deformed – myths and symbols lacking in their original substance. The 'Churchillism' of the political élite in the 1980s is seen as a result of degeneration and decay of the ideology. What Barnett fails to do is to locate the contradictions of modern neo-Churchillism in the decline of military participation. Although all the symbols of the Second World War could be applied, as Barnett notes, in the Falklands case, the practical meaning of them was fundamentally changed. While Britain in the Second World War can be seen as the archetype of 'citizen war', of total war through 'democratic' mobilisation, the Falklands are the vindication of small, professional armed forces, acting on behalf of the nation but needing no real mass participation to carry out their tasks. British civilian involvement was little greater than that of the tiny Falklands population itself. For the vast majority, it was limited to the utterly passive, vicarious consumption of exceptionally closely filtered news, and the expression of support in the opinion polls. Far from the Falklands representing a renewal of the 1940–45 type of participation, the war was a victory for the modern type of militarism, which as Mann suggests (1985) is based on a fundamental division between the 'deterrence-science' militarism of the professional élite and the 'spectator-sport' militarism of the mass. Tens of millions of people in Britain glued to their TV sets for scanty news of the few thousands tossing in the South Atlantic 'on their behalf', is as clear a picture as one could want of this divide.

The connection between military participation and social participation can be seen quite clearly in the contrasting results of 1939–45 and the Falklands. In the Second World War, social reform, the welfare state and full employment were quite clearly core parts of the Churchillian consensus; in the Falklands, Mrs Thatcher's 'Churchillism' is quite clearly an alternative to such social goals. The spirit of sacrifice in the Second World War was turned into national unity for social and economic advance; the 'spirit of the Falklands' is turned immediately against 'the enemy within', the war itself proving an ideological and practical inspiration for the political war against the miners in 1984–5. As Barnett (1983) put it, 'Thatcher's form of Churchillism (has turned) against its social legacy the name of Churchill himself'. The reality of participation in 1939–45, and its lack in 1982, go some way to explaining the paradoxical contrast between Churchill's landslide defeat in 1945 and Thatcher's landslide victory in the 1983 election.

CONCLUSION

The Thatcher government in Britain has been widely recognised – indeed, to a large extent, declares itself – as the end of the post-war 'settlement' of British society. The socio-economic basis of post-war democracy is under sustained attack, although even Mrs Thatcher's political will may be insufficient to destroy it altogether. What remains – or would remain, if she were successful – are the political and ideological forms of parliamentary democracy, emptied of most of the content of economic and social rights deriving from 1945, and combined with fundamentally undemocratic forms of militarism and state power.

What this chapter has done is to argue that a missing link in many explanations of this process is an understanding of the relationship between post-war democracy and the Second World War model of military participation. Once this is grasped, in its contradictory character, it becomes easier to understand both the limitations of that democracy and the reasons for its decline. It becomes possible to see that the nature of modern militarism is not incidental to the social and economic problems; it also becomes possible to explain how the ideology of wartime participation is being misused in justification of contemporary war and war-preparation.

As has already been remarked, the centralist, statist character of post-war democracy, with its roots in war-mobilisation, has been widely challenged. A successful strategy for social and economic democracy today will not simply be a defence of welfare state forms, still less of their wartime roots in military participation, but an elaboration of new forms of democracy based on alternative, non-military models of participation. A variety of social movements can contribute to this process, both those concerned with concrete economic and social goals, and those like the peace movement which can clarify the nature of contemporary militarism.

Although it is beyond the scope of this chapter to deal with all the political problems involved here, it seems important to stress that the shift in forms of war and war-preparation, away from those compatible with mass 'democratic' involvement and towards narrower, élite-based forms (already seen by C. Wright Mills nearly thirty years ago (1956, 1958)) is a fundamental one. If the historical memory of a more democratic form of militarism is an ideologically potent contrast to modern models, and can even generate some proposals for 'alternative' defence policies (Alternative Defence Commission, 1983; Tatchell, 1985), there can be no serious question of reverting to historically obsolete forms of militarism. Thinking about defence, as well as thinking about democracy, will have to move beyond the framework of war and war-preparation which has dominated in the twentieth century.

NOTE

1. This chapter has benefited from critical comments made on earlier versions given at the School of Peace Studies, University of Bradford, in November 1984, and at the conference on the Warfare-Welfare State, organised by Anthony Giddens and David Held at King's College, Cambridge, in January 1985. It is based on part of the argument to be contained in my forthcoming book, *The Dialectics of War*, Pluto Press.

REFERENCES

Addison, P. (1975) *The Road to 1945: British Politics and the Second World War*, London: Jonathan Cape.

Alternative Defence Commission (1983) *Defence Without the Bomb*, London: Taylor and Francis.

Andreski, S. (1968) *Military Organization and Society*, 2nd edition, Berkeley/LA: University of California Press.

Barnett, A. (1983) *Iron Britannia*, London: Allison and Busby.

Brooks, S. (1983) *Bomber: Strategic Air Power in Twentieth Century Conflict*, London: Imperial War Museum.

Bukharin, N. (1976) *The Politics and Economics of the Transformation Period*, London: Routledge & Kegan Paul.

Calder, A. (1969) *The People's War*, London: Jonathan Cape.

Coates, D. (1984) *The Context of British Politics*, London: Hutchinson.

Giddens, A. (1985) *The Nation-State and Violence*, Oxford: Polity.

Hall, S. (1985) 'Authoritarian Populism: A Reply', *New Left Review*, 151, May–June.

Hintze, O. (1975) *The Historical Essays of Otto Hintze*, ed. Felix Gilbert, New York: Oxford University Press.

Lenin, VI (n.d.) *The State and Revolution*, Moscow: Progress Publishers.

Leys, C. (1983) *Politics in Britain*, London: Heinemann.

McLennen, G., Held, D. and Hall, S. (1984) *State and Society in Contemporary Britain*, Cambridge: Polity.

Mann, M. (1980) 'State and Society 1130–1815: an Analysis of English State Finances', in M. Zeitlin, (ed.), *Political Power and Social Theory*, Connecticut: JAI Press.

Mann, M. (1984) 'Capitalism and Militarism', in M. Shaw, (ed.), *War State and Society*.

Mann, M. (1985) 'The Roots of Modern Militarism', unpublished paper at Conference on Warfare-Welfare State, Cambridge.

Marwick, A. (1968) *Britain in the Century of Total War*, London: Bodley Head.

Marwick, A. (1977) *War and Social Change in the Twentieth Century*, London: Macmillan.

Middlemas, K. (1979) *Politics in Industrial Society*, London: Deutsch.

Mills, C. W. (1956) *The Power Elite*, New York: Oxford University Press.

Mills, C. W. (1958) *The Causes of World War Three*, London: Secker & Warburg.

Nairn, T. (1977) *The Break-up of Britain*, London: New Left Books.

Pierson, C. (1984) 'New Theories of State and Civil Society: Recent Developments in Post-Marxist Analysis of the State', *Sociology*, vol. 18 (4), November.

Pearton, M. (1982) *The Knowledgeable State*, London: Burnett Books.

Pimlott, B. (1982) 'Trade Unions and the Second Coming of CND', in B. Pimlott and C. Cook (eds), *Trade Unions*, London: Longman.

Shaw, M. (1981) *Socialism and Militarism*, Nottingham: Spokesman.

Shaw, M. (1984a) 'War, Imperialism and the State-System: A Critique of Orthodox Marxism for the 1980s', in M. Shaw (ed.) *War, State and Society*.

Shaw, M. (ed.) (1984b) *War, State and Society*, London: Macmillan.
Shaw, M. (1985) 'Marxism, the State and Politics', in M. Shaw, (ed.), *Marxist Sociology Revisited: Critical Assessments*, London: Macmillan.
Skocpol, T. (1979) *States and Social Revolutions*, Cambridge: University Press.
Tatchell, P. (1985) *Democratic Defence*, London: Heretic Books.
Thompson, E. P. (1982) 'Notes on Exterminism, the Last Stage of Civilisation', in E. P. Thompson *et al.*, *Exterminism and Cold War*, London: Verso.

8 The People's War and the People's Theatre: British Socialist Theatre 1939–45

Don Watson

> The Second World War was, uniquely, a world-wide anti-fascist war involving millions of people. For many no doubt the political aspects of the struggle were largely abstract – it was a fight merely to stay alive. And yet the general thrust of this anti-fascist war was unmistakable: a war against fascism, against the old order of poverty and unemployment, a war for a more egalitarian and just tomorrow. (Davies, 1984a, p. 74.)

This judgement by a modern historian was not exactly the theme of the official British commemoration of the fortieth anniversary of VE Day in 1985. This is one illustration of the conflict at the heart of the sociology of the Second World War. On one hand the war years continue to supply powerful images and evocations for the contemporary political arena, as well as a rich source of material for commercial popular culture. At a certain level peace movements are charged with 'appeasement' and opposed by 'Churchillian' qualities of leadership, just as the demands of organised labour can be countered at times of crisis by appeals to the 'Dunkirk spirit'. This rhetoric serves to attack contemporary radicalism by the invocation of an assumed and constructed national memory. Similarly, if less obtrusively, the steady output of war films, novels, comics and television programmes in Britain supports this; when the war is treated solely at the level of individual actions, the concept of 'fascism' is generally submerged and the role of collective struggle dismissed. By these means popular memory and history are constructed, establishing a dominant consensus which systematically suppresses the radical meanings which these years clearly contain.

On the other hand, historians such as Calder (1971), Davies (1984b), and Grafton (1981), in advancing the idea of the 'people's war', counter this by examining how the circumstances of ordinary people in or out of the forces caused radical and socialist values to occupy the mainstream of British life. As this chapter hopes to demonstrate this is not only an academic exercise but one which has an important role in contemporary political affairs. Furthermore, whereas a discussion of socialist theatre between 1939 and 1945 – which immediately suggests that there was more going on than the received image of Vera Lynn, ENSA and Workers' Playtime – may seem marginal to the main effort to recapture the popular radical meanings of the war years, this chapter also hopes to demonstrate that the socialist theatre was a central part of their expression.

Cultural histories of the 1930s such as those by Clark *et al.* (1979) show that the outbreak of the war found the Left theatre innovative and flourishing. Associated with the Popular Front campaigns in solidarity with Republican Spain and opposing unemployment, appeasement and fascism at home, the Unity Theatres and the Left Book Club Theatre Guild had established networks of amateur theatre groups in many of the major towns and cities. They had pioneered forms such as the American-inspired 'Living Newspapers', documentary plays using several media, 'mass declamations' which dramatised verse to a heightened effect, and a form of writing and staging for plays like the famous *Waiting for Lefty* which lay between agitprop and traditional psychological realism. These groups performed at any possible venue in the context of these campaigns, and had built up a formidable body of production and touring experience.

However, the entry of socialist theatre into the war was conditioned by the setbacks initially sustained by the parent organisations which had set its agenda. Attfield and Williams (1984) have compiled the details but here it is enough to note that after early support the Communist Party – the dynamo behind the 1930s campaigns – soon complied with the Comintern to denounce the war as 'unjust and imperialist'. What the Party lost in members it gained in public hostility and isolation; the Left Book Club continued publishing until 1948 but it was finished as a political force from then on. Until 1941 when the Nazi attack on the Soviet Union caused it to reverse its approach the main activity of the CP was to promote the 'People's Convention', a broad organisation demanding adequate air-raid shelters and precautions, the defence of living standards and trade union rights, and a 'people's peace that gets rid of the causes of the war'. Constant attacks on the coalition government on this basis led to the banning of the *Daily Worker* in 1941.

In 1939 London Unity Theatre had scored its greatest success with *The Babes in the Wood*, by Geoffrey Parsons and Berkley Fase, which was a biting satire in pantomime terms of the process of appeasement. In the altogether different political atmosphere of Christmas 1940 the same authors tried to repeat this success with another pantomime, *Jack the Giant Killer*.[1] This featured a Wicked Baron (Mouthpiece of Capital), the Two Bad Boys (leaders of the trade union and labour movements), and the Home Front Fairy as well as Jack, Jill and the pantomime Dame. The songs and dialogue are largely satirical verbal sparring about wartime conditions and bureaucracy, and it closes with Jack and Jill refusing to climb the beanstalk (the social ladder) but determined to get rid of the Giant, capitalism, who has caused another war. Perhaps the 'collective' (i.e. Soviet) workers will help them?

> Jack: They are helping us, but they're not going to help the Baron, and it wouldn't be helping us if they did. They can't do everything for us, we've got to get rid of our own Giants like they did. They took the opportunity last time and we've got to take it this time.

The same questioning attitude can be seen in another genre in the Living Newspaper: *UAB Scotland*, performed by the Glasgow Workers' Theatre Group also in 1940.[2] Using a large cast and containing rapid scene, lighting and sound effect changes, the play follows the progress of a family through the unemployment and poverty of the 1930s by means of documentary material, cartooning, satire and social naturalism. It concluded with a complex mass declamation on the theme of class, power and nationalism in Scottish history:

> Fifty thousand families in houses
> unfit for habitation?
> A land fit for heroes to live in.
> Defeat Hitler and build a new Europe.
> What about a new Scotland?
> Half a million new houses needed.
> What do you say? When do we begin?
> Stop building. There's a war on.
> WHOSE WAR?

Another Living Newspaper on life and politics in the 1930s, *Last Edition*, had been toured up to 1939 by Ewan MacColl and Joan Littlewood's Manchester Theatre of Action. Goorney (1981, p. 22) describes how a new scene was added arguing that the only war should be the class war and that imperialistic conflicts such as this only served capitalism.

These three examples illustrate the socialist theatre by 1940, setting out the issues around which the CP was campaigning, and in the case of *UAB Scotland* articulating them through a socialist Scottish republicanism. There is no evidence that it was any more successful than the wider campaigns themselves: there is only one recorded performance of *UAB Scotland*, the tour of *Last Edition* was closed down by the police, and the role of *Jack the Giant Killer* seems to have been confined to providing a confirming function for isolated and embattled activists.

It is also worth noting that the Labour Party, as Hinton (1980), comments, was deprived of its sole activity – electoral politics – by the coalition government, and thus it faded away as a political organisation on the ground at this time. In any event the very conditions of life imposed by the early stage of the war at least were hardly conducive either to theatre-going or much traditional political activity. Air-raids, black-outs, restricted transport labour transfer and long working hours as facts of life soon exerted their effect. However, as regards theatre at least state intervention soon made a remarkable difference.

The Council for the Encouragement of Music and the Arts (CEMA) was formed somewhat casually by the government in 1939, and from 1941 to the end of the war it sponsored exhibitions, concerts and theatre tours by non-profit-making bodies. Particular encouragement was given to performances which fitted the factory shift arrangements of munitions works and other essential war industries. The Old Vic and Saddlers Wells, for example, toured successful performances of Shakespeare, Isben and Shaw through Lancashire, South Wales and County Durham, and observers commented on the shows given to munitions workers in their specially erected and often remote hostels. Mary Glasgow wrote:

> It is a startling fact that, at the beginning, only about two per cent of these hostel audiences had ever seen a stage play before. . . . They hardly seemed to realize that the peopled stage before them was not an inanimate cinematographic screen. Gradually they acquired a theatre etiquette and ceased to talk, walk about and

> drink tea during the performances. They came to know the actors who stayed in their hostels and they came in this way to have an opportunity of learning what few citizens in ordinary times ever know, that the people in the theatre are expert craftsmen in their trade, trained and disciplined to difficult tasks. (1949, p. 44.)

The Australian-born communist writer Jack Lindsay was less patronising:

> The ordinary barriers between audiences and performers are broken down. The actors live and eat among the workers; workers may look in on rehearsals and the plays form a basis for discussion with the audiences, who show an intense spirit of participation. The lack of scenery and heavy props gives a freedom of method and approach. The audiences are mostly unused to theatrical convention, but know the cinema with its quick transitions, its unfettered range over space and time; and so they will accept any dramatic method that can convince them on its merits, and the dramatists have full scope for any they can use with skill. (1945, p. 21.)

In this, an official publication which is also one of the very few comprehensive accounts of wartime cultural developments from a socialist perspective, Lindsay described how in some areas these tours led to amateur dramatic groups forming amongst the workers, with the appointment of full-time directors to work with groups of factories. This pattern was repeated with many Civil Defence groups, fire stations and ambulance centres as well as in industry. Much was the comment on the limitless possibilities which were being opened up, and a group around the Marxist journal *Our Time* both recorded this 'cultural upsurge' and pursued its importance.

This, then, was the cultural context in which the socialist theatre operated after those three early plays: one of accelerating public interest and participation in theatre on which it was soon able to build. This was possible when the political context changed in 1941 following the Nazi invasion of the Soviet Union. The CP now wholeheartedly supported the war effort in industry, called for a declaration on the aims of the war, agitated for the lifting of the ban on the *Daily Worker* and also for the opening of a 'Second Front' in Europe to ease the pressure on the Soviets. Events like the siege of Stalingrad and the epic resistance of the Red Army created tremendous public interest in and enthusiasm for Russia, sentiments which seemed to be supported by the government. Domestically also, as Hinton (1980) points out, the CP was able to dovetail into the popular view of the war by fusing immediate economic demands with demands for planning and efficiency in industry and society, support for the war effort and the Soviet Union into a production drive which expanded Party membership and workplace organisation.

The War Cabinet was therefore faced with a political quandary. Internationally, as Davidson (1980) argues, the Allies had to square their desire for a return to the pre-war status quo in Europe with the military need to support the anti-Nazi partisans – who, like Tito in Yugoslavia, owed their strength to their role as revolutionary movements of national liberation. Domestically their need was to support the Soviet ally without encouraging an interest in communism itself. McLaine's use of released files from the Ministry of Information (1979) describes many efforts to keep the initiative away from the CP when it came to organising officially blessed events like Aid to Russia Weeks and Stalingrad Festivals. Another quandary developed over 'war aims'. Public opinion was visibly pressing for a discussion of the various aspirations for the post-war world, as can be seen in the controversies over the modest proposals for social welfare contained in the Beveridge Report. The faction around Churchill, however, saw all this as a politically dangerous digression from the military tasks at hand.

In summary then the political tasks for the Left were clear, and coupled with this major opportunities were open to the socialist theatre. Three strands can be identified amongst its efforts to seize these opportunities, strands linked by common themes and personnel as CP theatre workers active in the 1930s became part of the political mainstream.

Anne Davies, a lead player with Unity Theatre in the 1930s, has described how a group played in the tube shelters during the London blitz, having first become involved in the local shelter committees:

> Sunday came and six of us set out for Belsize Park. We arrived too early and went for a coffee . . . and had a narrow shave when the back of the cafe was blasted when several bombs fell just behind it. In the tube . . . they were anxious to forget the horrors outside and were ready for anything. Some songs got them interested . . . prepared the way for a couple of sketches, solos, songs and jokes.

> Ten minutes at one end of the platform, and finally a show at each end of the lift shafts. Even when those items had to be done sideways on, with occasional trains roaring through, they went over big, and the crowd was almost as pleased as we were. I say almost, because to us this means a tremendous step forwards. Something has been done, and we know better now how to work, and most important of all, we had found that our work fits in with the feelings of the people, and the work of their committees. (Travis, 1968, p. 103.)

This work seems to have been both well organised and effective by 1942, as this review of sketches, obviously including one on the 'Second Front' demand, illustrates:

> The Germans are fighting the Russians/The Russians are very hard pressed/The Germans are fighting the Russians/So why don't we strike in the West? . . . The chorus roared out with such zest that I feel sure that some of the sleepers in Whitehall must have stirred uneasily in their strange dreams. These performances are determined by their audiences and their success is due to their masterly handling of people's desire to help create their own amusements. People would indignantly repudiate any attempt at self-conscious education – political or otherwise – . . . but encouraging people to sing the nonsense they all want to sing anyway and then showing them how to voice their back garden opinions in the same tuneful jingles produces results. (Brown, 1942, p. 28.)

On its own premises London Unity Theatre produced topical plays like *Lift the Ban* (against the ban on the *Daily Worker*), *The Yellow Star* (on Jewish oppression and resistance in occupied Europe), *Get Cracking* (on Russia and war production), and, on the Second Front, *Let's Be Offensive*. The theatre soon resumed its pre-war role of providing material, practical advice and assistance to amateur socialist theatre groups round the country: by 1942 Unity Theatres had opened or re-opened in Leeds, Oxford, Cardiff, Birmingham and Glasgow; Bristol and Liverpool continued from the 1930s. Angela Tuckett has described how her group in Bristol used *Buster*, a play following a family through unemployment and then war, in 1943:

> it shows a family reaching out from the appalling position of being not wanted – having no place, no opportunity – through the

> sacrifice and struggle shouldered in the war towards new possibilities. . . .
>
> . . . with only a dozen in the cast *Buster* could and did go everywhere. During August and September Bristol Unity Players toured Southern Command Ack Ack batteries, army camps and hostels as well as factories, works canteens and community centres. It was a tremendous effort in war conditions. Many of the cast were working long hours. Travelling conditions were exhausting and leading characters had to be changed at short notice; yet somehow *Buster* was kept going. (1980, p. 22.)

She goes on to describe how the BUP alone had plays about modern Russia for events like the Mayor's Aid To Russia week, a pageant on labour history in Bristol which played to 7000 people in Queen's Square on May Day 1944, pageants on women and fascism and *Landmarks of Liberty* (on the European anti-Nazi resistance) which played around Bristol parks in 1942 in collaboration with Co-op youth clubs and Women's Sections. According to Hill (1977) Glasgow Unity was moving at this time on from short sketches for troops and trade union branches to full-length plays by local people on Scottish working-class life.

Unity activist Anne Davies became the director of the People's Entertainment Society formed by the Co-operative Movement. This was designed to liaise with every area with strong Co-op Societies to finance and promote plays in conjunction with CEMA tours, leading to the purchase and running of theatres under democratic worker and consumer control. By the end of the war the PES had bought two theatres and built another; it had also formed a professional company which toured plays with Co-op themes such as *The Rochdale Pioneers*.

The manifestos of groups like Bristol and Glasgow Unity declared a clear purpose: they were out to build a theatre of progressive ideas and action for audiences of working people who so far had never seen any use or relevance in the theatre. They saw themselves as a counterpart of a 'people's war' in which the mass involvement of ordinary people in every aspect of the war rendered them leading actors in their own history.

A second and parallel strand is found in the plays organised by the Russia To-Day Society. A pamphlet, *The Theatre is Our Weapon*, carried a comment in 1943 by André Van Gyseghem (himself an expert on the Soviet theatre and a professional producer who had worked with Unity before the war) on the much greater willingness to absorb ideas which was evident, 'the alert and critical understanding with which audiences meet any comment on life by our theatre'. The pamphlet urged readers to use the two sketches it contained with Co-op Guilds, YCL branches and amateur dramatic societies in their areas; one of them, 'According to Plan', was written by Geoffrey Parsons, the co-author of Unity's *Babes in the Wood* and *Jack the Giant Killer*. This latest sketch featured some German soldiers stranded in a barn near Smolensk; a mixed bag of characters amongst whom the best lines are reserved for a cynic who gradually develops a political edge to his disillusionment in argument with the others. The sketch ends with their surrender, once the Nazis in the group have been overpowered, and a curtain speech of grim hope and certainty by a Red Army soldier. At a time of fierce fighting and tremendous sacrifice in Russia the poet Nancy Cunard described the impact of this sketch as 'little short of devastating emotionally' (1941, p. 25).

Another example, linked again to the Co-op, was the mass pageant or 'spot-lit commentary' presented by the Co-op at the Empress Stadium in Wembley in 1942 and then repeated around the country. This was *An Agreement of the Peoples* by the Unity Theatre veteran Montagu Slater, resuming an old collaboration with the composer Benjamin Britten. It opens[3] with a fire-watcher on a spot-lit podium who is approached by Jonathan Swift's Gulliver. He is keen to investigate why 'much of England's life and expectations for a year now have turned on its alliance with a certain Union of Soviet Socialist Republics'. What is going on? The fire-watcher recounts the exploits of the Russian war effort, and a series of mimed actions by industrial workers, ATS anti-aircraft crews and medical units take place in the main stadium area in preparation for an air-raid. Mime actions featuring dockers, transport workers, munitions women and the Merchant Navy continue, as Gulliver learns that an agreement of the peoples has taken place whereby the manufacturing nations of the West are supplying the Russians with the materials needed to finish the job. Voices from Europe tell of their oppression and the urgent nature of what that job is.

In the midst of a ballet celebration of Russia we learn that their resistance is based on their will to preserve a way of life they value, as distinct from the Nazi war effort based on terror, and the fire-watcher makes a series of pledges:

That we shall attack, and that quickly. That we shall maintain this Alliance and build on it not only in the confident expectation of an early overthrow of Hitler and fascism, lasting and complete, but also in the hope of a good life for ourselves and our children.

The last strand, itself one of the most fascinating episodes of British political theatre, took place within the army itself.

In 1940 the Central Council for Army Education had been empowered to establish programmes of discussion-based courses in civic studies and current affairs for the troops. The background material for these weekly sessions was prepared by the Army Bureau of Current Affairs (ABCA) and by 1943 some 60 per cent of home-based units were operating the scheme with varying degrees of success. Seeking more effective ways of presenting material than lectures, an ABCA Major who had been a producer in civilian life approached Unity Theatre personnel on the basis of their experience with the Living Newspaper method.

Thus began the ABCA Play Unit, and its first production, although not a Living Newspaper, was very much in the genre established by Unity. This was *What's Wrong With The Germans?* by International Brigade veteran Miles Tomalin (*c*. 1944), who had resisted efforts to turn his script into a quasi-racist perspective on the German people.[4] As the play opens[5] a nervous officer is addressing the audience of soldiers who are under the impression that they are about to hear a lecture. Their discussion of the Germans is interrupted by two actors planted in the audience, one of whom describes his own warm feelings about the ordinary German family he was billeted with in 1918. We see them all on the stage area and a series of scenes explain what happened to this family during the rise of Hitler. The son became politically active, and we see him making a speech which is suddenly interrupted:

(Commotion at the back of the auditorium. Men in Nazi uniform push in. There is some argument and shouting. From the intruders comes a Nazi official, who strides down the centre gangway.)

Nazi (half-way to stage): Silence! Everybody is to stay in their places. (Someone rises. Nazi swings his truncheon ostentatiously.)

Nazi: Sit down, you. (To all) The exits to this theatre are guarded. If anybody is lucky enough to get that far there are plenty of my men to deal with them at the door. (Muffled scream.) You will leave when I permit you. Everyone will be searched at the

> door, where German patriots will be sorted out from those who feel otherwise Heil Hitler!

A protestor is dragged on to the stage and beaten up, and the scene ends with a vicious Nazi speech.

The discussion group sees – and, by this use of planted actors and the whole auditorium, becomes involved with – scenes including the views of anti-Nazi partisans in Europe and the Mayor of an occupied town. Ideas about revenge, fascism, and the notion that 'the European family of nations is a family and must be given the means of living and working together' are given free flow, and although one character argues that the real danger is not the Germans 'but this idea they've got hold of', the conclusion, as befits a discussion tool is open-ended.

The impact this play's techniques could have has been recalled by one of the actors

> When the Nazis came into the Nissen hut it really was quite frightening because it gave the audience in that hut the feeling of what it's like to be in a police state, when a peaceful political meeting can be suddenly broken up by armed men. The Nazi chief was terrifying. . . . One place we did it, a young soldiers' unit, they were all really very young, I thought there was going to be a riot because they booed when he shouted his Sieg Heils and they were about to get up on the stage and get him. It was an astonishing piece of audience participation. (Goldmann, 1975.)

What's Wrong With The Germans? survived, as did ABCA itself, an inquiry into 'political bias' instigated by the Churchill faction of the War Cabinet. The Play Unit went on to constitute a permanent full-time company of thirteen soldiers and five ATS women; eventually one company toured home units whilst another toured overseas. The groups were responsible for the final scripts along with any necessary research, as well as their own set construction, transport, lighting and electrical work. Besides Miles Tomalin and the screenwriter Bridget Boland, the Unit attracted experienced theatre workers not only from the ranks but also from the pre-war socialist theatre movement: Jack Lindsay, André Van Gyseghem, Ted Willis and the Indian Communist novelist Mulk Raj Anand.

Their scripts synthesised different dramatic forms in order to develop suitable treatments for the themes they pursued. An example is *It Started As Lend-Lease*, which besides Jack Lindsay's mass declamation work used realism, cartoons and:

> explained in simplified and stylized documentation the multi-national co-operation involved in the building of war materials. Stylistically bare and expository prose briefs the audience on the complicated military and economic equations, and then a British vernacular voice interrupts the American narrator from the audience. Then poetry was used to go beyond the merely quantitative arguments. . . . *Lend Lease* was effective through the simple exposition of complex arguments and the use of symbolism. It used poetry to put the human side of the whole question, the split between vast economic schemes and simple human needs which the play tried to conclude in harmony. The troops didn't know they were hearing poetry, they were just straight emotional statements. (Goldmann, 1975.)

Within six months and a basic repertoire of five plays (the others included themes of world trade and hunger, a political analysis of Japanese culture and, on the issues of the war, J. B. Priestley's *Desert Highway*) the ABCA Play Unit gave around sixty performances to 20 000 troops, in anything from well-equipped garrison theatres to cramped Nissen huts. A feature of their style, one which came directly from the Unity of the 1930s, was 'cinematic writing'; points made and situations developed by quick scene changes achieved through timing and lighting. From Unity again came the experience of touring literally anywhere to 'non-theatrical' audiences. A participant commented at the time:

> We have given the troops verse at two o'clock in the afternoon and heard them applaud it to the echo; we have made them leap in their seats with realistic dive-bombing and listen, hushed, to a Japanese cradle song. We are still learning and, we hope, still shaking them. (Hawkins and Brimble, 1947, p. 172.)

A significant play was *Where Do We Go From Here?* which dealt with the troops' views on the future of the post-war world. It was performed in the context of public debate over the Beveridge Report and the possibility of a welfare state. The Conservatives' claim to support these proposals was greeted with cynicism in the country and the Beveridge pamphlet for ABCA discussions was withdrawn on government instruction. This reflected Churchill's deep hostility to anything approaching political discussion in the forces; this recollection of the impact of *Where Do We Go?* suggests that the hostility may have been well founded:

The officers always used to occupy the front rows and we were in our own uniforms, whatever unit we'd come from, and so we were all other ranks and we were sitting behind them, and so eventually, of course we used to get very adept at it, and we'd place ourselves just two or three rows behind the last row of officers and then we'd start heckling. We'd keep on heckling and going harder and harder to force the officers to turn round and actually do something about us. We'd wait until we were almost arrested, you see, before bursting through and jumping on the stage and then everybody realised that although we were troops we were part of the performance. The play was about class distinctions and already we'd created one within the audience because the troops sitting behind the officers were in a way being made a fool of by us. (Goldmann 1975.)

Despite the massive forces vote for Labour in 1945 commentators such as Addison (1975) are agreed that it is difficult to identify any precise contribution to it by ABCA, although the wartime phenomenon of organised current affairs discussion groups and 'brains trusts' of which ABCA is a prominent example made a major contribution to political awareness and education. Certainly on specific occasions their role within the armed forces justified the comparisons which the Left were quick to draw with the Putney debates of Cromwell's New Model Army: Leo Abse (1973) has described how his own group, having elected a socialist government to a simulated parliament, was suppressed and himself arrested by the RAF authorities; Davidson (1980) has an account of how another was forcibly dissolved following its support in India for militant actions by the Congress Movement. These may be isolated examples. Nevertheless it remains the case that ABCA education played an important part in the articulation of hopes for the post-war world; within this, in turn, an important part was played by the dramatisations and active audience participation achieved by the ABCA Play Unit.

These three main strands therefore demonstrate how the political developments, analysed by historians of the 'people's war', which culminated in Labour's electoral triumph in 1945 were accompanied throughout by a radical 'people's theatre'. This successfully maintained some central issues in the arena of public debate. These included the view of the war as one against fascism rather than Germans; an explanation of the strength of the Soviet war effort in terms of the defence of a system, a country genuinely, it was claimed, belonging to the people. Above all it helped to clarify and to strengthen popular demands for a clean break with the injustice, poverty, anti-Sovietism and free-market incompetence of the 1930s – 'the hope of a good life for ourselves and our children'.

Only a brief account of this theatre has been possible here, one which has not been able to deal with wider aspects of theatre and other wartime social change. In any event these six years contain a wealth of radical cultural material which repays examination. In the theatre the achievement was not in formal developments. The dramatic forms of the plays described had largely been pioneered by the socialist theatre of the 1930s, and as we have seen it was that movement which was able to respond to events with the necessary skills and experience acquired in pre-war campaigns. The real achievement lay in building a mass audience, a radical popular theatre, to an extent which had never proved possible during the struggles of the 1930s. Those involved felt they had participated in a cultural revolution which, like the political change offered by the new Labour Government, would leave both theatre and society transformed.

It is worth noting that some of these practitioners were also trying to translate their experiences into creative theoretical contributions. Jack Lindsay for example, simultaneously an important contributor and one of the few historians of how the people's war had engendered a people's theatre, used this and his 1930s experience to present a theoretical paper to a Communist Party Writers and Historians Group meeting in 1945. In this he argued[6] that the mechanistic notion of 'base and superstructure' should be rejected in favour of the more accurately Marxist idea of culture as a productive force in its own right. These may be uncontroversial propositions in 1985, but in 1945 they were badly received. The point, however, is that 1945 was when they were argued, and argued from the practical experience of the interface between artistic and political events. Here again the horizon was full of possibilities.

The socialist theatre shared the euphoria which followed the 1945 election, and at first it appeared that its hopes were to be fulfilled. In London the ABCA Play Unit took over a civilian theatre for a season; the AUEW sponsored 'Theatre 46' to produce topical plays, including work by Jack Lindsay; in 1947 the Ministry of Fuel and Power sponsored a Unity Living Newspaper on the then serious fuel crisis. Elsewhere Glasgow Unity achieved both a local popular audience and eventually national success with plays by local writers such as *The Gorbals Story*. Manchester Theatre of Action was reformed by Joan Littlewood and Ewan MacColl after the war as Theatre Workshop, which toured *Johnny Noble* (on the 1930s, the war and after), and *Uranium 235* (on the atomic bomb) around the country. According to Goorney (1981) the apex of this tour was the impact they made on audiences at the Butlins holiday camp at Filey in 1946. Successes such as these, as well as the experience of the war audiences they had built, prompted London Unity to amalgamate the Unity Theatres into a national society. The aim was that instead of touring each branch was to sustain its own professional company on its own permanent premises. The showpiece was to be London Unity, which turned professional in 1946. Soon, however, these exciting developments were thrown into reverse.

The professional company soon proved to be a mistake; the small premises could not support it and after a year the project collapsed in serious debt. This in turn prevented the development of the pre-war basis of a London centre being able to advise and support a network of regional groups. One reason for this failure was that there had been a general overestimation of how far the new audiences attracted during the war could be sustained in peace-time conditions, as Landstone (1953) recognises. But whereas this was inevitable to some extent what was not inevitable was the failure of the Labour Government to build on or consolidate the wartime experiments; instead, it systematically dismantled them.

ABCA and its Play Unit, like the documentary Crown Film Unit in civilian life, were disbanded, thus leaving information and discussion of public affairs entirely in the hands of the commercial newsreels and the press, and a bland diet soon pervaded the commercial theatre. CEMA became the Arts Council of Great Britain and rapidly adopted an approach which had always been present, but apparently missed by the Left, during the war. Those tours of the hostels and works canteens had caused a fear in the cultural establishment that a debasement was occurring, whereby audiences with no standards of their own passively accepted everything they received regardless of quality. Therefore in 1942 the decision was taken to concentrate funding on already established professional companies and not the multitude of amateur groups which were arising from amongst ordinary people. This 'few but roses' philosophy caused the Arts Council to abandon plans for regional offices and community arts centres; despite international critical acclaim Glasgow Unity and Theatre Workshop were denied funding on grounds of their 'artistic standards'. By 1950 this had led to the bankruptcy of Glasgow Unity and the start of Theatre Workshop's move to the West End, and another type of theatre. At the same time one quarter of the entire budget of the Arts Council was being spent on the Royal Opera House, Covent Garden.

The point to be made here is that under this Labour Government the cultural field parallels the industrial field. Just as nationalisation left existing management and control intact and thus frustrated the hopes which had been held for it, so the Arts Council became yet another distant bureaucracy which excluded effective participation by ordinary people.

The favourable political climate which the socialist theatre movement had largely enjoyed since 1941 was short-lived also. The processes of the Cold War, lucidly summarised by Davies (1984b), soon exerted their domestic consequences. Orchestrated anti-Communism accompanied expulsions from the Labour Party and trade union officialdom, employer blacklisting and attacks on workplace organisation. Hewison (1981) notes how a wartime phenomenon of active disengagement from public affairs on the part of new writers (again, apparently, not sufficiently understood by the Left), continued and was fuelled by this political climate into a conformist and quiescent attitude amongst intellectuals. Perhaps the best concluding comment has been provided by Goorney's account of the failure of the cultural Left to mount a 'people's' alternative to the first Edinburgh Festival in 1948. Quite apart from Arts Council hostility to the very idea of socialist theatre being represented on this auspicious occasion, he recalls that 'any suggestion of commitment was suspect in those days' (Goorney, 1981, p. 79). That this could be said so soon after the 1945 election is itself a definite sign that an era had come to an end. It is difficult to escape the conclusion that the enthusiasts of Unity and so forth had suffered from a naive view of the nature of the state and of the impending relations between the West and the Soviet Union. In any event the 'people's theatre' could not survive the contrived indifference of the Labour Government and the ideological assaults of the Cold War.

This chapter has been concerned to demonstrate how one example of the cultural life of the war presents an alternative to the received images of these years. As was pointed out initially, the sociology of the Second World War has a role in contemporary political affairs, and this is equally true of these remarkable efforts to build a 'people's theatre'. The theatrical descendants of these touring groups have again had to grapple with the ingrained élitism of the Arts Council in their own efforts to build a popular radical theatre. It is important to make it clear that this is no new debate, and that the consequences of the Arts

Council position in the past have seriously damaged the achievement of its stated objectives. This is a case which must be taken into the political arena again.

In the current Cold War it is important to remind Europeans at least that in the recent past they were encouraged to view the Soviet Union with enthusiasm and not hostile suspicion. Asserting and examining the bases of that wartime enthusiasm is one step towards beginning to heal the divisions of forty years and strengthening impulses for disarmament.

Finally, it can be argued that the ideas engendered by participation in this theatre have made an enduring contribution to British Marxism. At the conference in 1945 where Jack Lindsay argued his paper on Marxism and culture his only supporter in the audience, he has said,[7] was E. P. Thompson. Such ideas about the nature of culture as a productive force have of course informed not only Thompson's own work subsequently but also that of Raymond Williams. They remain live theoretical issues today.

These are merely three examples of how an understanding of the role of the 'people's theatre' in the 'people's war' can enhance both an alternative account of the general thrust of the Second World War and theoretical and political practice in the present.

NOTES

1. Unpublished. The text used is the copy held by the Morris Library, University of Southern Illinois at Carbondale.
2. Unpublished. The text used is the copy held by the Scottish Playwright's Association Archive in Glasgow.
3. Published in *Our Time*, vol. 2, no. 4, July 1942, pp. 1–11.
4. Miles Tomalin, letter to the author.
5. Unpublished, shown to the author by Miles Tomalin.
6. This episode is recorded, and the ideas refined, in Lindsay's *The Crisis of Marxism* (1981).
7. J. Lindsay, *Life Rarely Tells* (1982, p. 801).

REFERENCES

Abse, L. (1973) *Private Member*, London: Macdonald.
Addison, P. (1975) *The Road to 1945*, London: Cape.
Attfield, J. and Williams, S. (eds) (1984) *1939: The Communist Party and the War*, London: Lawrence & Wishart.

Brown, F. (1942) 'Let the People Sing', *Our Time*, vol. 1, no. 10, January, p. 28.
Calder, A. (1971) *The People's War*, London: Cape.
Clark, J. *et al.* (eds) (1979) *Culture and Crisis in Britain in the 1930s*, London: Lawrence & Wishart.
Cunard, N. (1941) 'According to Plan', *Our Time*, vol. 1, no. 9, December, p. 25.
Davidson, B. (1980) *Special Operations Europe: Scenes from the Anti-Nazi War*, London: Gollancz.
Davies, A. (1984a) 'Jack Lindsay and the Radical Culture of the 1940s', in R. Mackie (ed.), *Jack Lindsay: The Thirties and Forties* (University of London Centre for Australian Studies).
Davies, A. (1984b) *Where Did the Forties Go? A Popular History*, London: Pluto.
Glasgow, M. and Evans, B. (1949) *The Arts in England*, London: Falcon Press.
Glasgow Workers Theatre Group (1940) *UAB Scotland* (Scottish Playwrights Association Archive, Glasgow).
Goldmann, A. (1975) *A Theatre at War* (BBC Radio 4, 13 March: BBC Radio Play Library, London).
Goorney, H. (1981) *The Theatre Workshop Story*, London: Eyre Methuen.
Grafton, P. (1981) *You, You and You! The People Out of Step with World War Two*, London: Pluto.
Hawkins, T. H. and Brimble, L. E. J. (1947) *Adult Education: The record of the British Army*, London: Macmillan.
Hewison, R. (1981) *In Anger: British Culture in the Cold War, 1945–1960*, Oxford: University Press.
Hill, J. (1977) 'The Rise and Fall of Glasgow Unity Theatre', *Theatre Quarterly*, vol. 7, no. 27, Autumn, pp. 61–70.
Hinton, J. (1980) 'Coventry Communism: A Study of Factory Politics in World War Two', *History Workshop Journal*, no. 10, pp. 48–71.
Landstone, C. (1953) *Offstage*, London: Elek.
Lindsay, J. (1945) *The British Achievement in Art and Music*, London: Pilot Press.
Lindsay, J. (1982) *Life Rarely Tells*, Victoria: Penguin Books.
Lindsay, J. (1981) *The Crisis in Marxism*, Bradford-on-Avon: Moonraker Press.
McLaine, I. (1979) *Ministry of Morale: Home Front Morale and the Ministry of Information in World War Two*, London: Allen & Unwin.
Parsons, G. (1943) 'According to Plan', in A. Van Gyseghem (ed.), *The Theatre is Our Weapon*.
Parsons, G. and Fase, B. (1940) *Jack the Giant Killer*, Morris Library, University of Southern Illinois at Carbondale.
Slater, M. (1942) 'An Agreement of the Peoples', *Our Time*, vol. 2, no. 4, July, pp. 1–11.
Tomalin, M. (*c.* 1944) 'What's Wrong with the Germans?', unpublished, author's copy.
Travis, R. (1968) *The Unity Theatre of Great Britain 1936–1946: A Decade of Production*, University of Southern Illinois M.A.

Tuckett, A. (1980) *The People's Theatre in Bristol 1930–1945*, London: Communist Party History Group, Our History Pamphlet No. 72.
Van Gyseghem, A. (ed.) (1943) *The Theatre is Our Weapon*, Russia Today Society pamphlet.

9 What did you do in the War, Mam? Women Steelworkers at the Consett Iron Company during the Second World War

Kath Price

During the Second World War more women were brought into the workforce than ever before and into a wider range of occupations and industries. The role women played in some of these industries, such as munitions and aircraft production, has been well documented; while in others like the iron and steel industry there has been very little recognition. But many accounts, especially media reports at the time, often embellished the facts and romanticised the situation. They also exaggerated the social changes as a result of women's entry into the workforce, stressing the achievements for women. There is also a tendency for some historians to generalise about the extent of social change affecting women in the post-war reconstruction (Marwick, 1968).

There were some writers at the time who considered in detail the jobs women were doing, paid attention to important issues like equal pay for women, evaluated men's attitudes to women at work and offered interpretations. Some of these were traditional, stressing that war work was only temporary and that women would be glad to return to their 'real role' as wives and mothers based in the home (Scott, 1944); others offered feminist interpretations and were aware and critical of male prejudice and power that reduced women's opportunities (Douie, 1950). Douie outlines the efficiency of women as workers and especially the speed with which they learnt new jobs that would normally be entered into by a long apprenticeship. Furthermore, she explains much of the confining of women to low grade labouring roles in industry to men's desire to keep the more difficult jobs for themselves coupled with their patriarchal view that women could not undertake such work and should mainly be used for 'fetching and carrying' for the men (this being an extension of the domestic role). Stronger criticisms of the role of the Government and unions and concern for future opportunities in employment for women are revealed in her book *The Lesser Half* (Douie, 1943). However, she over-optimistically concludes that men's attitudes generally and those of the unions in particular will have changed sufficiently during the war to enable women to participate more fully in the post-war reconstruction. After all: 'Our women tipped the scales of war' (Ernest Bevin, Minister of Labour and National Service, 1943). Though women received much praise, they did not achieve equal pay or opportunity during the post-war reconstruction and it took a further thirty years before such legislation came into effect. Women lacked the power and men did not change their attitude towards women.

However, feminist writers such as Betty Friedan (1965) did see the Second World War as a time of positive changes for women – for example, in terms of childcare policies – that were then reversed after the war. This is contradicted by other researchers who have noted that, even during the war, the patriarchal view of the real role of women (as wives and mothers in the private realm) persisted, resulting in the government adopting childcare policies and employment policies, such as the registration and conscription of women, that were less effective than they might otherwise have been (Allen, 1980; 1983; Summerfield, 1984). Furthermore, the resilience of such patriarchal ideas that appear to transcend both class and political ideologies can be seen when analysing women's war work 1914–1918 and the post-war situation of the 1920s (Braybon, 1981).

Much of this contemporary research has tended to emphasise the development of social and economic policies and the role played by the government, employers, trade unions and the labour movement generally for which a great deal of documentary evidence is available. But their different perspectives do not present a total picture when assessing and interpreting change. Sherna Gluck (1982) criticises approaches that see women simply as 'passive victims' of patriarchal society and focuses her research on individual women's work experiences during the war in the Los Angeles aircraft industry using oral history techniques. For her, 'life histories with their description of personal life over time, help to recast the question of how we evaluate social change' (Gluck, 1982, p. 110).

There does appear, therefore, to be a need to reconcile general theoretical perspectives with the subjective perspective provided by the individual, giving the latter greater emphasis and assessing the interaction between, for example, the 'constraints' imposed by the other 'actors' in society and the way women actually experience them and make their choices within these constraints.

Gluck differentiated her sample's experiences at work and home in terms of the women's pre-war workforce status, their family status and age. The operation of similar factors such as pre-war work and marital status will be considered when analysing the personal experiences of women steelworkers at the Consett Iron Company in County Durham during the Second World War. Before considering these findings, documentary evidence on the iron and steel industry will be reviewed followed by discussion of the oral history methods adopted.

MAKING STEEL DURING WARTIME

The general literature on women's war-work neglects the role women played in the iron and steel industry. Although *The Consett Story* notes:

> Women and girls played a vitally important part in the war effort. At one time between six hundred and seven hundred women worked for the Iron Company, releasing men for the services and for heavier duties. (The Lion's Club, 1963, p. 22.)

that is the end of the matter as far as that source is concerned. However, Vera Douie (1950) proves to be an exception to the general rule. She notes that by September 1942, women were doing about 950 different jobs in the iron and steel industry and describes some of them:

> One of the most skilled jobs was that of the deseamers, whose work was to burn away defects in steel billets by means of the flame of an oxyferrolene jet. A few were bar examiners – a job calling for judgement and needing exceptionally good eyesight. (1950, p. 99.)

Though the making of steel during wartime was shrouded in

secrecy, the British Iron and Steel Federation did release publications in 1945 to show the labour situation in the industry and their view of the role women played. Regarding labour, up to the end of 1944, 90 000 of the industry's younger men were called up and women were recruited in accordance with female labour agreements made with the union (the Iron and Steel Trades Confederation) that stressed the temporary nature of the arrangement.

> In normal times there are, of course [sic] few female process workers in the industry, except in some of the lighter trades, but it will be seen that the percentage of women employed as process workers rose to nearly 20% in 1943 and 1944 spread over every branch of the industry. (British Iron and Steel Federation, 1945a, p. vi.)

But facts and figures such as these cannot tell us the effects on employees of, for example, working longer hours in adverse circumstances such as during blackouts. Such hazards were being faced by the new recruits who were increasingly being employed on jobs described as follows:

> The daemonic setting of the melting shop (steel-making area) is perhaps the place one would least expect to find women, but there are a good many of them even there; in a typical large plant 150 are employed on the three shifts in this shop alone.
>
> In the scrap yard you may see girls high up in the overhead cranes; this is a job the younger women do exceedingly well and there is hardly a male crane driver in the works. On the stage others are unhooking the chains as the boxes of scrap and ore are delivered ready for the furnaces, weighing out the different materials . . . carrying out practically all the labouring jobs; dressing and laying bricks. The last is particularly dirty work and hard on the hands but suitable women have learnt very quickly and become skilled workers. (British Iron and Steel Federation, 1945b, pp. 46/7.)

This, then, gives some background information; it is to the ways in which personal evidence was obtained that we shall now turn.

METHODOLOGY

The initial problem was how to reach women who worked at the Consett Iron Company (usually referred to by them simply as 'the Company') during the war. Therefore, an article was written for the local newspaper which resulted in several telephone calls from people in the Consett area. After a couple of informal preliminary discussions, taped interviews were conducted with sixteen women and two men. Although Thompson (1978) suggests that interviews should generally be conducted on a one to one basis, many of my interviews did not turn out that way. To some extent interviewees played a part in selecting the methodology since between my initial contacts and the actual taped interview, one man and three women chose to involve others, so that a group interview took place. On only four occasions was there only the interviewer and the respondent present; at other times, daughters, husbands or other visitors would also be in the room.

The loosely structured questions which covered the respondents' background, schooling and pre-war work, their job at the Company and post-war occupations were organised onto four index cards. The idea was to go through the questions systematically but it rarely worked out that way particularly in the group interviews and what really occurred were 'semi-structured' conversations. Although the taped conversations lasted from between three-quarters of an hour and two hours I was often in the company of a respondent for an hour or two longer than that as it was very much seen as a social event. Contact with the women has been maintained. A booklet based on the conversations was sent to each respondent to 'give the history back to the people in their own words' (Thompson, 1978, p. 226). The next section tells just part of that history.

WOMEN OF STEEL

'Consett Iron Company has been my life. I can't believe it's wiped off the face of the earth.'[1]

Before describing some of the jobs undertaken by women at the Consett Iron Company some background information on them will be presented. Table 9.1 illustrates the age distribution as well as their marital status when they started war-work.

Table 9.1 Women steelworkers: age and marital status

Year of birth	*No. of women*	*Age in 1984*	*Age in 1943*[2]	*Marital status*		
				Single	*Married – no children*	*Married – with children*
1906–1910	3	78–74	37–33	—	—	3
1911–1915	3	73–69	32–28	1	—	2
1916–1920	4	68–64	27–23	—	1	3
1921–1925	6	63–59	22–18	4	2	—
Total:	16	Age range = 19 years		5	3	8

Of the eight women who had children, four had one child, aged between one and two years old, three had two children mainly or nearly of school age and one had eight children. None of these women was doing paid work prior to taking up employment at CIC; neither were two of the three married women who did not have children. All the single women were working immediately prior to joining the Company. It should be noted that while virtually all women were required to register at employment exchanges during the war, women with children under 14 living with them were not required to take up employment. The fact is that many women did, often out of economic necessity, as their husbands were away and only sending home 'a private's pay' (five of the eleven married women had husbands in the Forces). The young, single women were conscripted into the forces or directed to do war-work often away from home. However, the women who worked at the Consett Iron Company were local, living within a few kilometres radius of Consett; the women interviewed mainly came from one of the several semi-separate settlements that comprise the Consett district and steelmaking community: Blackhill, Bridgehill, Benfieldside, Leadgate and Delves Lane.

Most of the women had strong family connections with the Company with fathers, uncles or brothers working there; two had husbands in the works during the war. There were similar strong links with the pits (coal-mining and steelmaking being the major male employers).

Regarding the types of employment available to women pre-war, that there was only a narrow range of low paid options is very apparent. Half the women interviewed entered domestic service of various kinds, mainly outside the immediate locality: either in the Newcastle upon Tyne area or further away at Manchester, Bradford or London. Several women recalled their domestic duties.

> I went into service . . . well, you had to . . . well, I started at a local house and then I went into service at Newcastle, you see . . . I worked for a Mr T . . . and I got four shillings a week for seven days a week; 6 o'clock at night from 7 in the morning. . . . There was a lot of girls; we all used to travel together when it was our half days, you know, come home and go back together. . .. Then I worked for two doctors and then me other two friends worked for another two doctors further down. I got twelve shillings a week then.

Two women also went away to work in ice-cream parlours. This was seasonal employment, so they were unemployed during the winter months. Next to domestic service, shop-work, usually in grocers or drapers, was the main alternative employment for them. One woman was a delivery driver for a local baker; another was an usherette in what was virtually a 'family concern'. There was very little manufacturing employment available in the area apart from a hosiery factory. The evidence suggests that the girls had to be of necessity highly mobile in terms of distances travelled to work, more so than boys of the same age who could obtain an apprenticeship or work their way up at the Consett Iron Company or go down a local pit (and there were seven owned by the Company at this time) both of these options being facilitated by extensive family connections and were, of course, sources of local employment.

There are several ways in which these pre-war experiences may have influenced how women viewed their jobs at the Company, such as comparisons made over pay and conditions and working relationships; their comments will be examined later.

CALL UP

The reasons why women came to work at the Company in the first place are worth examining. It would appear that the Government's press releases and radio broadcasts about registration were not always reaching their intended targets, so that even women with small children feared that they would be sent away. Therefore, this may have precipitated their entrance into war-work locally. Economic considerations were also important reasons especially for women whose husbands were either semi-invalids or in irregular employment. Despite the fact that most of the married women had small children, they did embrace these new, if temporary, employment opportunities at the Company; however, they generally needed the support of another woman in the family as wartime nurseries were not available at Consett. Such provision elsewhere was sparingly provided and generally withdrawn after the war – the patriarchal assumptions being that women should remain at home to look after children and that they should be supported financially by their husbands. However, such assumptions have always underestimated the extent to which working-class women have taken on paid work and when opportunities arose such as those offered by the Company, they were only too willing to take them up.

Whilst most of the married women knew that they would not be sent away (the two married women without children were directed to do war work locally) the position for single women was rather different, as their experiences reflect, since they seemed to meet more directly with officialdom. On the one hand, in some households when several members of the family had already been called up the thought of losing another daughter brought additional stress. On the other hand, some of the single women did seek a move by trying to get into the Forces. They remembered queueing outside the recruitment offices in Newcastle upon Tyne; two of them were rejected through ill-health and detailed into the Company; the other decided upon munitions work in the Midlands instead, but with the onset of bombing there, was recalled by her father and through him obtained work at the Company. This once more attests to the strong family connections there.

Therefore, single women were conscripted into the Forces or into war-work. They heard about these opportunities from the Ministry of Labour and National Service or from family. Similarly, married women with children heard that the Company were 'setting the women on' from a relative or a friend. In some cases women went with their friends for a job 'on the spur of the moment' or came into the Company 'by chance' thus attesting to the many informal ways women obtain work which is still true today.

'WOMEN'S WORK' AT THE CONSETT IRON COMPANY

During the early part of the war (1940–early 1941) women supervisors had not yet been appointed so that the women were engaged by the various managers. It was clear that there were no set procedures and that they did not always know what to do with the women when they got them. In some cases, the women did not have any idea about what jobs they were going to do:

> [The supervisor said] There's a vacancy for this, that, welder. Oh, I hadn't a clue—welder—but I said, Oh, I'd like to be a welder. (Electric welder, born in 1919.)

> We didn't know the right end of a machine or an ingot when we went in. The only thing we knew the right end of was a sweeping brush, and that's what we thought we'd be going in for, sweeping the floors up and that . . . (Machine turner, born in 1910.)

Most women did, in fact, undertake labouring or semi-skilled work. They worked at the blast furnaces, where the iron is made, either at the top, in the open air, where the coke, iron ore and dolomite are added, or at the bottom of the furnaces, of which there were eight at this time. Some worked in the 'melting shop' where the iron is made into steel. Other women worked as labourers on the many railway lines in the works, clearing the tracks of debris. Also, women acted as labourers to the bricklayers. However, there was a greater variety of jobs for women in the 'finishing off' processes where the steel, now in the form of ingots, is shaped into bars,

Table 9.2 Women steelworkers: classification of occupation

Occupation	*Number of women*
Labourer	4
Crane driver	3
Van driver	2
Operator	2
Stocktaker	2
Electric welder	1
Billet inspector	1
Supervisor	1
Total	16

billets and plates in the various mills. Here women were operators, crane drivers and stocktakers, for example. Table 9.2 classifies the first job the 16 women did at the Company. (Several women changed their jobs during the course of their wartime employment.)

Some of these jobs will now be described by the women who did them to give some idea of the nature of the work, of their attitude to it and to other work-related aspects such as pay and men's attitudes to women at work.

LABOURERS, CRANE DRIVERS AND VAN DRIVERS

> We just had to go on and sweep; you didn't need any training for it; it wasn't like crane driving. You see, the men . . . the men used to go to the coke kilns and fill the barrers with coke and obviously there was so much of the coke spilt all around and when they were wheeling their barrers from the kilns to the weigh machine and then from the weigh machine down to the bogey,[3] all the coke – a lot of it – would drop off. Well, we had to sweep that up to make the road clear for the men bringing the barrers backwards and forwards . . . (Labourer, born in 1922, describing one aspect of her job on the 'blast top' which meant working in the open air.)

Crane driving in the old angle mill is described as follows:

> Well, it's like driving a car . . . The middle – the centre was the handle – now that was to take you up and down the bay, you know. A larger handle, just like a ratchet handle, not a wheel . . . and these [gesticulating with hands] were two smaller ones . . . the one at this side took the chains out to wherever you wanted it and the other one (on the left), when the men – the slingers – put the chains on the load, the other lifted it and then you come back to this one to bring your load back in and, of course, it was sloped like this, your window, so you had to look down to wherever you wanted to put it . . . on to your wagon or wherever and then you dropped it and the slingers . . . (took the chains off) and that was it; it was simple . . . I worked with good men. I worked with them all the time I was there – the same men.
>
> Question: It was a gang of you?
>
> Yes, one stocktaker . . . I had him all the time and two slingers.

Three of the women interviewed were involved in driving various vehicles in and around the Company; one came to this job via labouring and another left to work in the plate mill as an operator. She explained why she changed her job.

> I was a driver in the fitting shops for a year and then I found out I could get more money working in the mills. This was the only reason . . . because, well, your mother and father didn't have anything . . .
>
> I was getting three pounds at the fitting shop. Why mainly, why I *left* the fitting shops which is more or less what it is today, is feminine equality, you know? I was off work for a week – I was ill for a week – and I went back to the shop – fitting shop – and the fella that was on my job for that week got twelve pounds and I was only getting the three and I *said* why should he – I mean, sort of *then* there were the heckles up, you know; I was doing the same job as him exactly. I had the same responsibility – in fact, I had more because it *was* my job and why couldn't I have that? They just pooh-poohed and laughed, you know, and threw you out.

These feelings of injustice, indeed the power with which they were communicated more than forty years after the event, are very apparent.

Although the main steel union (The Iron and Steel Trades Confederation) paid equal wages to women doing men's work, in fact it is likely that the proportion of women receiving equal pay was small; women were concentrated in labouring and operating jobs previously undertaken by boys aged under 21 so that they would be paid that rate. But it should also be recognised that, during the war, the iron and steel industry provided women with employment in areas of the country where there had been few opportunities before and that they were obtaining wages several times higher than they had been receiving in their pre-war employment. However, this does not mean that they were unaware of the differences between men's and women's wages or totally acquiesced in these anomalies as the above quotation shows.

It was also noted that driving offered a lot of freedom and variety; many other women mentioned these aspects in their jobs at the Company compared with the jobs they had done before; they felt that their time was less rigidly structured.

OPERATORS, STOCKTAKERS AND WELDERS

Operating and stocktaking jobs were undertaken mainly in the plate mill and old angle mill. One of the women interviewed learnt to operate all the various machines in the former and described the whole steel finishing process there; she acted as relief when people were absent. Stocktakers had to watch the progress of steel plates or bars and see that the correct sizes and quantities were made for each customer, checking the sheets that had come from the offices and calculating the weight of each plate.

Probably the only woman electric welder at the Company received the longest training and attained a high degree of skill, of which she was rightly proud. She trained at Wallsend for three months alongside women recruited into the shipyards. She describes aspects of her job.

> You see, there were lots of other welders but they were all flat welder, as you know. But, I mean M—— will tell you, I had to go up on to the coke ovens and weld on the top of them, you know? . . . All the flux was coming off, you know, overalls were burnt to devil – well I used to go to the Fell to get the second-hand overalls.

BILLET INSPECTORS AND SUPERVISORS

The job of billet inspector also appeared to need a high degree of skill, but like many of the other jobs described above, women got the hang of it very quickly.

After a dispute with a male worker in the larger billet section over wages, Mrs F was transferred to the chipping bay and worked among a group of girls 'where there was none of this piecework lark'.

The women worked in pairs, one at each end of the billets that were arranged on rails, turning them over with tongs and looking for cracks in the metal. Fine cracks were ignored but the cracks that went deep were marked out with a tin of paint on the billet itself and then thrown over to the deseamers and grinders.

She went on to explain that their group of eight did have a bit of power and refused to do menial tasks expected of them by the men simply because they were women. This group of women also took on additional work calculating the whole tonnage for their shift. Here is an example of women modifying their job by taking on more work rather than less (many jobs during the war were 'diluted' for women, that is, simplified, to enable new inexperienced recruits to do them).

The Consett Iron Company appointed women supervisors, as advised by the Government. Apart from the Head Supervisor of the Ladies Welfare Department, there were seven others: one on permanent day shift and two on each of the other three shifts (most people and two-thirds of those interviewed worked shifts: 6 am–2 pm; 2 pm–10 pm; 10 pm–6 am). Some of the supervisors were related to the managers that worked there and there was an element of 'class distinction' here. For example, some of the older women referred to supervisors as 'gaffers' wives'. There was a wide range of duties some of which are described here:

> Well, it was definitely, in one respect, a welfare job; to see the girls were made as comfortable as possible while they were at work such as their toilet facilities, for washing, and that there was a place for them to have their meals (the rest rooms) and that that was kept right and also their welfare on their jobs . . .
> We didn't just go into the rest rooms, we had to see the girls at work . . . I think really you used your common sense more going around these places . . . as long as you had a bit of humanity about you.

WORKING RELATIONSHIPS

Many of these accounts, parts of which are quoted above, not only give an insight into some of the jobs undertaken by the women but also reveal more personal views which indicate their pride in their work, the ease with which the jobs were learnt, the conviviality of working in a regular gang, the fun and the humour, as well as the conflicts over such issues as pay and men's expectations of women at work. It is clear that not all women acquiesced in all aspects of the 'patriarchal belief system', even if there was little they could do to change it overall; as individuals, several women tried to alter their circumstances within these confines.

While there was a consensus view that 'the men were all gentlemen' and 'never swore in our presence', this would be contradicted, often within the same interview, by such comments as 'some of them could be awkward, you know' but it is likely that this was mitigated to some extent by the presence in the Company of other male relatives of the women.

Apart from some direct antagonism, there were other 'lighter' aspects of working relationships that should be mentioned. Stories about the jokes played by the men on the women (and vice versa) are legion. The men must have had a field day (for several years) with all the new women coming into the works instead of the smaller number of boy apprentices who would normally bear the brunt of this as part of their initiation. Several women mentioned that they were asked to fetch 'a long stand', a barrow of steam or left-handed screwdrivers from the pattern shops! One woman recalled being given a nickname by a male worker which stuck for the whole time she worked at the Company; another remembered a foreman who called every woman in the works 'Mary'.

However, apart from the money (the 'little bit of independence the money gave you' as one married woman put it) and the freedom at work, most women mentioned the 'friendliness' as being the best aspect of being at the Company. Some friendships made then among the women have lasted for over forty years and former workers, female and male, are often recognised in the street or on the bus. Consett has remained a fairly close-knit steel oriented community; even though most of the women left the Company after the war, there were still strong ties, since many had husbands, sons and daughters who worked there until the closure in 1980. On the other hand, for many women, finishing at the Company also meant that all social ties were ended too, as they returned to or commenced family/domestic duties. To quote Mrs H talking about the time her husband returned from the Forces:

> At first, there's so much to talk about and a lot of years to make up, you don't realise that you have to settle down . . . when all the glamour's over, of the reunion and everything, after that, you miss the company you had, you miss all those women.

However, the fact that women had worked there provided a common bond when making new friends later on. Two former workers from the Company, who did not know each other during the war because they were on different shifts, were able to form a stronger bond as neighbours through recalling their experiences of war-work. These experiences, therefore, may have had a variety of long-term effects in the community.

AFTER THE WAR

As the men returned, fewer and fewer jobs were available for women at the Company. Demobilisation, however, took a long time, demand for iron and steel products continued and expansion occurred at the Company. This meant that it was 1955 before women were virtually eliminated, in accordance with union policy, from the jobs described in this chapter. The reasons the women gave for leaving the Company will be explored in detail; in the main they reflect their marital status and stage in the family life cycle, but many of their statements reveal more complex issues reflecting their self-image and perceptions of their future employment role which will be discussed.

Regarding the five single women, one (a labourer) was laid off.

> Well, we all had to leave when the men came back. We knew it was only for the war. . . . So many of us got finished at a time. You just had to go on the dole.

Similar views of acceptance were asserted by two of the married women with children who were also 'finished'.

However, of major importance to three other single women was the fact that they were leaving to get married; rather than leaving purely of their own accord, they were acquiescing in their husbands' view that they should not work. 'He didn't want me to work among men . . . it was just men's minds.'

The older single woman continued in the same job as a stocktaker in the plate mill after the war until 1947 when she was switched to the angle mill in 1951. As with the immediate post-war situation the men eventually reclaimed all these stocktaking jobs and, having been offered alternative office work which she declined, she left. It would appear that older self-supporting single women and widows with work experience were retained but in the final analysis gender prejudice would override even economic needs.

Many women were offered alternative jobs when the men came back. Immediately after the war a range of operating/technical jobs were available and a few women switched to these; but when a job usually designated 'women's work' such as clerical work or cleaning was offered several women turned them down and left the Company. And yet these jobs were either similar to ones undertaken before the war or were the jobs they were originally seeking when they first applied to work at the Company. This would suggest that, during the course of their war-work, there had been a reassessment in terms of their self-image and/or future employment goals. For example, the electric welder did try to get another welding job in the 1960s. However their employment goals were reappraised and changed, they were stifled or did not come to fruition because the actual employment opportunities for women did not themselves change. Women lacked the power to bring about such changes though the potential for social change was there in the individual appraisals that had been made. This evidence would appear to contradict those commentators who made simplistic assumptions about the real role of women and their post-war preferences for employment.

All the married women left the Company after the war; some were laid off or were pregnant; others left in anticipation of their husbands returning from the Forces. However, they all returned to paid employment later on, usually full-time and for up to twenty years, when they retired on their own pension. Cleaning and clerical work became the main 'openings' for women in the Company after the war. Five of the women interviewed worked for the Company again as cleaners or clerks with the exception of the older single woman who remained as a stocktaker.

The other main source of employment for women was at Shotley Bridge Hospital; several of the women became cleaners or auxiliary nurses there. Retailing was the other main occupation; this narrow range of opportunities was, therefore, very similar to the pre-war position although over the last twenty years there has been an increase in manufacturing industry in the area, but women are often restricted to working in areas like the clothing sector (Price, 1984).

Therefore, the women's work experiences during the Second World War at the Consett Iron Company did not result in increased opportunities for them or others to enter this male domain post-war and this clearly contradicts some of the myths developed by the wartime media and other commentators, who exaggerated the changes that would be brought about for women especially in the field of employment. It is clear that the union tended to operate a 'blanket' policy of excluding women, however much they enjoyed the job, however skilled or competent they were, from continuing in what were traditionally seen as men's jobs. But, for the women who did those labouring, operating and welding jobs, it broadened their experiences, gave them good wages for the first time and a certain amount of independence. Also, as a result of these work experiences, it is evident that some women's employment goals were changed, but ultimately, in a patriarchal society, which ascribes to women a domestic role, underestimates the extent to which working-class women take up paid work, and sees the preservation of men's jobs as a priority, these goals were not realised.

Subsequent government and union policies that could have facilitated these women's changed goals and self-perceptions resulting in real social changes via increased employment opportunities for women and economic emancipation, were not provided. It seems that the individual will or potential for change (in this case, taking on jobs other than those traditionally ascribed as 'women's work') was there: the social will of a powerful patriarchal society to facilitate this was not (though they were quite willing to pretend that there had been more social change than there was in fact).

The actual extent to which individual women were changed by their war-work is difficult to determine overall; short-term benefits in terms of good pay, freedom and independence compared with their pre-war work were in ample evidence. More long-term effects upon the individual, her family and community can more ably be ascertained by studying women's life histories to consider, for example, how such employment might influence later friendship formations, other work experiences or relationships with daughters, some of whom were eventually allowed to become operators thirty years later. Then management and unions chose to recall the care and conscientiousness with which women had done their jobs in the iron and steel industry during the Second World War but in the main their contribution has been neglected and its wider significance and potential for social change has been ignored.

NOTES

1. From conversation with Mrs T.
2. 1943 was the peak year in terms of total female employment in the iron and steel industry.
3. Hoist mechanism.

REFERENCES

Allen, M. (1980) 'British Women at Home in World War Two', *Second Women and Labour Conference Papers*, Melbourne, pp. 437–48.

Allen, M. (1983) 'The Domestic Ideal and the Mobilisation of Woman Power in World War II', *Women's Studies International Forum*, vol. 6, no. 4, pp. 401–12.

Braybon, G. (1981) *Women Workers in the First World War: The British Experience*, London: Croom Helm.

British Iron and Steel Federation (1945a) *Statistics of the Iron and Steel Industry in the United Kingdom*, Warwick: Castle Press.

British Iron and Steel Federation (1945b) *The Battle for Steel. A Record of the British Iron and Steel Industry at War*, Farfare Press.

Douie, V. (1943) *The Lesser Half*, Women's Publicity Planning Association.

Douie, V. (1950) *Daughters of Britain*, Oxford: George Ronald.

Friedan, B. (1965) *The Feminine Mystique*, London: Penguin Books.

Gluck, S. (1982) 'Interlude or Change: Women and the World War II Work Experience', *International Journal of Oral History*, vol. 3, no. 2, pp. 92–113.
Lion's Club, The (1963) *The Consett Story*, Consett: Ramsden Williams Publications.
Marwick, A. (1968) *Britain in the Century of Total War: War, Peace and Social Change 1900–1967*, London: Macmillan.
Ministry of Labour and National Service (1941) *The Employment of Women: Suggestions to Employers*, London: HMSO.
Price, K. M. (1984) 'Women's Employment and Unemployment in the Current Recession: Facts or MisInformation?', *Built Environment*, vol. 10, no. 1, Alexandrine Press in association with the Regional Studies Association, pp. 53–60.
Scott, P. (1944) *They Made Invasion Possible*, London: Hutchinson.
Summerfield, P. (1984) *Women Workers in the Second World War*, London: Croom Helm.
Thompson, P. (1978) *Oral History – The Voice of the Past*, Oxford University Press.

Part III
The Sociology of Peace Movements

10 The Sociology of CND

John Mattausch

INTRODUCTION

This chapter is divided into three parts. In the first part I give a critical overview of three of the major academic analyses of the British Campaign for Nuclear Disarmament (Parkin, 1968; Taylor and Pritchard, 1980; Nias, 1983). In this overview, I am particularly concerned with the analysts' theoretical perspectives and their limitations. It is argued that their various theories are inappropriate and give rise to misleading portrayals of the Campaign and its members. In the second part of the chapter, I briefly outline an alternative theory to account for the form which the original Movement took, a theory which sheds some light on its social base. In Part 3, I will discuss some preliminary findings of my own research in progress in which I utilise the theory discussed in Part 2 of this paper, to investigate sociologically the recent revival of the Campaign.

1 MIDDLE CLASS RADICALS?

Published in 1968, Parkin's *Middle Class Radicalism* has become widely known and has the distinction of being the only major sociological study of the first Campaign; the title has entered into the sociologist's lexicon. Based upon 358 mail questionnaires completed by randomly selected adult supporters, 445 mail questionnaires completed by youth supporters initially contacted at the 1965 Easter March, and an unspecified number of interviews with various branch secretaries and other supporters, Parkin sought to provide 'a study of the social bases of support for a political mass movement – the Campaign for Nuclear Disarmament'. Parkin was not concerned with the Movement's 'general aims and strategies', nor with giving 'an historical narrative'. Instead, 'The political movement which resulted is examined here for the light it throws on certain problems of current interest in the sociology of politics . . .' (1968, p. 1).

In this study, Parkin hoped to shed light upon the hitherto neglected 'small minority of the middle class which endorses left wing political and social views', a small minority which, he felt, was the analogous obverse of working-class Conservatives. Furthermore, Parkin wished to examine the supporters' 'perception of the social structure and their place within it'. He believed that 'CND also provides a useful test case for current propositions in political sociology concerning the sources of recruitment to mass movements'; this question of recruitment is considered mainly in terms of theories of alienation.

The following picture of CND members emerges from Parkin's study: the members are drawn from the educated middle class, they hold a consensus view of society, they tend to be located in the 'creative and welfare' professions and they are likely to endorse left-wing politics. The youthful supporters are portrayed as following in the adult mould. Parkin argues that the middle-class CND supporters were alienated from certain dominant social values and were motivated by psychological forces, that their form of political activity is best characterised as 'expressive' (rather than working-class 'instrumentalist') and that they derived 'emotional or psychological' rewards from such activity. Importantly, for Parkin, such political activity represented, for the middle-class radical, not merely a protest against the Bomb but, in addition, a protest against a whole array of issues for which CND became a focus and a symbol.

What were the theoretical assumptions and concomitant methodological procedures which led Parkin to these conclusions? First, Parkin decided to ignore the Campaign's aims and strategies and does not discuss the Movement's historical evolution[1] from the early days of anti-testing protests. Secondly, he characterises CND *a priori* as 'a mass *political* movement' (my emphasis). Thirdly, he implicitly reifies CND – partly as a legacy of his ahistorical perspective – to the status of an independent entity. Parkin's analytical stance is that of a neo-positivist social scientist explaining a social phenomenon: this stance is reflected in the language he employs; for example, CND will be a 'test-case', a 'useful laboratory' for his scientific analysis.

Unfortunately, Parkin chose not to justify this stance. The onus is upon Parkin to justify his characterisation of CND as a mass *political* movement rather than, say, a 'non-political' single-issue pressure group. Similarly, it is reasonable to expect Parkin to explain his unwillingness to consider CND's 'aims and strategies' as these would seem, at the least, pertinent analytical factors. However, Parkin is not particularly concerned with Campaign members' own avowed reasons for their actions.

Instead, Parkin uses his superior sociological knowledge to explain CNDers' motivations. Thus, for example, when he analyses why some individuals become recruited to the Campaign, his explanation is couched in terms which derive from his theoretical model rather than from asking the supporters the reasons for their recruitment. Briefly, Parkin argues that CNDers are 'alienated'[2] from certain dominant normative values. This normative alienation is deduced by Parkin from his samples' responses to a series of questions relating to the monarchy, to nationalisation, and whether they considered themselves as belonging to various religious denominations or were non-believers. However, there is nothing in these answers which, by themselves, tell us *why* they agreed/disagreed, or why they considered themselves religious. Rather, their responses are only interpreted within an explanatory paradigm of alienation as evidence for a cause of recruitment to 'the Movement'.

Parkin initially assumed that the concept of alienation would allow us to explain recruitment to CND and evidence of such alienation was then sought. Is it reasonable to employ the 'evidence' in this manner? The responses are taken as evidence of a psychological state, alienation, which the respondents make no claim to possess and which is presented as affecting all the respondents in a similar fashion. Could not 'alienation' be experienced in different ways by different people? And why, even allowing that the respondents are 'alienated', do they opt to join CND in particular and protest in a particular way? And what is the connection between stating disagreement with a proposition and alienation from a value?

Underlying Parkin's theoretical approach, and generating many of the problems encountered in his work, is a reifying, essentialist position. Thus, he attempts to discover why people become recruited *to* the Movement and he attempts to identify a *common* causal impetus (the psychological motivation resulting from 'alienation'). However, it will be readily appreciated that CND is a social praxis and not an entity. CND has no objective existence, nor is there any reason to believe that there is any one common reason which impels every new recruit to join the Campaign.

Parkin's research methodology reflects his 'social scientist' approach. There are a number of criticisms which can be made. First, the adult sample were *activists* over the age of 25 selected primarily by their local branch secretaries on the grounds of whether the secretary considered them to be activists. I am unhappy with this equation of 'radical' with activism, especially as the bulk of CND members are not activists; is this a study of middle-class activists? Secondly, and most importantly, the adult sample was initially contacted in February 1966. By this time, CND had evolved from small anti-testing groups, through a large non-membership Movement, and was on the verge of becoming a disillusioned and diminished membership Campaign.[3] Quite simply, CND was a very different Campaign in 1966 from that which it had been in its 1958–61 heyday. At the very least, Parkin should have qualified his conclusions in the light of these historical developments.

I hope that the foregoing critique[4] of Parkin's study at least highlights some of the problematic consequences of his theoretical perspective and stance and that his methodology will be seen as one of these, equally problematic, consequences.

Perhaps not surprisingly, Parkin did not suggest any campaigning strategies or tactics for the Movement; indeed, the whole issue of nuclear weaponry and peace is never mentioned in his book. For Parkin, CND is to be analysed as an ahistorical entity, defined in *a priori* terms, whose members are drawn from the ranks of the psychologically motivated, alienated middle class. It is my contention that this portrayal is, at best, misleading and is based upon a set of dubious theoretical premises and an inadequate methodology.[5]

In contrast to Parkin, the writings of Richard Taylor are informed by a comprehensive and thorough knowledge of the historical development of CND[6] and the socio-political milieu in which the Campaign arose. Moreover, and again in contrast to Parkin's study, Taylor is deeply concerned with the anti-nuclear cause and has a clear political standpoint. For the purposes of this chapter, I shall be concentrating upon *The Protest Makers* (1980), Taylor's retrospective study of activists in the first Campaign, which was written in collaboration with Colin Pritchard. However, it should be recognised that Taylor's other, valuable writings on the past and present Campaigns are also informed by the analytical and political perspectives which are employed in this study.

Taylor and Pritchard were unfortunate in the timing of their study. Published in 1980, their research was mainly carried out in

1977–8 shortly before the recent, dramatic revival of the Movement. At this time, it did appear that the Campaign was defunct, and this would have given credence to Taylor's basic belief that the first CND was a *failed* Movement. Nevertheless, this belief is, as I will discuss, a reflection of Taylor's overall political analytical stance: for Taylor, the first CND failed because it did not find adequate political articulation and, concomitantly, the present CND will experience a parallel failure, he argues, unless the Movement adopts a particular New Left ideology.[7]

In the preface to their study, Taylor and Pritchard declare that their focus is 'political and sociological rather than historical', and that they intend 'to explore the political and ideological dimensions of the Movement and the problems which its experience has posed for achieving radical change in modern Britain, and to analyse the current attitudes and activities of Movement supporters some twenty years on' (1980, Preface). The data for their research was comprised of 'in-depth interviews with leading figures of the Movement' and 400 mail questionnaires completed by 'core activists'. In common with Parkin, this study is of activists rather than 'ordinary' members.

.Taylor and Pritchard's study is essentially the analysis of what they take to be a failed social movement, and much of their work is concerned to show that, because of the internal conflicting ideological components contained within the Movement, CND was unable to develop an adequate *political* strategy with which to secure their disarmament objectives. Crudely summarised, it is the author's contention that none of these ideological factions was able to formulate a political strategy which could secure support from the membership and the general public and could effect the necessary *political* changes. Neither the advocates of Direct Action, nor the New Left (as it was then[8]), nor the Labour Party supporters of the Movement, were able to overcome the inherently middle-class nature and moralistic character of the Movement in order to build a Campaign involving mass working-class support which appreciated the need for economic realities to be incorporated within disarmament strategy. CND failed because it could not find a viable socialist expression for necessarily political action: 'The great moral and emotive spasm which gave rise to the Movement in 1958 did not find adequate political expression' (1980, p. 131).

This portrayal of CND as a failed social movement is less credible in 1985 following the impressive resurgence of both interest and activity. But, as I have already noted, it should be remembered that Taylor and Pritchard carried out the bulk of their research in 1977–8 and felt able to state that 'its days as a *mass movement* had ended by 1965–6' (1980, p. 131). However, such unfortunate statements are not merely the result of poor luck; rather, I feel, they are partly a consequence of the authors' theoretical paradigm.[9] In order to fully understand why Taylor and Pritchard regarded CND as failed and defunct, it is necessary to examine their arguments regarding the Movement's origins. Basically, the authors believe that the impetus for the original CND arose not only because of a greater appreciation of the nuclear threat in the late 1950s, but also because certain political and social events had left a lacuna within British political life. The failure of the Labour Party to radically restructure Britain in a truly socialist mould, the 1956 Hungarian uprising and the Suez fiasco had produced 'an increased scepticism and mistrust of the old ideologies and the old institutions' combined with 'a heightened political atmosphere' (1980, p. 3). Thus, *historically specific* events had engendered a distrust of existing politics and an increased political consciousness. In addition, the authors also cite two other related, historical, contributory factors; 'the growth of a new and unique youth culture' and the publication of the Sandys White Paper on British defence policy. So, 'by 1956 the time was indeed ripe for "a new kind of politics" to rekindle the idealism and commitment of the radical strata in British society' (1980, p. 5).

These events of the late 1950s created a political vacuum, 'a vacuum which CND was shortly to fill'. Taylor and Pritchard go on to list four events which occurred in the autumn of 1957 and which acted as catalysts in the formation of the Movement: first, the launching of the Russian Sputnik; second, Professor G. F. Kennan's Reith Lectures arguing against Dulles' Cold-War stance; third, Aneurin Bevan's denunciation of unilateralist policy at the 1957 Labour Party annual conference; and fourth, J. B. Priestley's seminal article in the *New Statesman*.[10]

These historically specific events, it is argued, formed the socio-political milieu which spawned CND. However, such historical factors are necessary rather than sufficient conditions for the present CND, which is remarkably similar to the original Campaign, and has revived without these *specific* generative events being present.[11] Nor does the identification of these events, by itself, allow theoretical purchase on the question of why the Movement 'failed'. Although Taylor recognises that a set of historical events contributed to CND's decline, his main argument remains that the Campaign could not translate its 'emotive and moral' impetus into tangible political reality. This argument introduces a teleological aspect into Taylor's analysis which is based upon the author's, albeit convincingly presented, political predilection.

Nevertheless, and as Taylor acknowledges, it is clear that, for a large number of CND supporters, the Campaign was not a political enterprise but, rather, a moral movement. How, then, do the authors characterise these moral beliefs? Because of the authors' political convictions and their imbricated teleological perspective, such moral factors have ultimately to be seen as inadequate because they hinder a development of the New Left political consciousness which, it is argued, is necessary for CND if it is to achieve its objectives.

Leaving aside the validity of Taylor's political beliefs,[12] it is worth questioning the legitimacy of denigrating moral reasons for campaigning. It is by no means clear that CND 'failed' except in the sense of not achieving unilateral disarmament; as a *protest* movement it was highly successful, i.e. many tens of thousands of people staged, often very imaginative, protests. An act of moral protest is complete in itself, regardless of the outcome, and it is nonsensical to try to assess its success or failure by reference to future events. At this point it is worth noting that some of Taylor and Pritchard's 'respondents strongly disagreed with [the] statement', 'I believe that the disarmament movement failed because . . .' which formed question 19 of the questionnaire. It is only within the authors' analytical framework that the achievements of CND assume such importance; presumably, if you are a 'protest maker' you could be as interested in the quality of protesting as much as in the effects of such protest.

The studies of Parkin and Taylor and Pritchard are the only major analyses of the first CND:[13] to date, and to my knowledge, only Peter Nias has carried out any substantial study of the present movement. Nias's study (1983) is rather more descriptive than analytical and has the great merit of drawing upon large-scale survey data.[14]

Nias argues that in the 1970s a number of events and influences emerged which provided an atmosphere conducive to the growth of 'protest movements in general and nuclear disarmament movements in particular'. In addition, following the arguments of Tony Benn, Nias cites the demise of 'consensus politics' in the 1970s as responsible for provoking a re-examination of political ends as well as political means. No truly sociological analysis of the Campaign and its membership is offered, rather Nias characterises the membership in terms of the data drawn from his surveys. He concludes his thesis by suggesting that the disarmament movement has, so far, been successful in raising the public consciousness to the dangers of nuclear weapons but has, except when working in alliance with other groups, achieved little else and that neither 'the nuclear disarmament movement in general' nor any of its component parts, can 'legitimately be called a mass movement, partly because the membership is too narrow' (1980, p. 3).

Before moving on to Part 2 of this chapter, I want to summarise the main points which I have made in the foregoing overview of these studies of CND. My argument is not that their analyses or conclusions are wrong, rather, that they are at times misleading. I have tried to show that the various theoretical models and perspectives are problematic and can, on occasion, lead to suspect portrayals of CND and its members. Many of the observations of the aforementioned writers are both pertinent and valuable: it would seem that the first CND did (and I think still does) represent a symbolic protest against a whole range of issues as Parkin noted and, as Taylor in particular is aware, the first CND had a peculiarly moral flavour to it. And as all the writers acknowledge, the social base of the Campaign was narrow and socially specific, which as Nias's research confirms, is a characteristic of the present Movement. What is needed is a new sociological heuristic which permits an *understanding* of these defining characteristics, rather than an explanation which may lead to such characteristics becoming devalued. Such a heuristic should go some way to answering the questions: Why is it that only a minority of the population feel it incumbent upon them to protest against nuclear weapons? and Why is it that CND appears to be particularly attractive to those individuals who, as Chris Rootes has recently written, are drawn from 'the highly educated practitioners of the service, welfare and creative professions of the non-market sector of the economy'? (1984, p. 5).

2 BEVERIDGE AND THE BOMB

In this section of the chapter I will briefly outline the theoretical heuristic which informs my own research in progress (which I discuss in Part 3). I want to begin with a couple of premises: first, my own belief in the real danger inherent in our present policies of nuclear 'defence'; second, that nuclear weapons and weapons systems are *State weapons*. Clearly, it would be foolish to deny the importance of the profit motive and the 'military–industrial complex' when considering the historical development of the arms race. Nevertheless, right from the earliest days of the M.A.U.D. Committee, it has been the State which has initiated and controlled the production of nuclear arms. Weapons programmes have always been conceived in the light of inter-state politics (for Britain, especially in terms of the Anglo-American 'special relationship').[15] In terms of legitimation, social presentation and political control, *the bomb is a State weapon*.

Curiously, this facet of the State's role, the external defence role, has not been subject to the same amount of ideological and political debate as has its internal welfare responsibilities. It is a sad historical irony that the period which saw the most progressive internal policy changes, the establishment of the Welfare State, also witnessed the equally important decision to produce the British Bomb. However, for this latter decision there were few witnesses.[16] Indeed, with the honourable exception of some small groups who, with foresight, were concerned mainly with the effects of nuclear weapons testing, the Mr Hyde of the British State managed to remain hidden and unchallenged. Political debate focused on the management of the Welfare State and on foreign policy issues, not on the wisdom, or otherwise, of Britain possessing a nuclear arsenal.

But by the mid-1950s, events conspired to bring the nuclear issue to the public attention. As Taylor argues, a vacuum had existed on the British political Left, for in a period of comparative affluence and economic growth, and at a time of disillusionment with conventional politics, ideological causes were in short supply. Moreover, it appeared as though the basic principles underpinning the Welfare State were workable, if in need of better management. However, the international events of this period began to bring the credibility of the British State's legitimation into serious question.

These catalystic events, in particular Hungary and Suez, occurred at a time of disillusionment with conventional politics and at a time when the effects of nuclear testing had begun to provoke worry and debate. The legitimating rationale of the State, as a moral defender of national interests, was called into question. Suez in particular had suggested to some observers that Britain was capable of ethically suspect diplomacy and was not the autonomous superpower of pre-War years.[17] Those who identified most strongly with the aims and spirit of the Welfare State were likely to be most shocked and alarmed at the newly revealed failings. Not surprisingly, their protest and politics were couched in the language of the ideology of the State itself; i.e. the early CNDers were acting in the common interest and were seeking to rectify the moral failings of the State's policies.[18] Hence, the first Campaign was 'above' politics, as supposedly is the State, moral and disciplined. Its members, rather than just 'middle class' were drawn from those sections of this nebulous stratum who were cushioned from the realities of capitalism but were imbued with the State's ideology; e.g. teachers, students, nurses, social workers, lecturers etc. These were individuals who were commonly employed and entrusted to carry out State policy and were personally involved and responsible for the work of the State. The size of this social class, the *State class*, was, at this time, growing and its constituent members were fortunate in that they did not have to worry over much about their immediate needs, such as employment.

Furthermore, there was a perverse affinity between the issue of nuclear weapons and the legitimating ideology of the bourgeois State; whereas its legitimation rested on the notion of acting for the common good, its armaments threatened mass extinction. In this sense, protest against nuclear weapons also challenged the ideological cornerstone of the State itself. However, such a potentially revolutionary issue was bereft of a political voice, for the mainstream parties were committed to working within the constraints of the capitalist State.

In summary, historically specific socio-political events had called into question the ethics of Britain's nation-state position and a greater awareness of the character of its nuclear arsenal, and of the effects of testing, had provided an alarming affinitive substantiation to these concerns. Those individuals who were most susceptible to alarm over these problems were likely to be personally affected and committed to the ideological buttresses of the State. However, these issues were difficult to articulate politically through partisan political parties; the Campaign expressed itself through legal protest (with minor infringements) and sought its strength in education and persuasion rather than confrontation. The contradictory socio-political forces which had given rise to both Beveridge and the Bomb had also engendered a State class which was to be the sharpest critic of the State's defence posture. In their attempt to actualise the State's moral legitimation, the State class sought to give a unilateral moral lead to other, benighted nations. Even if such protest was ineffective in terms of achievements, it was still morally right.

Moreover, seen in this way, one can understand why protest against the Bomb assumed symbolic importance (as noted by Parkin): protest against the Bomb was also, perhaps unwittingly, protest against the State itself and a reclamation of usurped moral authority. Furthermore, CND was naturally to act as a political nursery for those who came to realise that their concern over nuclear weaponry implied a critique of other State policies.

In the foregoing paragraphs, I have been forced to overstate and simplify my arguments in order to succinctly convey the thrust of my theoretical position. In short, the above discussion of the first Campaign is supposed to be a description of the 'form of life'[19] in which the Movement arose; the Campaign's social context. By placing the first CND in its 'form of life' we can *account* for the form of protest in which CNDers engaged and shed some light upon the Campaign's social base. In particular, the heuristic permits an understanding of the moral character of the first CND and why it was that disarmament protesting represented more than just a protest against the Bomb. In the final part of this chapter I intend to discuss a few of the findings[20] of my own research wherein I am employing the theoretical position I have outlined in order to sociologically investigate the Campaign's recent revival. In this final section, I shall be concentrating on the relationship of my respondents to the State which, I have found, is considerably more complex than the above theoretical sketch would suggest.

3 STATE CLASS RADICALISM

CND has always embraced a very diverse group of individuals and ideologies. My own impression of the revived membership is that they are at least as diverse as their predecessors; this diversity is as important as any similarities and should not be neglected for the sake of analytical convenience.

In my interviews with samples of CND members[21] I was especially interested in their relationship to the State; whether this relationship was important in politicising them and whether it coloured their political and ideological beliefs (as suggested by my understanding of the first Campaign). Consequently, in the interviews I tried to elicit a biographical sketch focusing upon when and how they became politically aware and when they joined CND or the Peace Movement in general. In addition, I became interested in whether particular relationships to the State engendered particular political perspectives both in terms of general political orientation and in terms of political strategy for CND. It would seem that such relationships are complex and individual, as the following two illustrative examples show.

Colin and Ian are both 32 years old and both men have left the Royal Air Force because of their moral and political beliefs. However, this seemingly common experience was, in fact, markedly different for each man and they both hold very different views of what CND is and should be. For Ian, joining the RAF was an alternative to unskilled dead-end jobs in New Town where he lived with his working-class foster parents. When he entered the Force, Ian was already a 'Labour man' and saw himself as a bit of a rebel ('a biker'). He served his apprenticeship and worked as a propulsion engineer and by the time he had to leave the RAF he had become a self-taught socialist. His political views proved unacceptable to the Air Force: 'They threw me out, they don't like socialist thinkers.'

Ian's social perspective, and his views on the Campaign, are directly related to his 'hard Left' political views. He sees his neighbours, and the working class in general, as unthinking, over-materialistic and embourgeoisified. Similarly, he believes that his former RAF colleagues were 'brainwashed'. For Ian, the local CND is a 'middle-class clique': 'I think that a lot of them are middle-class, semi-professional, teachers, doctors, that sort of thing'. He disagrees with CND's non-political stance and thinks that if the members 'really thought about the issue' they'd join the Labour Party of which he himself is a member. Apart from the occasional payment to Oxfam, Ian has no involvement with any charity or any other campaign or group; nevertheless, he tries to live out his political beliefs (for example, shopping only at the Co-op and making his own wine to avoid donating money to the Conservative Party). Although opposed to all nuclear weapons, he is in favour of retaining conventional arms. For Ian, nuclear disarmament is a political issue which can only be achieved by political means.

For Colin, on the other hand, disarmament is primarily a moral issue. Joining the RAF had been a boyhood ambition and, at first, the job seemed to live up to his expectations: 'wearing a uniform, strutting about, people saluting you, that sort of thing'. However, after a while, Colin found himself teaching new recruits and his views changed:

> when I had to teach new people when they came in as new recruits, I began to question what I was actually teaching. And at the end, I just *could not* teach what I did not believe in and did not agree with and I had to leave. If I had not sat down and thought about it [he pauses], I was teaching and I had to plan out the lessons and things, and I thought 'I don't *believe* in this' so I'm damn well not going to teach it.

The final straw came on the day of the Queen's Silver Jubilee Celebrations at Colin's camp:

> when I heard the attitudes, the sort of attitudes I was actually helping to develop, y'know, it was time to get out.

On leaving the Air Force, Colin travelled to both the USA and the USSR 'to compare the goodies and the baddies'. He has been unemployed since returning to Britain and although not a member of any other organisation, Colin buys Campaign Coffee, goes to Chilean Aid concerts and Anti-Apartheid meetings. Not a member of any political party, he sees CND as a 'one-issue' campaign which should not align itself to any one political party for fear of alienating potential supporters. He believes that the majority of the British population do not belong to CND because they are apathetic and he does not think that the members of CND are 'stuck to any one particular class'. For Colin, disarmament is 'a moral issue. For me, disarmament is tied in with the ethics and morals of violence'.

Clearly, for both men, their experiences of the State, in the form of the RAF, was highly important in their lives and in the formation of their views. Nevertheless, the effects of their contact with the State were disparate: for Ian, it resulted in a hardening of his nascent socialist politics, for Colin, it provoked a reassessment of his beliefs and attitudes. Ian sees disarmament as a political issue to be fought for, by and through the Labour Party whilst Colin hopes a 'build-down' to a 'less deadly level' can be achieved by a single-issue mass Movement. Rather than a single causal relation leading to a single effect, their contact with the State acted as a catalyst in their personal development; for Colin, nuclear disarmament is something for which he has become inadvertently personally morally responsible.

Similar diversity can be seen when considering the effects of the education process and in particular higher education upon CND members. All the studies of CND have commented upon the fact that members of CND tend to be highly educated and that teachers, lecturers and students have a high profile in the Campaign. And yet, there exists no necessary relation between higher education and CND membership; many highly educated people do not belong to CND. My own two samples of CNDers contained a large number of highly educated members, teachers and lecturers and, once again, I was interested in how their experiences of the State education process had shaped their views.

For Gerry, a gas-fitter from Scots City, a day-release ONC course proved to be instrumental in his joining CND:

> One of the instructors was a member of CND, [he wore] peace badges and that white dove, and I was, huh curious at the time and I didn't understand anything about it or know anything about it which is why I joined CND. The instructor brought in the magazine and it had the address in and I filled it out.

Gerry's account of how he joined CND is, I think, not uncommon; opportunity leading to curiosity. However, Gerry's contact with State education was comparatively slight and short-lived and does not appear to have significantly changed or shaped his opinions or political views. In contrast, the lecturer who influenced Gerry has had most of his opinions formed by his experiences in education. Nigel started life as a miner, from a Northern mining family and is now a lecturer in a large technical college in Scots City. Nigel is aware of the effects of his personal social mobility which he thinks 'made me smoother, more middle class' and gave him the opportunity to mix with people from other backgrounds with different views from his own. He sees his role as teacher as being very important and he tries to help his students resolve their own moral dilemmas. At the same time, he tries to make his students aware of wider social and sociological issues:

> I teach a lot of technologists and scientists, I make a point and I think that's quite a powerful situation to be in, I teach about war and the economy and I've actually been accused by the students of putting a particular perspective across! As a liberal, I immediately put another perspective across.

Both Gerry and Nigel think that the Campaign should be non-political. However, for Gerry, this is because he distrusts politicians and is only interested in the issue of law and order (for which he thinks Willie Whitelaw is a good politician). For Nigel, a politically aware lecturer, CND's non-political stand 'gives you an enormous moral authority, which we're pretty short of in Britain' and this moral authority is

CND's 'greatest strength'. Whereas Gerry thinks that joining CND is the duty of the individual ('otherwise you deserve all that's coming to you'), Nigel believes that he has a duty, because of his relation to the State, to – at least – bring the issue to the attention of his students. This is not surprising, for part of what it means to be a teacher, the ideology of the profession, is the sense of duty.

This notion of a duty to campaign and protest was present in many of my interviews with teacher members. For example, for Philip, a 38-year-old foreign languages teacher, being a university student convinced him that his 'major interest was really social service' and after spending some time doing VSO abroad, and after a short spell working with physically-handicapped children, he became a teacher which he sees as, properly, performing a very important social role. Philip is frustrated by the government's lack of appreciation of this role; he believes that they should 'enlarge the scope of social education, bringing peace studies into the curricula' as he himself has attempted to do at his own school (in the face of strong opposition from other teachers and some parents). He thinks that the majority of the population do not belong to CND because they 'are too ready to pass on their responsibility to others'; for Philip, because of his State experiences, it is not so easy to shirk what he has come to see as his own responsibility. Nor is it easy for other State employees whose work demands from them a high degree of personal involvement and imbues them with a sense of responsibility for their clients and the State's policy.

In this brief discussion of these few examples drawn from my research in progress, I have tried to show, first, that the notion of a State class is a viable and helpful heuristic and, secondly, that in practice, relations to the State and effects of such contact are varied and complex. The argument is *not* that contact with the State *causes* people to join CND, or that it causes them to hold one definite view of the Campaign: rather, I am suggesting that their involvement with the State helps render them *susceptible* to becoming CNDers. There is no thing which exists which is called CND; the Campaign is a social praxis, existing in a social context, created by people. Consequently, it is a fallacious enterprise to seek to discover the *one* defining common quality which all CNDers share which makes them CNDers; in actuality no such essential quality exists. To suggest, as Parkin did, that all members of CND are 'middle-class radicals' deriving psychological rewards from their 'expressive' politics is misleading. CND campaigning, and the Campaign itself, have different meanings for different individuals. CND is not a 'test case'; it is a continually *created* social praxis which can be understood but not explained. Such a sociological understanding requires CND praxis to be located within its generative and historically-specific social context. This is the purpose of the State class heuristic.[22]

ACKNOWLEDGEMENTS

I would like to thank Frank Bechhofer, Donald Mackenzie and Richard Smith, all at Edinburgh University Sociology Department, for their constructive comments on the conference version of this chapter. Special thanks are due to Dipti Pandya without whose help this chapter could not have been written. As usual, all errors and deficiencies are my responsibility.

NOTES

1. Excepting some brief discussions of the historical involvement of particular factions such as the Church and the Labour Party.
2. Parkin opts for this definition of 'alienation' after rejecting two other, for him, unproductive definitions of alienation as either powerlessness or social isolation.
3. CND became a membership Campaign in January 1967.
4. I have undertaken a much more detailed and comprehensive critique of Parkin's study as part of my research in progress. The discussion which I present here is merely a condensed outline and, consequently, may appear unduly critical of his research which remains a valuable resource.
5. Unfortunately, Parkin's data is unavailable for secondary analysis (private correspondence between Parkin and author).
6. To my knowledge, Taylor's doctoral thesis: 'The British Nuclear Disarmament Movement of 1958 to 1965 and its Legacy to the Left' (1983a) is the best available political history of the first Campaign and an invaluable reference work.
7. This is Taylor's basic position on CND. See Taylor (1983a) and Taylor, R. 'The British Peace Movement and Socialist Change' (1983b) and Taylor, R. 'The British Peace Movement and the New Left 1950–1980' (1984).
8. Taylor sees the humanistic New Left of the period as the best possible vehicle for politically articulating CND's objectives. But, he argues, it was unable, at that time, to realise its potential and failed to attract sufficient working-class support.
9. Taylor does discuss the revival of CND (1980, p. 137) in an appendix. However, I feel this discussion only amounts to an afterthought and the revival has not caused Taylor to alter his basic arguments. Taylor was not the only one to be surprised by the revival; in 1979, Bruce Kent also

thought that CND was finished as a mass movement (see Martin Ryle, 1981, p. 26.)

10. This article contained the call for a 'new kind of politics' (Priestley, 1957, pp. 554–6). *The New Statesman* of this period had begun to regularly carry articles on the nuclear issue, in particular Russell's correspondence with Kruschev and announcements of the inaugural meeting of CND.
11. Although it could be argued that there were *similar* events in the late 1970s which acted as comparable catalysts. Taylor seems to be arguing this in 'The British Peace Movement and Socialist Change' (1983b, pp. 139–40). Moreover, he argues in this paper that a 'crucial development in the 1970s . . . has been the expansion' in 'the number of radical, tertiary educated, professional and intellectual employees, whose public-sector occupations and general background of "critical thinking" have resulted in an ideological stance opposed to the market individualism of competitive capitalism' and that this section of the middle class has become increasingly important in radical politics and political movements (Taylor, 1983b, p. 139). This observation is, I believe, crucial for an understanding of the social base of CND (see Parts 2 and 3 of this chapter). However, Taylor's analysis juxtaposes this expanded social group to the, for Taylor, more important working and capitalist classes and their concomitant ideological domains. In contrast, I am arguing that this social group derives its 'form of life' from the social production of the *State* and that the post-war British State fulfils a dual role of welfare and defence which leads to problems of legitimation. For further discussions of this social stratum see Coates (1984, esp. p. 135) and Cotgrove and Duff (1980, pp. 333–51) – both cited by Taylor (1984, p. 139).
12. For an analysis in a similar vein, although much less well developed, see: Groom (1974, p. 393). Groom argues that a major cause of the decline of CND was its inability to overcome internecine disputes and capitalise on the 1960 Labour Party's Conference decision to adopt a unilateralist policy. Groom's analysis is, by comparison, slender, and relies heavily on Parkin's work.
13. With the addition of Taylor's (1983a) doctoral thesis on the present Campaign, mention should be made of Bartlett, *The Nuclear Disarmament Movement* (1983). Bartlett concentrates on the revival of the Campaign in Scotland and the study is, perhaps, a useful corrective to London-centric analyses of CND. It is worth remembering that peace initiatives can originate outside London and the Home Counties. In the early days, autonomous Scottish anti-testing groups, pre-dating the formation of CND existed and actively campaigned (documentary evidence held by author).
14. Copies of summaries of these surveys (of CND members, END members and of marchers on the 6 June CND London Demo.) are available, for a small charge, from: Peter Nias, Research Surveys, 48 Victoria Road, Madeley, Telford, Shropshire TF7 5EU.
15. On the historical development of this 'special relationship' see: Gowing (1974); Malore (1984); and Baylis (1981).
16. This decision was taken by members of Attlee's Cabinet Defence Committee. The decision was not made public knowledge.

17. Despite the possession of an 'independent' nuclear deterrent. The retention of superpower status in the post-War world was one of the main arguments behind the decision to build the British Bomb.
18. This is clearly reflected in Priestley's (1957, pp. 554–6) moral call to arms.
19. The allusion is, of course, to Wittgenstein's mature philosophy. For the activist's own views and impressions of the first Campaign see: Duff (1971); Collins (1966); Russell (1969); Minnion and Bolsover (1983); and Boulton (1964).
20. The tape-recorded interviews which I will refer to in Part 3 were only transcribed shortly before I wrote this chapter. This, combined with shortage of space, means that I am only in a position to illustrate my argument by reference to particularly illuminating examples.
21. As part of my research in progress, I interviewed randomly selected samples of members of two CND groups; one group from a large Scottish city and one Home Counties group (total, to date, 64). Both activists and lay members were subjected to a semi-structured tape-recorded interview lasting, on average, an hour. All names in the text are uninspired pseudonyms.
22. For some campaigning implications of my argument see: Mattausch (1985).

REFERENCES

Bartlett, P. (1983) 'The Nuclear Disarmament Movement', unpublished MSc. thesis, Dept. of Politics, University of Strathclyde.

Baylis, J. (1981) *Anglo-American Defence Relations 1939–1980*, New York: St Martin's Press.

Boulton, D. (1964) *Voices from the Crowd Against the H Bomb*, London: Peter Owen.

Coates, D. (1984) *The Context of British Politics*, London: Hutchinson.

Collins, Rev. Canon, L. J. (1966) *Faith Under Fire*, London: Leslie Frewin.

Cotgrove, S. and Duff, A. (1980) 'Environmentalism, Middle Class Radicalism and Politics', *Sociological Review*, vol. 28, no. 2.

Duff, P. (1971) *Left, Left, Left*, London: Allison and Busby.

Gowing, M. (1974) *Independence and Deterrence: Britain and Atomic Energy. Volume I*, London: Macmillan.

Groom, A. J. R. (1974) *British Thinking About Nuclear Weapons*, London: Frances Pinter.

Malore, P. (1984) *The British Nuclear Deterrent*, London: Croom Helm.

Mattausch, J. (1985) 'The Peace Phoenix: Will the Revived CND Fail Again?', *Natur Och Samhalle* (Sweden), vol. 11, no. 33.

Minnion, J. and Bolsover, P. (eds) (1983) *The CND Story*, London: Allison and Busby.

Nias, P. (1983) 'The Poverty of Peace Protest', unpublished MA thesis, Postgraduate School of Studies in Peace Studies, University of Bradford.

Parkin, F. (1968) *Middle Class Radicalism*, Manchester: Manchester University Press.

Priestley, J. B. (1957) 'Britain and the Nuclear Bomb', *New Statesman*, vol. LIV no. 1390, pp. 554–6.
Rootes, C. (1984) 'Protest, Social Movements, Revolution?', *Social Alternatives* (Australia), vol. 14, no. 1.
Russell, B. (1969) *The Autobiography of Bertrand Russell, Vol. 3, 1944–1967*, London: Allen & Unwin.
Ryle, M. (1981) '*CeNDing*', *New Statesman*, vol. 105, 14 Jan. 1981.
Taylor, R. (1983a) 'The British Nuclear Disarmament Movement of 1958 to 1965 and its legacy to the Left', unpublished PhD thesis, Dept. of Politics, University of Leeds.
Taylor, R. (1983b), 'The British Peace Movement and Socialist Change', in *The Socialist Register 1983*, London: Merlin Press.
Taylor, R. (1984) 'The British Peace Movement and the New Left', *Social Alternatives* (Australia), vol. 14, no. 1.
Taylor, R. and Pritchard, C. (1980) *The Protest Makers: The Nuclear Disarmament Movement of 1958–1965 Twenty Years On*, Oxford: Pergamon Press.

11 Activists for Peace: The Social Basis of a Local Peace Movement

Graham Day and David Robbins

CND AND THE 'NEW POLITICS'

Part of the disarray – or, to put a more optimistic gloss on it, the regrouping – of the British Left following the collapse of social reformism and the Butskellite consensus of the 1950s and 1960s has been a revived interest in questions of political organisation, which has brought with it a new awareness of the importance of a strategy of coalition-building. Talk of a 'new politics' has been in the air for some years, as in the pages of *New Socialist* and *Marxism Today*, and one or two exemplary models of the new politics in practice are held out – the GLC and other 'local socialisms' (Sheffield, West Midlands) – but a great deal of the discussion is at a highly general level and has little substance to it. In this chapter we intend to examine some features of the peace movement as it appears at local level, to see how far it can be said to exemplify the 'new politics'.

Support for the Campaign for Nuclear Disarmament has grown very rapidly in the past two or three years, outstripping the resources of the campaign to keep up with it; estimates put the figure at 110 000 members in 1985. By any standard, this is a major contemporary social movement, yet there is a striking paucity of research on it; at most a handful of articles and papers. The most substantial discussion is still that of Frank Parkin (1968) which deals with the previous wave of peace activity in the 1960s.

Parkin's discussion is a solid piece of political sociology, but has certain limitations. Parkin carried out questionnaire research on two samples of CND activists derived from local membership lists and from names collected during a youth demonstration, yet most of his discussion is not drawn from these, but consists of a review of published literature and public statements by key figures in churches and political parties from which Parkin 'reconstructs' motives and real aims. The upshot of this is that Parkin treats support for CND as more or less entirely symbolic of other things.

Not only is attachment to CND an *index* of other commitments ('a capsule statement of a distinct political and moral outlook', 1968, p. 3) but the campaign is seen as *used*, more or less consciously, as a vehicle in order to further aims to which people are more committed than they are to unilateralism. If we subtract all those who 'use' CND in this way – i.e. 'pacifists, the New Left, Communists, Anarchists, Quakers, the Labour Left and so on' (p. 5) little if anything remains. Young people, for example, join CND because doing so symbolises their rebellion against the older generation; Christians see CND primarily as a means of revitalising their churches; and the Labour Left uses CND for 'a language or dressing to cover other deepseated conflicts unrelated' to its objectives (p. 113). There is a consistent unwillingness to take CNDers' motivations on their own terms, which is partly explicable in terms of the thinness of the questionnaire material and the limited use Parkin makes of those interviews he did carry out with local secretaries and other (unspecified) activists. A later retrospective survey of CND members, twenty years on, found that only 18 per cent put their commitment to CND at the time below other commitments in terms of importance – the vast majority, long after the event, when there was no particular reason for deceit, said their prime loyalty had been to the movement (Taylor and Pritchard, 1980, p. 27).

The methodological bias in Parkin's work goes with a more fundamental restriction arising from the imposition of a particular conception of political action which he shares with many others. When he tells us for example that young CND supporters would find it hard to give 'expressly political' reasons for their behaviour (p. 158), or that CND 'bypasses the orthodoxies of the political process' (p. 10), it is obvious that he has a view of what 'proper' political action looks like: namely, conventional, organised, *party* politics with relatively clear objectives that are capable of attainment. CND failed to conform to this model in that it brought together a set of disparate causes, uniting people whose main preoccupation was with 'unrelated' issues; it represented a 'cause without an ideology' (p. 56) or as we would now commonly describe it, a single issue campaign around which otherwise unconnected or even antagonistic forces could temporarily unite. Indeed, the lack of a clear and achievable objective is understood by Parkin as the movement's major asset, since it appeals to the 'expressive' gestural politics of those who pursue principles, rather than joining in the pragmatic instrumental politics of conventional parties – essentially, the radical middle classes whose expressive orientations neatly correspond to the symbolic nature of support for nuclear disarmament.

However, the picture of CND activity as a single issue, unrelated to other commitments except as a convenient symbolic vehicle is hard to reconcile with the recognition of a 'distinct moral and political outlook', and 'a constellation of predictably radical attitudes and beliefs' which accompany involvement (p. 39). Here one suspects the coherence and integrity of a political outlook and set of political meanings simply eluded the methods of research.

A certain convergence on a model of 'correct' or properly 'political' organisation is manifest elsewhere. It surfaces in David Bouchier's work on the women's movement, in which he appears to deny its real achievements on the grounds that 'a movement which speaks with many voices . . . cannot be identified in the public mind as one movement. Nor can it act together towards goals which are so variously defined' (1984, p. 5). More explicitly it pervades Alain Touraine's research (1983), in which the French anti-nuclear power movement is evaluated in relation to a paradigm of politics as class struggle in which two principal antagonists (ruling class and subordinate class) organise themselves into coherent, formalised, political structures and contest a well defined objective (the transfer of power). In contemporary 'post-industrial' society, according to Touraine, this would situate the 'people' against the 'technocracy'. Political bodies and ideologies would have a clear 'class meaning', corresponding in one-to-one fashion with underlying class 'interests'.

Different though they are in many respects, the idea of politics which underpins the work of Touraine, Bouchier and Parkin might be termed the *Old Politics*, of formalised bureaucratic institutions, systematised doctrine, and strategic policy formulation. It is arguable that from this point of view all politics is 'essentially' about 'class' issues, and the examination of political movements deals with the forms of representation through which class interests are expressed. Certain kinds of political activity – broadly understood – have been awkward to fit into these pigeonholes: such as feminist politics, 'ethnic' and national politics, black political action, and, it seems, the Peace Movement.

THE 'NEW' POLITICS

Increasingly the framework of the old politics has come into question, and attempts have been made to construct an alternative 'new' politics. Theoretically a major impetus came via the work of Poulantzas (1980) and others in 'loosening up' the connections between determining conditions and political outcomes: the 'relative autonomy' of the political argues the need to pay attention in detail to the way the political is constituted. Ultimately, the new politics stems from Gramsci's critique of orthodox Marxist (Leninist) conceptions and has played an important part within the framework of 'Eurocommunist' thought, as it has developed in Britain for instance since the publication of the 1977 *British Road to Socialism*; but there is certain common ground with other, Weberian, traditions.

Once the possibility is allowed of detaching political commitments from 'class' position, a range of issues opens up, such as the significance of 'non-class' movements, or movements which straddle class boundaries ('pluriclass' groupings). Urban sociologists have suggested that alongside class politics, to do with accumulation and struggle between capital and labour, there are to be found crucial struggles around 'consumption' issues, and conflicts involving consumption sectors (Cawson and Saunders, 1983) or grassroots organisations and demands (Castells, 1984).

These examples are of course still concerned with arenas of struggle focused on distribution of economic resources of one kind or another; they are relevant because they begin to pose the question of *how* popular alliances are assembled, cemented, and maintained. In this respect, much of the literature is quite disappointing: for example, Raymond Williams' article on 'Splits, Pacts and Coalitions' (1984) despite frequent references to 'new political directions' does not go beyond stating a need for a novel but basically electoral coalition, and various other writers seem to think it is enough to list the constituent parts for an alliance to spring into action. Others are, however, more aware that extensive work is involved in bringing alliances together, that 'Social alliances do not simply happen, they are brought into being by a common political discourse' (Stedman Jones, 1982, p. 15). Some, like the authors of *Beyond the Fragments* (Rowbotham *et al.*, 1979), believe that such alliances are well on the way to crystallising, through practical political activity and 'struggles on the ground' which already outstrip existing party political structures. The 'new politics' is characterised by a concern with such issues: the formation of coalitions within flexible, movement-style structures which will allow the coordination of struggles and the building of relevant majorities. Behind this lies the recognition that it is no longer possible – in all probability, it never was – to assume that automatic majorities for particular positions (such as socialism) will be delivered by social conditions. If one cannot read 'politics' from economic structure, then the *processes* of political mobilisation take on great importance.

Alliances and political groupings have to be put together from existing resources, resources which are already 'structured' in a variety of ways within society, for example according to such characteristics as gender, age, race, region, national/ethnic identity, some of which bear a very loose relation to the fundamental class structures of capitalism. Hence there is always a diversity of bases upon which individuals may mobilise, as social subjects. Furthermore, the effectiveness of such mobilisation is mediated through the forms of organisation, and the availability of practices, symbols and rituals, in society. The significance of forms of political organisation has been stressed by Barry Hindess and fellow authors (Hindess, 1983), to the virtual exclusion of the 'structuring' factors already mentioned (which are dealt with more adequately by Urry (1981). Rather than interests existing prior to political action, and being brought to it, Hindess stresses how interests are constructed in the course of mobilisation and activity; political majorities are built around programmes and objectives to include non-class, non-economic forces whose aims are constituted *through* practice. 'Parties' are made up of classes in alliance. Nevertheless it is admitted that although there is space for constructing a diverse set of alliances, the ingredients or component parts are not infinitely malleable, since the process will be subject to some structural constraints.

In short, both theoretically and practically, the 'new politics' is alert to the importance of limited, transitory, shifting struggles of highly disparate kinds, and the need for continuing efforts to achieve some sort of controlling direction over the diversity of practices, ideas and groupings. The lesson is well stated by a theorist in END (European Nuclear Disarmament), that 'social movements are not driven by some pregiven "essence" but . . . are typically fragmented and divided internally, their infrequent unity always being a temporary result of political mechanisms such as compromise, tolerance, repression and strategic choices and judgements' (Keane, 1984, p. 6).

The relevance of these considerations for CND and the Peace Movement is firstly, that it is itself just such a 'coalition' of heterogeneous elements; secondly, that the peace movement is invariably included in the lists of the component 'fragments' from which the wider alliance of the Left might be formed – along with women, blacks, unemployed youths, gays, nationalists and others. The peace movement therefore provides a context in which to explore some of the substance of the new politics. But the 'coalitions' and 'alliances' of which people have been writing are intended to be more than bargains and trade-offs between leaders and public figures, of the kind Parkin considered; they have to do with the formation of real bonds, shared objectives, and common ideologies among grassroots activists. It is at the local level that the new social alliances should be taking shape, where Hilary Wainwright suggests 'people will tend to build these wider links with people they know and trust; and they will do so in ways that are close to their own experience' (Rowbotham *et al.*, p. 11). Unlike Parkin, and most other studies of the Peace Movement, this implies an interest in its local base.

A PROFILE OF LOCAL ACTIVISTS

Judging by the turnout at national demonstrations and local public meetings the Peace Movement enjoys considerable backing in the Aberystwyth area of mid-Wales. While much of this support is not formally organised there is a core of activists totalling perhaps 80 fairly actively committed local people. We have conducted 47 detailed interviews with such local activists. Our aim has been to see to what degree this core displays the 'new political style' of a coalition in the making. The central questions have to be: what are the strands that make up the local movement, how do they come together and with what degree of unity do they pursue their aims? How far does the common experience of participation in the movement weld them into a collectivity, a political force?

In terms of length of involvement, it is fairly easy to distinguish three political 'generations', which only roughly correspond with the age of the respondents. There are those for whom activity in CND and in the present upsurge of peace protest is merely a continuation of earlier, more or less life-long, commitments. These can take the form of engagement with pacifist/religious traditions – such as Peace Pledge Union, Fellowship of Reconciliation; or ties with the Welsh/nonconformist social milieu – for example, *Urdd* (Welsh League of Youth) internationalism, and Chapel societies; or political beliefs (Marxist or Labour Left, Left Book Club, trade union leftism). Individuals who belong in this category provide the long-term backbone for peace campaigns; their commitment over time has been steady, and they were ready to 'surface' again when peace activity picked up in the 1980s.

Secondly, there are those whose 'career' has been roughly coextensive with the history of CND: they became active in the 1960s, and when CND faded they took this activism into other channels – anti-Vietnam struggles, local party or pressure group activity – resuming in the 1980s more or less where they left off.

Finally, about half our informants have been drawn in during the last four or five years. While a few were too young to have been active previously, the rest were not sufficiently caught up in the issues to become involved – although mostly they claim to have taken informed interest in the debates.

Given this generational formation, the average age of activists is quite high: 18 are over fifty, and only five under thirty: the prominence of older people at local meetings presents a contrast with the 1960s image of a 'youth' rebellion, although it is likely that the core of *organised* support was then also relatively old. As will be shown below, differences in political style between these categories seem to present some problems for those concerned.

Whatever the continuity and level of involvement in the movement, we find a notable absence from the scene of the working class. In occupational terms, CND activists belong squarely to the intellectual/artistic/educational middle class: getting on for half (43 per cent) of our respondents are teachers, lecturers, researchers or involved with the arts. The remainder includes nurses, secretaries, librarians, civil servants, ministers and students. In common with other recent studies (see Mattausch in this volume, ch. 10 and Nias, 1985) we find that those in waged work are overwhelmingly employees of state agencies concerned with health, education or welfare. The educational profile is remarkable: only three have not been involved in further or higher education, one of whom is now entering university as a mature student: 37 (77 per cent) are graduates.

They are highly articulate, very capable of manipulating ideas and concepts, and well suited to the task of innovating new types of social and political outlook. They are also quite firmly cut off from the less educated, from manual workers and also from the business and commercial middle class – except for one former shopkeeper and the wife of a banker. Furthermore, when we asked about ways of increasing the effectiveness of the movement, there was a general lack of perception of this limited social range as a problem, and very few displayed any conception of either the need, or the means, for making links with the working class. In Aberystwyth, at least, CND does not gather the support of the public sector trade union activists who are said to form a part of the contemporary left coalition (Coates, 1984).

PEACE MOVEMENT IDEOLOGY: COHERENCE AND DIVERSITY

To the extent that political movements are an alliance of diverse groupings, then ideology must play an important role in cementing the fragments together. The main thrust of Parkin's argument is that the Peace Movement of the 1950s and 1960s represented a temporary alignment of groups with quite diverse objectives and ideologies. In contrast, those who see the Peace Movement as an exemplar of the 'new politics' are arguing that the movement has made considerable progress towards uniting its component parts at the level of ideology and political strategy. In view of this the extent of ideological coherence among Peace Movement members is a matter of empirical and political significance.

While exploring the ideological outlook of Peace Movement activists we detected a number of distinct orientations, various permutations of which define the position of individuals. When they are examined we find that in some ways the field of political action has moved on from the 1960s.

Half our respondents are women. In contrast the retrospective study by Taylor and Pritchard of CND in the 1950s and 1960s drew a sample which was 65 per cent male. The impact of *feminism* is evident even if several of our female respondents distance themselves from the label 'feminist'. Local women were among the original group of Welsh women who went to Greenham Common, many respondents since have visited Greenham, and there is universal admiration for the Greenham women: all those we have spoken to see them as the major force behind reawakened public awareness, any criticisms made of their actions are carefully hedged about with expressions of support, and many make an explicit connection between peace campaigning, the women's movement, and changed attitudes to gender roles. Activity in CND obviously precludes a militantly 'separatist' standpoint and we have not interviewed anyone who could be described as *primarily* feminist in orientation; nevertheless feminism provides an important input into the field of peace politics, and its influence is quite pervasive.

A second set of orientations are primarily *political*. Not surprisingly political leanings are to the left: voting goes Labour (47 per cent); Plaid Cymru (21 per cent); Liberal (14 per cent); Nothing/Floating (17 per cent). Only two had ever voted Conservative. Party members are in a minority (40 per cent) and with the exception of a lone Communist belong either to Labour or Plaid. While most of the politically orientated members of the Peace Movement have links with these two parties, a small number have been involved with or attracted towards the Ecology Party. Although local Communists can be counted on for support in activities such as the annual Peace Festival they do not play an organising role and Trotskyite organisations, such as the SWP, make no appearance other than on the larger, national marches. Parkin's suggestion that membership of CND is used by political factions to advance wider political aims is not borne out among our sample. More usually, support for the Peace Movement is seen as part of a seamless web of political commitments, in which it is actually rather difficult for the people concerned to order their priorities.

Although many respondents would describe themselves as 'socialist' this can mean very different things. This highlights the fact that different ideological orientations do not consist of discrete bundles of attitudes and concerns that can be readily picked out by content analysis of questionnaire responses. There is a range of cultural resources to which most Peace Movement supporters have access and ideas about socialism are part of this shared repertoire. Following structuralist reworkings of Gramsci (Laclau, 1977; Mouffe, 1979) we would suggest that the meaning of a concern with socialism will be given by the way in which it is linked or articulated to other ideas and concerns within the activists' world views.

For 17 respondents (36 per cent) *socialism* acts as the articulating principle around which a whole range of other elements is arranged and made intelligible. In this case issues of peace, the arms race, inequality, civil rights or the environment are consistently linked with questions of economic ownership and control, as are solutions to such problems: e.g. 'My motivation is left-wing socialist: anything that frustrates the present economic system is supportable, so I would support all disarmament . . . we're victims of an outdated economic system'.

For respondents adopting other orientations, however, socialism can play a role as simply one element in an ideology which derives its meaning from an alternative articulating principle. '*Libertarianism*' is one such orientation, adopted by a significant proportion of activists (17 per cent) among whom stress is placed on the connection between peace activity and other elements within a comprehensive 'life style' or 'totally interconnected philosophy of living'. According to Taylor and Pritchard, people on the libertarian/anarchist wing of CND in the 1960s were the most likely to drop out of political activity subsequently. Segal and Rowbotham argue in *Beyond the Fragments* that 'many libertarians have overstressed the prefigurative lifestyle element. This has led many of them to retreat from public activity and class politics into rustic bliss, or mysticism, or whole foods or ghetto-ised coops' (1979, p. 198). If so, the retreat is not total, because such people, for whom peace activity is a 'life stance' (or, part of it) are prominent in local activity.

Aberystwyth has three whole food shops/cafés each of which is a point of dissemination for news of peace activities: one is in many ways the key focus since apart from displaying literature and advertising events, it provides a centre of personal contacts which run through much of the movement; the owners are leading activists engaged in withholding taxes, and taking a prominent part in local demonstrations. These illustrate the contrast between the 'expressive' political style of the libertarians, with its reliance on symbolism and theatre, and the 'instrumental' approach of more conventional left politics. Bernice Martin has identified the 'expressive revolution' of the 1960s as the point where the modernist movement in art converged on popular culture (Martin, 1981). A 'die in' in Aberystwyth's main street, the symbolic burial of a cruise missile on the beach and the production of dyed 'blood money' to pay taxes are part of the political legacy of the counter-cultural 'happenings' of the 1960s; there are supporters of the Peace Movement who do not feel comfortable with such tactics, finding them personally embarrassing, and who prefer more formal, more 'respectable' types of activity. This relates to a tension about organisation and 'style' which we discuss below.

Libertarianism harbours a hostility to organised politics and none of the libertarians are deeply involved with any of the local parties. Typically, one anti-nuclear activist who had been very involved in establishing a local branch of the Ecology Party explained that he had left, partly because of the Party's lack of concern with issues of social justice but also because

> given current political structures, I haven't much faith in working within them, Eco was placing too much emphasis on a formal party political approach . . . the reason why I haven't joined another party is that I'm dubious of their effectiveness.

For such activists the relatively informal structures of many of the peace and anti-nuclear groups provide a more congenial political milieu. For a few even these structures are seen as compromising the individual's freedom of action:

> it is important to have a group, I can see that, otherwise you get nowhere, need to join with like-minded people, but groups always tend to be dominated by those with stronger convictions, you might have to do something the group decides but you don't agree with.

Whether political or not, in 'party' terms, the Libertarian element is important in bringing to the modern peace movement a much 'greener' tinge than it had before: concern with environmentalism, and with ecological issues, connect to enthusiasm for rural community, alternative technology, and, of course, opposition to nuclear energy. Libertarians tend to be critical of organised socialism as represented by the Labour party and a number, even though English, more readily support Plaid and its programme of decentralised socialism. One such respondent successfully learned Welsh and became a member of Cymdeithas yr Iath while others reported attempts to learn. *Pacifism*, whether justified in religious or secular terms, also forms a crucial component of this orientation. Respondents object to far more than just nuclear weapons. The military itself, representing order, hierarchy, aggression and traditional masculinity, stands for virtually everything that they most abhor.

Our third significant political orientation includes those who would attach their position much more firmly to '*Welshness*'. Of the activists interviewed 17 (36 per cent) came from Wales and six of these were local (from Ceredigion). Welsh speakers comprise 31 per cent of the sample and six had 'Welshness' as their primary concern. For them peace activity is closely associated with commitment to Welsh language and culture, particularly within the rural community, only part of which can be shared by 'English' members of peace groups: 'the peace movement is a natural extension of my concern with community, Wales and self-government; peace is central to *Plaid Cymru*, almost *the* most central thing'. In fact the ideological positions adopted by members of this group tend to be more consistent and integrated than those of any other group. Around the axis of Welshness a set of commitments are tightly arranged: non-conformist Christianity, pacifism, decentralisation, Welsh language, community and, more contentiously, socialism. The discourse functions as an integrated structure to signify the underlying Welshness of which the Peace Movement is a natural outcome. This web of concerns is exemplified by a non-conformist Minister who explained that his commitment to peace, to Wales and the language and to the Third World was

> all part of the struggle for justice and dignity. Wherever man's dignity is threatened, God is threatened – as in the miners' strike (which is) a just struggle for their communities. The struggle for the Welsh nation and language is part of the same struggle . . .

It is difficult to assess the extent to which the language division constitutes a real 'frontier' within the movement and a possible source of friction. Advocates of separate Welsh language organisations believe that the movement is strengthened by the existence of both Welsh and English speaking groups and suggest that cooperation between them works well. But not all the Welsh activists favour separate organisation. Some advocate mixed groups in each of the local villages, and others expressed concern that the movement seemed to depend heavily for its 'rank and file' upon immigrants to the area. More than 60 per cent of our respondents have moved to mid-Wales from England; 22 had lived in the area for ten years or less.

Feminism, socialism, libertarianism, environmentalism and Welshness stake out much of the territory within which peace groups move. There is one other significant thread, *religion*. Our study includes ten individuals (21 per cent) for whom Christianity is the driving force behind their involvement, though Christianity also forms an element in the world view of others whose major orientation is towards socialism, Welshness, or libertarianism. Indeed, almost half our respondents declared themselves to be members of churches and chapels (non-Conformists fourteen, Catholics three, Anglicans/Church of Wales four, Christian Buddhist one). Three respondents had actually been trained for the Ministry. This compares with Taylor and Pritchard's observation that 41 per cent of CND supporters in the 1960s agreed with Christian beliefs (1984, p. 39). The prevalence of religious connections in our sample obviously owes something to the Welsh, rural context, but at least argues against any obvious secularisation of the movement over time.

Some of the Christians, most obviously the non-Conformists, are accustomed to an environment in which religion and politics are threaded together, whereas others see their involvement and the prospects of the movement's success in purely religious terms. One Catholic explained

> CND is not a political thing, but a human survival thing; the evil of nuclear weapons is just wrong, against love of any kind, it's very hard to say in this country but we must turn to God.

For such people a Christian commitment is taking them into a world that is unfamiliar and perhaps threatening. The recently formed 'splinter' Christian CND in Aberystwyth represents a way of coping with the threat by providing, as one Anglican puts it 'a safe home'. Advocates hope that it will be a centre of attraction for Christians who find it beyond them to enter the 'less respectable' world of CND (just as the women's group seeks to draw in women who feel excluded from existing organisations). Such fragments, which seem to be proliferating, mark out the borders of the political space which an alliance must embrace.

As for the others, among whom religious and political commitments are linked, this articulation takes place in a broadly consistent way. *All* those concerned with the defence of 'Welshness' had non-Conformist links and pacifist convictions, while the religiously inclined libertarians leaned towards the Quaker tradition or 'Gandhian' practices of non-violent direct action. The sample was evenly divided between pacifists and those who have no absolute objection to military preparedness. Pacifism is most closely related to Welshness and libertarianism, and to a lesser extent Christianity. It is least related to socialism.

It is perhaps difficult to disagree with the characterisation of this whole set of orientations and commitments as 'an amalgam of various types of middle-class radicalism' (Taylor and Pritchard, p. 29) except that we would not want to underestimate the consistency with which views are held. While differences in orientation are significant, they should not be allowed to obscure the shared commitments that bring peace activists together. Hardly any of our respondents see the issue of peace as an isolated problem; most link it with a range of other issues. A moral concern with inequality and social justice, particularly in relation to disparities between rich and poor nations, is a distinctive feature of activists' ideologies. A majority of activists extend this concern with inequality to domestic issues: unemployment, poverty, cuts in the welfare state and 'the rise of the right'. Almost all make connections between the arms race and these problems on moral and economic grounds, though the majority tend to see solutions in terms of changing values and attitudes rather than social structures. This radicalism extends to their view of the state, which is seen as increasingly repressive and decreasingly responsive to democratic forces and popular needs. The indifference of the government to public opinion polls showing opposition to Cruise and Trident is often cited in this context. Television coverage of peace issues is almost universally considered to be inadequate, biased or downright distorted and the producers are assumed to be subject to political pressure or covert censorship. In addition the security services are widely believed to be actively involved in the surveillance of the movement and the disruption of its activities. The state is increasingly seen as a threatening presence: 'I used to think that the police were impartially keeping the peace but the miners' strike has undermined my faith in these principles'.

In other respects too, the Peace Movement seems to be moving beyond the limits of the 'social democratic consensus'. 'Legitimate' pressure group politics (lobbying MPs, demonstrations etc.) are widely felt to be useful tactics but insufficient in themselves. The overwhelming majority (94 per cent) endorse at least some form of non-violent direct action, only three respondents being wholly opposed. Some were more enthusiastic about such action than others who gave it qualified endorsement. This goes hand in hand with an emphasis on grass-roots activity – 'getting out and doing something'. Existing political structures, particularly the Labour Party, are indicted for their inability to operate as active, campaigning organisations. For some this even extends to CND itself. Contrary to Parkin's argument that middle-class radicals find their rewards in action itself, rather than in what it achieves, our respondents showed a capacity to distinguish clearly between the value of symbolic actions in raising consciousness and improving morale, and the long-term objectives which still had to be achieved. They approached the issue of direct action in a carefully calculated way.

This array of radical concerns with inequality, social justice and the state constitutes the raw material from which the ideologies of Peace Movement activists are constructed. As such it is consistent with the ideological values institutionalised by the post-war growth of the Welfare State and known to be attractive to the professionals of the health, education and welfare agencies (Cotgrove and Duff, 1980) who provide such an important source of Peace Movement support. The very specific nature of the social base from which activists appear to be drawn leads us to qualify Mattausch's emphasis on the relationship between the emergence of a 'state class' and the growth of CND (see Mattausch, this volume, ch. 10). It is important to avoid a reified conception of the state. Some of our respondents do not work within the state, and, of those who do, others would not see themselves as 'state' employees. Furthermore, it is not the case that employees of the state have a single set of economic and social interests. The mobilisation of welfare professionals must be seen in the context of the crisis of social democracy and the sharpening conflicts within the British state, between its repressive and reproductive arms. There has been a shift of resources from welfare services to the police and the military, and an accompanying tendency to legitimate the role of the state in terms of 'law and order' rather than social welfare. In the face of this material and ideological threat it is hardly surprising that the Peace Movement provides an avenue of mobilisation that is particularly attractive to members of the 'caring' professions.

While peace activists share a common concern with social justice, inequality and the state, they differ in the ways that these raw materials are assembled into distinctive ideologies. For some of the less politically inclined such concerns are articulated at the surface level around an axis of general moral concern, lifestyle or diffuse religious commitment. For others they are the manifestations of deeper structures: discourses embracing some combination of Welshness, socialism, libertarianism and Christianity, with different orientations having one or other of these elements 'structured in dominance'. These deeper discursive structures vary significantly in the extent to which they are able to combine the various elements and the coherence of their combination. Even activists primarily concerned with 'Welshness' who exhibit the most inclusive ideologies experience tensions around the concept of socialism, which may be omitted or rendered equivalent to 'community'. Conversely many of the socialists display an antipathy to religion and find the theatrical style of libertarian politics uncomfortable. One general and significant absence (even amongst some of the socialists) is a lack of awareness of a need to establish links between peace politics and the economically oriented and collectively based politics of the labour movement.

Suggestions are being made within the peace movement nationally that the survival of the campaign will require a broadening of perspectives beyond the nuclear issue alone. John Keane, for example, argues the movement must strengthen its grip on social life 'by elaborating hithero untreated issues, such as unemployment, gender discrimination, North–South relations, environmental degradation, and the war in Ulster' (1984, p. 10). The local membership seems to accept they are in for a long haul; they would also, more or less, endorse some sort of concern with the issues indicated by Keane – but they certainly would not all go all the way with all of them; nor should they, for there is no reason to see the Peace Movement as the place within which all the pressing issues must be solved. Yet it belongs to a political universe within which these issues have to be addressed. The crucial question is how far it can carry how many of its members towards some resolution of them.

ORGANISATIONAL DILEMMAS

Within local CND certain issues have proved controversial. There is, for many members, a point at which peace issues become over-'political', that is, seized within party struggles. Divisions have emerged over questions of whether the movement should publicly support the miners' strike and whether party political banners should be displayed at public meetings. Underlying the differences between those for or against a higher political profile is a recurrent, if often implicit, debate about organisation which various respondents have been eager to discuss.

Certain members favour a 'loose' unstructured and undirected form of movement and a corresponding style of meeting: without an agenda, or leaders, and without formality. This model, as recommended by the representative of national CND at the founding meeting of the Aberystwyth branch in 1982, resembles the pattern of Quaker meetings, and also the approach adopted by feminist groups. Greenham Common is cited as evidence for the capabilities of non-hierarchical, spontaneous, organisation and the nucleus of the

Peace Network (the Aberystwyth Peace Group) already followed this style, in which 'consensus' emerges through a relaxed, fluid exchange of views. The opposite view is expressed by those who feel CND got off to a false start, and who want structure, definite tasks, a sense of progress and coordination. They complain that without this necessary planning and control, decisions never become clear, responsibilities are confused, and that you do not 'learn' anything from attending meetings.

A number of our informants – mainly drawn from the more elderly – tended to see this as a 'generational' problem: the young took a joky, casual standpoint, as when they suggested that Peace Festival activities should include children's games, face-painting etc., whereas the older members were more earnest, staid, and respectable, regarding peace as serious business. Generation, or age, does not, however, fully explain the problem which results from the existence of different perspectives within which are embedded distinct senses of 'proper' organisation. Some members take these from their current and past involvements in political parties, and churches, whereas others derive their ideas from experience in other 'movement' situations. Whereas the former complain that a whole generation is having to learn the lesson of political organisation from scratch, their opponents might view this as a re-assertion of the 'old' politics within the new. What is striking is that disagreements are expressed much more readily in terms of *style* than content: disputes about organisation indicate the practical limits to drawing together individuals who come from such different origins. For instance, the gulf between those activists who consider that peace objectives form part of a whole life-style, which as it evolves carries them through 'formal' organisations and out into 'exemplary' patterns of living, and those who see the future development of the movement as bound up with increased 'respectability' and the ability to lobby the powerful, is considerable.

CONCLUSION

Similar organisational tensions to those we have commented on have been observed by David Coates, who looks to the formative experience of common work within organisations to bridge this gap. We would support the view that those concerned do *learn* from one another. Organisational problems and difficulties were spontaneously mentioned quite frequently as one area within which people were trying to draw lessons, and to find some common ground, even if at times they found the practical questions of joint action frustrating. While it is difficult to pinpoint where exactly an exchange of political and social views takes place, it is also apparent from our interviews that people do become aware, through their activity in the Peace Movement, of connections between issues, or problem areas, which previously did not engage them. Thus during 1984 awareness of the miners' strike, and a general sympathy for their case, was virtually universal among the peace activists, regardless of their various backgrounds. Day-to-day involvement with the strike overtook peace activity for certain individuals: they did not bring the strike into the Peace Movement, except in carefully controlled ways; rather, they carried their Peace Movement commitments with them into other forms of organisation. Both locally, in the Miners Support Group, and eventually nationally, in the Wales Congress in Support of Mining Communities, CND had a 'natural' presence. The Congress brought together NUM, Plaid, Labour, CP, Welsh language campaigners, Farmers' Action groups and church representatives, along with CND, in a quite new coalition. Present indications are that the Congress will remain in being despite the return to work. CND was among the movements which had prepared the ground for this political development within Wales (see Francis, 1985).

The 'new' politics is perhaps not that new: the New Left of the 1960s and onwards was seen as introducing a 'new style of politics' and many of its key figures (Thompson, Williams, Hall *et al.*) are still there, plugging away at the old themes. Some comfort can be taken from the fact that, despite all the setbacks of the intervening period, and the current political and cultural ascendancy of the right, the Peace Movement is here again, and with it many of the people who were politicised by it in the 1960s. This is despite predictions that the contemporary CND would not again be able to mobilise mass support following the decline of the 1970s (Taylor and Pritchard, 1980, p. 128). This tendency to underestimate the staying power of the movement, and to dismiss it as a form of emotional 'politics of immaturity' arises, we would suggest, from the tendency to judge it against a preconceived yardstick of correct politics – the 'hard, committed political radicalisation' (Taylor and Pritchard, 1980, p. 111). An alternative interpretation, which would make sense of both the lack of ideological clarity and certainty within the movement, and the resurfacing of already experienced disagreements and debates about organisation, would be to see both as aspects of the *work* of political mobilisation, and as necessary features of alliance building. Our research suggests that in its attempts to bring together a variety of ideological themes and negotiate appropriate organisation structures, the Peace Movement is rehearsing many of the problems that will be faced by any broader alliance of the left. The success or failure of such efforts will determine the fate of the new politics.

REFERENCES

Bouchier, D. (1984) *The Feminist Challenge*, London: Macmillan.
Castells, M. (1984) *The City and the Grassroots*, London: Edward Arnold.
Cawson, A. and Saunders, P. (1983) 'Corporatism, Competitive Politics and Class Struggle', in R. King (ed.), *Capital and Politics*, London: Routledge & Kegan Paul.
Coates, D. (1984) 'Radical Hopes Revived by a Middle Class Left', *Guardian* Agenda, Nov. 30th.
Cotgrove, S. and Duff, A. (1980) 'Environmentalism, Middle Class Radicalism and Politics', *Sociological Review*, vol. 28, 2.
Francis, H. (1985) 'Mining the Popular Front', *Marxism Today*, Feb.
Hindess, B. (1983) *Parliamentary Democracy and Socialist Politics*, London: Routledge & Kegan Paul.
Jones, G. S. (1982) 'Marching into History', *New Socialist*, 3.
Keane, J. (1984) 'Civil Society and the Peace Movement in Britain', *Thesis 11*, Feb.
Laclau, E. (1977) *Politics and Ideology in Marxist Theory*, London: NLB.
Martin, B. (1981) *A Sociology of Contemporary Cultural Change*, Oxford: Blackwell.
Mouffe, C. (1979) 'Hegemony and Ideology in Gramsci', in *Gramsci and Marxist Theory*, London: Routledge & Kegan Paul.
Nias, P. (1985) 'The Poverty of Peace Protest', paper at BSA Conference, Hull.
Parkin, F. (1968) *Middle Class Radicalism*, Manchester: Manchester UP.
Poulantzas, N. (1980) *State, Power, Socialism*, London: Verso.
Rowbotham, S. *et al.* (1979) *Beyond the Fragments*, London: Merlin.
Taylor, R. and Pritchard, C. (1980) *The Protest Makers*, Oxford: Pergamon.
Touraine, A. (1983) *Anti Nuclear Protest*, Cambridge: University Press.
Urry, J. (1981) *The Anatomy of Capitalist Societies*, London: Macmillan.
Williams, R. (1984) 'Splits, Pacts and Coalitions', *New Socialist*, 16.

Index

Aberystwyth, peace movement in, 223–36
aboriginals, Australian, 18
Addison, Paul, 145, 171
Agadir crisis, 60
aggression, 3
airborne warning and control aircraft (AWAC), 74–5
American Civil War, 65
Andreski, Stanislav, 145
Angola, 71, 100, 107, 109, 110
  MPLA, 109
  UNITA, 107, 110
animal behaviour, 20
anthropology, social, 2, 3–4, 17
  and ethology, 19–20
anti-fascism, 159, 166
Arabs, 42
  see also Palestinians
Argentina, 81, 90, 92
arms transfers, 86
Army Bureau of Current Affairs, 168–73
Arts Council of Great Britain, 173, 174
  see also Council for the Encouragement of Music and the Arts
Attfield, J., 160
Attlee, Clement, 148, 152
Austria, 60, 61, 63, 65

Baker Plan (US), 90
Barnett, Anthony, 154–5
Begin, M., 139
Belgrano (Argentine warship), 81
Beveridge, William, 149, 208
Bevin, Ernest, 179
Beyond the Fragments (Rowbotham *et al.*), 221, 227
Biafra, 92
Birmingham, 151
black politics, 220
Bolsheviks, 68
Botha, P. W., 101, 103, 109, 114, 115
Bouchier, David, 220
Briggs, J., 21
Bristol Unity Players, 165–6
Britain, 63, 143–56
  defence policy, 152–4
  democracy in, 9, 143–56
  economic supremacy, 55
  Falklands/Malvinas war, 80–1, 90, 92
  foreign policy, 64
  militarisation in, 9
  'military-democratic state', 143–56
  parliament, 64
  role in Palestine, 123
British Iron and Steel Federation, 181
British Road to Socialism, 221
British Sociological Association study group on war and peace, 11
Buddhism, 41
Bukharin, Nikolai, 149
Burch, E. S., 26
Bushmen, 18, 20, 21, 28
Butskellism, 218
  see also consensus
Byzantium, 47

Calder, Angus, 145, 159
Callaghan, James, 154
Campaign for Nuclear Disarmament (CND), 153, 199–214, 218–36
  and 'new politics', 218–20
  Christian CND, 230
  research on supporters, 199–206, 224–34
  see also peace movements
Canada, 19, 147, 148
  Canadian Eskimo, *see* Eskimo

capitalism
economic success, 69
transnationalism, 67
war, militarism and, 6–7, 52, 71
Carter, Jimmy, 71, 80
Central America, 67
Central Council for Army Education, 168
Chad, 81
Challenger (US space shuttle), 91
chauvinism, popular, 66, 67
child development, emotional training, 19, 20, 21–2
China, Imperial, 'capstone state', 37–41, 47, 52
Christianity, 42, 43, 46, 229–30, 232
Christian CND, 230
Churchill, Winston, 143, 144, 152, 154–5
'Churchillism', 154–5, 159
Cibulski, O., 129
cities
in Europe, 47
in Islamic society, 43
'citizen wars' (Mann), 146, 154
citizenship, and war, 65–6, 69
City of God (Augustine), 46
civil defence (UK), 153, 163
Civil War (US), *see* American Civil War
Civil War (Russia), 149
civil wars, *see* wars
class, classes
and rule, states, war, 63–4
chauvinism, 66
capitalist, 62–3
liberal/Marxian view challenged, 57–8
inter-national, 60, 70
middle, 63–4, 65–6, 199–206, 229
national, 60, 65, 67–8, 69, 70, 71
'state class', 206–9
struggles, 67–8, 71
transnational, 60, 63, 66, 67–8, 70, 71
violence between, 5
working, 65–6, 69, 200
Clausewitz, Karl von, 7, 146, 151
'Clausewitzian wars' (Mann), 146
Clark, J., 160
Coates, David, 234
cohesion, social, 5
Cold War, 144, 175
Comintern, 68
command, control, communications and intelligence (C3I), 79
communism, 69
Communist Party (CP), 160, 162, 163, 164, 226, 235
Writers and Historians Group, 172
conflict
inter-state, 6, 7
social, 4–5, 7
Conqueror (British submarine), 81
conscription (UK), 153
consensus (UK), 153–5, 218, 231
Conservative Party, 153, 200, 210, 226
Consett Iron Company, 178–94
Consett Story, The, 180
Co-operative Movement, 166, 167
Council for Encouragement of Music and the Arts (CEMA), 162, 166, 173
see also Arts Council of Great Britain
Cruise missiles, 154, 231
culture, and violence (Eskimos), 34
cultures, and states (Hindus, Islam), 44
Cymdeithas yr Iath, 228

Daily Worker, 163, 165
Davidson, B., 164
Davies, A., 159, 164, 166, 174
defence
and sociology, 12
and third World country, 83–4
defence policy (UK), 152–4
alternative, 156
defence studies, 1
Defence White Paper (1957), 153
democracies, war-proneness, 10, 12
democracy, and militarism, 9, 143–56
demography, and violence among Eskimos, 28–9

détente, 153
deterrence, deterrent (nuclear), 67, 153
Deutsch, Karl, 129
Dien Bien Phu, 91
diplomacy, 59
direct action, non-violent, 230, 231
Dominions, in Second World War, 147–8
Douie, Vera, 178–9, 180
Dresden, 147, 152
Durkheim, Emile, 5, 55

Ecology Party, 226, 228
education, and peace activists, 224–5
Egypt, 128
Eibl-Eibesfeldt, I., 22
El Salvador, 76
England, state formation in, 49, 51
Eskimos, 17–34
  compared with Yanomamö, 29, 33
  execution, 25
  family structure, gender roles, 22–3, 25
  female infanticide, 24–5, 32–3
  ideology in justification of violence, 31–3
  kinship, 23
  'peacefulness', 18, 28
  relations with Indians and Europeans, 26–7
  social structure, 22
  violence among, 17–34: frequency, 29; instrumentality, 30
  warfare among, 33
ethnic politics, 221
ethology, ethologists criticised, 19–20, 31–2
Eurocommunism, 69, 221
European Nuclear Disarmament (END), 222
Exocet missiles, 89

Fabianism, 149
Falklands/Malvinas war, 4, 5, 80–1, 89, 90, 154–5
family, in Eskimo society, 22–3
fascism, 159
Fase, Berkely, 161
Fellowship of Reconciliation, 224
feminism, 220, 225, 233
feudalism, 60–1
First World War, *see* World War I
Foreign Military Sales programme (US), 86
France, 51, 62, 63, 81, 84, 91
  Foreign Legion (Chad), 81
Frederick II (Prussia), quoted, 61–2
Friedan, Betty, 179

Gandhianism, 230
gender
  and militarism, 11
  in Eskimo society, 22–3
generations, in peace movement, 224, 234
geo-politics, 62, 64–5, 70–1
Germany, Germans, 55, 62–3, 147, 152, 168
  see also Prussia
Ghali, Brahim, 91
Giap, General, 91
Glasgow, Mary, 162
Gluck, Sherna, 179–80
Graburn, N., 27
Grafton, P., 159
Gramsci, Antonio, 221, 226
Greater London Council (GLC), 218
Greenham Common, 225, 233
Greenland, 18
Grenada, 76, 80, 92

Hall, Stuart, 143, 235
Hardenberg, 50
helicopters, 74–6
  Apache, 76–7
  Black Hawks, 75, 92
Hewison, R., 174
Hindess, Barry, 222
Hinduism, 'Hindu custodial state', 45–51
Hinton, James, 162, 164
Hintze, Otto, 56, 144

Hiroshima, 143, 147, 152
historical phases (war and society), 60–70
history
military, 6
oral, 2
social, 2, 6
theoretical, 2: *see also* sociology, historical
Hobbes, Thomas, 46
homicide, 21, 25–6
Hull, 147, 151

Ibn Khaldun, 42, 43
ideology
in justification of violence (Eskimos), 31–3
peace movement, 225–33
Improved Conventional Munitions (ICM), 77
India, 52, 88
see also Hinduism
Industrial Revolution, 62
industrialisation (W. Europe), 62
infanticide, female (Eskimos), 24, 31–3
'internal pacification' (Giddens), 4
Intercontinental Ballistic Missiles (ICBMs), 79
International Monetary Fund (IMF), 91
international relations, 2, 8
Iran, 67, 80, 90
Iron and Steel Trades Confederation, 181, 188
Islam, 'Islamic cyclical state', 45–51, 52
Israel
Air Force, 92
Arabs in, 135
democracy in, 9
immigration, 138
Jewish National Fund, 136
Jewish state, 123
land and settlement, 135–40
militarisation in, 9
'permanent war society', 121
politics, parties, 125, 139
repression in, 9
Zionists, 122, 123, 137
see also Palestine
Israeli–Arab conflict, 121–8
internationalisation, 125–6
occupied territories (West Bank, Gaza), 128, 136, 139, 140
phases, 122
'protracted social conflict', 121
role of Zionist settlement, 122
wars: 1948, 123–4, 135; 1967, 127–8; 1973, 74–5, 89, 127–8; 1976, 128; 1982, 74–5, 89, 127
Israeli sociology, 128–35
Arabs in, 129, 131, 132
as sociology of Jewish society, 130–1
classified, 130
military in, 132–4
neglect of Arab–Israeli conflict, 129
'settler-colonial model', 134
wars in, 133

Japan, Imperial, 147
Jews, extermination by Nazis, 125, 147
Junkers, 63

Kaldor, Mary, 7
Keane, John, 222–3, 233
Keynes, John Maynard, 149
'Keynesian welfare state', 144
Khadafy, M., 81
'kill ratio', 66
kinship, in Eskimo society, 23
Klare, Michael, 90
Kohn, Hans, 58

Labrador coast, 27
Labour Governments, 144, 149, 154, 172–4
Labour Left, 219
Labour Party, 154, 162, 210–11, 226, 231, 235
Landstone, C., 173
Lapidus, I., 44
Leacock, E., 27
Lebanon, 67, 74, 127
Lee, R., 21, 28

Left Book Club, 160
Left Book Club Theatre Guild, 160
legal systems, European, 48
Lenin, V. I., 149
Lesotho, 106
Lesser Half, The (Douie), 179
liberal/Marxian theory, 54, 55–6
Liberal Party, 226
libertarianism, 221–8, 232
Libya, 81
Lindsay, Jack, 163, 169, 172, 175
List, Friedrich, 55
Littlewood, Joan, 162, 172
'Living Newspapers' 160, 161, 168, 172
Los Angeles, 179–80

MacColl, Ewan, 162, 172
McNeill, W. H., 50
Machel, Samora, 109
Malan, General, 107, 114
Malaysia, 21
Malvinas, 92
  see also Falklands/Malvinas War
Manchester Theatre of Action, 162, 172
Mann, Michael, 144, 146, 148, 149, 150, 155
Marsland, David, 1, 12
Martin, Bernice, 227
Marwick, Arthur, 145, 178
Marx, Karl, 5, 41
Marxism, 37, 38, 52, 54, 55–6, 63, 144, 163
Marxism Today, 218
mass media, and war, 4–5, 154–5
Mattausch, John, 224, 232
methodology, 182, 199–206, 219–20
Middle Class Radicalism (Parkin), 199–202
Middlemas, Keith, 145
militarisation, militarism
  and capitalism, 71
  and democracy, 9, 143–56
  and gender, patriarchy, 11
  and repression, 9, 99–116, 121–40
  comparative sociology of, 9–10
  'deterrence science' (Mann), 67, 68, 155
  in Britain, 9, 143–56
  in Israel, 9, 121–40
  in South Africa, 9, 99–116
  mass, 66
  space, 73–93
  'spectator sport' (Mann), 67, 155
militarist pressure groups, 63
militarist theory, 54, 55–6, 63
Military Assistance Programme (US), 86
military expenditures
  S. Africa, 104
  UK, NATO, 154
  US, 73–4
military factors in history, 37
'Military Participation Ratio', 145
military power (Imperial China), 38
miners' strike (1984–5), 235
Miners Support Group, 235
Ministry of Fuel and Power, 172
Ministry of Information, 164
Ministry of Labour and National Service, 185
missiles
  anti-tank, 76
  cruise, 154, 231
  Exocet, 89
  surface-to-air, 74–5
Mongols, 38
Morocco, 91
Mozambique, 100, 106, 107, 109, 110
  FRELIMO, 109
  MNR, 107, 110
Mulley, Fred, 154
Multiple-Launch Rocket Systems (MLRS), 77–8

Nagasaki, 147
Nairn, Tom, 144
Namibia, 18, 100, 105, 106
  SWAPO, 109
  SWA Territory Force, 106
Napoleonic Wars, 64–5, 146
National Health Service (NHS), 144
national societies, 9
National Union of Mineworkers (NUM), 235
nations, nation-states, 4, 58–9

Nazis, 125, 147, 160, 163, 168–9
Nef, John, 37
New Left, 203, 219, 235
New Model Army, 171
'new politics', 218, 235
New Right, 113
New Socialist, 218
Nias, Peter, 205–6, 224
Nigeria, 92
nobility, feudal, 60–61
nonconformism, Welsh, 229–30
North Atlantic Treaty Organisation (NATO), 12, 92, 154
nuclear disarmament, 10, 211
nuclear weapons, 3, 78–9, 207–9
  as symbol, 209
nuclear war, 145, 152

Owen, David, 154

pacifism, 228, 230
Pajak, Roger, 90
Palestine, 122, 127, 135
Palestine Liberation Organisation (PLO), 92, 128
Palestinians, 122, 123
  national movement, 46
papacy, 46
Parkin, Frank, criticised, 199–202, 206, 209, 218–20, 223
parliaments, 48, 64
Parsons, Geoffrey, 161, 167
participation
  Falklands war, 154–5
  military and social, 155
  total war, 145–7, 150, 154–5
  war preparation, 150
pastoralism, 42
patriarchy, 11, 179
peace
  definition of, 2–3, 18
  in simple societies, 17–18
  since 1945, 10, 150–1
  sociology of, 1–2, 10–11
  strategies for, 71
peace movements, 3, 10
  British, 11, 199–214, 218–36
  ideology, 225–33
  international, 11
  local (Aberystwyth), 223–36
  methodology of studying, 218–20
  organisation, 233–4
  politics of supporters, 223–8
  religion, 229–30
  social bases of, 11
  women's, 11
peace studies, 1
'peaceful societies', 17, 20–1
  Eskimo society as, 18, 28
Pearton, Maurice, 150
'People's Convention', 160
People's Entertainment Society, 166
Philip II (Spain), 50
Philippines, 18, 22, 87
Plaid Cymru, 226, 228, 235
Poland, 147
Polisario, 91
political systems (militarism), 12
Popular Front, 160
Poulantzas, Nicos, 221
pre-Neolithic peoples, 18, 28
Priestley, J. B., 170
Pritchard, Colin, 202–5, 232, 235
Protest Makers, The (Taylor and Pritchard), 202–5
Prussia, 50, 61, 65
Pygmies, 18

Quakers, 219, 230

Reagan, Ronald, 54, 81–2, 86, 113
Red Army, 163, 167
religion, *see* Christianity
remotely piloted vehicles (RPVs), 74–6
research
  comparative, 9
  methods, 2, 182, 199–206
Roman Empire, 38, 46
Rootes, Chris, 206
Rowbotham, Sheila, 219, 227
Russia, 60, 65

St Augustine, 46
satellites, 79–81
Schneider, William, Jr, 86
'Second Front', 165

Second World War, *see* World War II
Segal, Lynne, 227
Semai, 21
Serbia, 60, 65
Silesia, 61, 62
Skocpol, Theda, 144
Slater, Montagu, 167
Smooha, S., 129, 134–5
socialism
  and peace activists, 226–7
  'local', 218
  'military-political expansionism' (Marsland), 12
  Soviet-style, 68, 70
socialist states, 67
socialist theatre, 159–75
Socialist Workers Party (SWP), 226
sociology, sociologists
  and defence, 12
  and peace, 10–11, 12–13
  comparative, 9, 17
  Israeli, *see* Israeli sociology
  military, 2
  of militarism, 9
  pacific view of, 55
  political commitments, 12
  urban, 221
sociology of war, war and peace, 1, 12
  as sociology of state, 6
  definition, 2
  historical, 5–7
  neglect, 1, 54
  role in sociology, 12
South Africa
  African National Congress (ANC), 107, 109, 110, 111
  Afrikaners, 101, 102
  black trade unions, 114
  blacks in army, 105
  Bureau of State Security (BOSS), 102, 106
  conscription, 105, 106
  De Lange Commission, 114
  Department of National Security (DONS), 106
  'instrumentalist' view of state, 110
  'liberalisation', 108
  militarisation in, 9, 99–116
  military, 100–4
  'military-corporate state', 100–4
  military expansionism, 104–7
  military expenditure, 104
  National Party, Nationalists, 101, 104, 108, 110, 112, 114, 115–16
  Riekert Commission, 113
  security forces and Bushmen, 18
  South African Defence Force (SADF), 101, 103, 104–7, 111
  South African Reserve Bank, 112
  State Security Council (SSC), 102–3
  'total strategy', 101, 110–15
  Urban Areas Act, 113
South Atlantic War, *see* Falklands/Malvinas War
Soviet bloc, 68
Soviet Union, 67, 70, 71, 82, 87, 89–90, 92, 147–8, 149, 160, 163
Soweto, 100
Spain, 48, 160
space militarisation, 73–93
Stalingrad, 163, 164
Stalinism, 147
'Star Wars', 54, 81, 82
states
  against reification of, 232
  and violence, 5
  capitalist, 67
  'capstone', 37–40, 48
  democratic, 9–10
  'European organic', 40, 45–51
  geopolitical aspects of, 59–60, 66
  'geopolitical privacy', 61, 67
  'Hindu custodial', 41–5
  'internalism' criticised, 99
  'Islamic cyclical', 41–5
  Marxist view, 5–6, 144
  'military-corporate' (S. Africa), 100–4
  'military-democratic' (Britain), 143–56
  'revisionist' view, 6, 144
  repressive, totalitarian, 10, 99
  socialist, 12, 67
  variety of forms, 48
  war and, 6, 9–10, 60–1

'state class', 207–9, 232
radicalism, 209–14, 232
state-system (international), 7–8
emergence of multi-state system (Europe), 51
Strategic Defence Initiative (SDI), 81–3, 90
strategic studies, 1
Sung, Southern (China), 38
superpowers, 66, 67, 69
Sweden, 148
Swirski, S., 134–5
Syria, 74–6, 89–90, 92

Tasaday, 22
Taylor, Richard, 202–5, 207, 230, 235
taxation, in pre-industrial empires, 38
technology (weaponry), 73–9, 92–3
Thatcher, Margaret, 4, 143, 154–5
theatre, socialist, 159–75
Theatre Workshop, 172, 173
Third World, 71, 73, 229
effects of space militarisation, 83–92
Thomas, Marshall, 20
Thompson, E. P., 150, 175, 235
Thompson, Paul, 182
Tomalin, Miles, 168, 169
total war
concept, 151–2
models of, 7, 146
S. Africa, 100, 101
totalitarianism, 10
Touraine, Alain, 220
Treurnicht, Dr A., 108, 114
trade unions, 154, 193–94
tribes, in Islam, 43, 45
Trotskyism, 226
Tuckett, Angela, 165–6
Tunisia, 92
Turnbull, C., 21

Umayyads, 42
United Nations, 100
United States, 21, 52, 55, 67
and Chad, 81
and Falklands/Malvinas war, 80–1
and Iran, 80
economy (cost of militarism), 90
high-technology weaponry, 73–9
military expenditures, 73–4
in Second World War, 147, 148
space militarisation, 73–9
Unity Theatres, 160, 161, 163, 165, 173
US Army, 73–9
USSR, *see* Soviet Union
Urry, John, 222

van den Bergh, General, 102
Van Gyseghem, André, 166–7, 169
vengeance killing (Eskimos), 25
Vietnamese, 91
violence, 3–5
and classes, 5
and gender, 11
and warfare, 3–4
and state (legitimate), 5
culture and level of, 34
imprinted in infancy (ethologists), 19
instrumental and expressive uses, 30–1
in Eskimo society, 17–34
in simple societies, 17–18, 22
internal social, 4–5
Vorster, J., 101, 102

Wainwright, Hilary, 223
Wales, 223–36
Wales Congress in Support of Mining Communities, 235
Welsh language, 228, 235
Welshness, 229, 232
war, warfare
absence (Eskimos), 17, 18, 33
and capitalism, 6–7
and democratisation, 10
and state, 6
as socio-historical problem, 2
civil, 6, 8
defined, 17
devastation (increase), 66
Marxist theories, 8
'mode of', 7
profitability, 61, 66

war, warfare – *cont.*
rationality, 61, 64, 66
role in rise of capitalism and West, 37–52
sociology of, 1–2
'space-dependency', 79
total, *see* total war
War and Human Progress (Nef), 37
war prevention, 3
as task for sociology, 12
Warsaw Pact, 92
weaponry, weapons
conventional, 78–9
costs, 90
high-technology, 73–9, 87
'kill ratios', 66
nuclear, *see* nuclear weapons
revolution in, 78
space, 79–83
Weber, Max, 5, 48, 56
welfare state, 143, 156, 207, 232
see also 'Keynesian welfare state'
West, Western capitalism, 37–52, 70–1
Williams, Raymond, 175, 221, 235
Willis, Ted, 169
women
and national chauvinism, 66
in Eskimo society, 25–6
war work (1939–45), 178–94
women's movement (Bouchier), 220
women's peace movement, 11, 225–6
'women's work', 186–7
working class, *see* class
working class movement, 67, 70
World Bank, 90
world order, society, 8
World War I, 62, 146
Marxist theory and, 8, 148, 179
origins, 60
'people's war', 65
'total war', 151
World War II, 66
aerial bombardment, 151–2
British society, democracy, 5, 143–56
comparison of war experience, 147
'people's war', 159–75
sociology of, 174–5
'total war', 151–2
women workers, 178–94

Yanomamö, 17, 29
Young, Andrew, 100

Zimbabwe, 100